Writing History 7–11

Writing History 7–11 supports students and primary teachers helping them to explore ways in which activities involving the talk that underpins historical enquiry can be developed into reading and exciting, extended, reflective writing.

The step that teachers and pupils take from 'talk for learning' to 'talk for writing' is a vital one. In this book the authors argue that all aspects of historical enquiry leading to writing involve discussion and dialogue which permeate every aspect of 'doing history'. From this perspective they set out a theoretical framework for understanding the role of talk and reading in developing pupils' critical thinking and confident reflective writing, then demonstrate through a series of case studies, in which teachers, university lecturers and pupils work together, how the theory is put into practice in the classroom.

Themes include:

- How to support children in writing in a variety of interesting genres
- How to make links between the National Curriculum (2013) for History and for English
- How to plan for breadth and depth studies in the new National Curriculum
- How activities in *History 5–11* can be developed into exciting extended writing.

The second half of the book draws upon case studies from a number of real primary classrooms with children of different ages. Each case study shows how teaching was planned to develop children's confidence and enjoyment in discussion and to scaffold reasoned, written explanation and argument. Topics presented are all relevant to the new curriculum framework and include talking and reading about:

- Time, change and significance over 6000 years – writing a television script
- Celtic Britain and the Roman Army – writing a travel brochure about Celtic Britain
- The destruction of Roman towns – writing a Saxon poem
- An archaeological investigation of a body in a Danish peat bog – writing a newspaper report
- Did any countries benefit from WWII? – writing an argued viewpoint
- The expansion westwards of European settlers – writing a flap book exploring different perspectives.

This indispensable book provides not only sources for pupils to use in their writing, but also models and exemplars of different styles and voices to draw upon.

Hilary Cooper is Emeritus Professor of History and Pedagogy at the University of Cumbria and co-edits the *International Journal of Historical Learning, Teaching and Research*. She has published widely and has an international reputation in her field. She is author of the bestselling *History 5–11* now in its second edition.

Writing History 7–11

Historical writing in different genres

Edited by Hilary Cooper

Routledge
Taylor & Francis Group

LONDON AND NEW YORK

First published 2014
by Routledge
2 Park Square, Milton Park, Abingdon, Oxon OX14 4RN

and by Routledge
711 Third Avenue, New York, NY 10017

Routledge is an imprint of the Taylor & Francis Group, an informa business

British Library Cataloguing in Publication Data
A catalogue record for this book is available from the British Library

Library of Congress Cataloging in Publication Data
Writing history 7–11: historical writing in different genres/edited by Hilary Cooper.
pages cm
Includes bibliographical references and index.
1. History—Study and teaching (Elementary) 2. Report writing—Study and teaching (Elementary) I. Cooper, Hilary, 1943- II. Title.
LB1581.W75 2014
372.89—dc23
2013050696

ISBN: 979-0-415-84259-4 (hbk)
ISBN: 978-0-415-84260-0 (pbk)
ISBN: 978-1-315-76779-6 (ebk)

Typeset in Bembo and Helvetica Neue
by Swales & Willis Ltd, Exeter, Devon, UK

Printed and bound in Great Britain by
TJ International Ltd, Padstow, Cornwall

Contents

Tables

Contributors

Jane Carter originally trained in law but soon became interested in teaching, through volunteer work with children in inner-city Bristol. Her teaching career has included primary classroom teaching, local authority literacy consultancy, in-service training and deputy headship of a primary school. Jane now leads the University of the West of England's English team on the Initial Teacher Education programmes. Jane was recently awarded a Higher Education Academy National Teaching Fellowship.

Hilary Cooper is Emeritus Professor of History and Pedagogy at the University of Cumbria. After many years as a primary school teacher, during which time she wrote a PhD on Young Children's Understanding in History, she became a lecturer at Goldsmiths College, London University, then becoming Director of Professional Studies in the Education Department at Lancaster University. She has published widely and has an international reputation.

Penelope Harnett is Professor of Education at the University of the West of England, Bristol. Her PhD is on the development of the history curriculum and its implementation in primary schools. She has researched and published widely in the field of primary education with an especial focus on history and citizenship education. Penelope is a former editor of *Primary History*. Recent publications include: *Understanding Primary Education: developing professional knowledge, skills and attributes* (Routledge 2008); two chapters, 'Investigating activities using sources' and 'Creative exploration of local, national and global links', in H. Cooper's (Routledge 2013) *Teaching History Creatively*, and chapters in *Shared Histories for a Europe without Dividing Lines* (Council of Europe 2014).

Hugh Moore is Senior Lecturer in Primary History at the University of Cumbria. He is a former museum educator and specialist in ancient history, with an interest in the use of sources and artefacts in the classroom. His publications include, Ancient history: things to do and questions to ask, in *Exploring Time and Play* (David Fulton 2004); 'Who are we?' in *Cross-curricular Approaches to Teaching and Learning* (Sage 2009) and 'Teaching World War I and Teacher professional development' in *Primary History* (Issue 54, Spring 2010). Hugh's doctoral research investigates children's understanding of chronology and of artefacts to create narrative.

Jon Nichol has been involved in the cutting edge development in the theory and practice of history teaching since the early 1970s. From 1991 he co-edited the Nuffield History Project for teaching National Curriculum history to 5–11-year-olds. For the past four years he has been editor of the Historical Association's journal *Primary History*, the country's leading publication in this field.

Sue Temple is a Senior Lecturer in Primary History at the University of Cumbria's Carlisle campus. Sue taught Early Years and Primary children for seventeen years before joining the University, including time as a nursery head teacher and working in a pupil referral unit, for children with speech and language difficulties. She is a member of the Historical Association Primary Committee and editorial team. Sue is currently working towards her PhD, researching the teaching of history to primary-aged children with a variety of Special Educational Needs.

Sarah Whitehouse is Senior Lecturer in Primary and Early Years Humanities and Education at the University of the West of England, Bristol. She is also the Programme Manager for the PGCE programme for Primary and Early Years. She has researched and published in the field of primary education with an especial focus on history and geography. Recent publications include: two chapters, 'Investigating activities using sources' and 'Creative exploration of local, national and global links', in H. Cooper's (Routledge 2013) *Teaching History Creatively*. She is currently working on publishing *Jumpstart History* and *Jumpstart Geography* (Routledge).

Acknowledgements

First, as editor, I must say how grateful I am to my colleagues, who have found time, amongst all their other commitments, to work with teachers on the case studies in schools, and to write about them, drawing on their considerable practical experience and up-to-date theoretical understanding. I feel that they have made an important contribution to our understanding of the rich variety of ways in which we support children in writing, with enthusiasm, in history, in ways which meet the requirements of the National Curriculum (DfE 2013) for history and for English.

I enjoyed working on chapter seven with Jen Ager and Jenny Charlwood at High Hesket CE Primary School in Cumbria and with their head teacher, Margaret Taylor. Thank you for making me so welcome. My colleagues would like to record their thanks to the head teachers, teachers and children with whom they worked, on the case studies in this book.

Penelope Harnett thanks Dee Wratten, the Year 6 class at Little Mead Primary Academy in Bristol and the German student teacher who worked with her, Laura Kringe. Sarah Whitehouse thanks Michelle Pugh and Becky Robbins, teachers at Penygawsi Primary School, Pontyclun, and Jane Carter would like to thank the children and teacher she worked with at Charlborough Road Primary School, Filton, in Gloucestershire. Penelope, Sarah and Jane are the authors of chapter 8. Sue Temple is grateful to the staff of Fellview Community Primary School, Caldbeck, Cumbria – in particular Debbie Graham, the Year 5/6 teacher and Norma Bagot, the head teacher, and to the children with whom she worked, to write chapter 9.

References

DfE (Department for Education) (2013) The National Curriculum in England. Available online at www.gov.uk/dfe/nationalcurriculum.

Preface

About eighteen months ago I was talking to a Very Important Person at a conference, (no, not Mr Gove). He was saying what a lot of learning in history was going on in primary schools, through visits and engaging activities, but that there was little evidence of discursive writing. Well, I suppose 'write it up' can be boring. But it should not be.

History 5–11 (Cooper 2012) analysed the processes of historical enquiry through which historians find out about the past, then considered how similar processes can be used by children, at different levels of complexity. Its companion book, *Writing History 7–11*, explores ways in which oracy and reading underpin critical thinking in history, and how this can be developed as extended writing. Since the 2013 National Curriculum (DfE 2013) makes it quite explicit that speaking and listening, reading and writing, should be developed across the curriculum, so this seems a very good time to consider how to extend history activities involving talk[ing] and reading into enjoyable and engaging writing.

Oracy

Oracy (listening, hearing, exposition, questioning, dialogue, discussion, argument, debate, presentation) permeates every aspect of 'Doing History' from the initiation of an historical enquiry, through questions and questioning, to the composition and presentation of pupils' extended reflective writing.

Reading

This book explains how reading is crucial to writing, providing not only information and evidence for pupils to use in their writing (i.e. factual content), but also models and exemplars of different styles and voices to draw upon (i.e. vocabulary, terminology, syntax, phraseology and genres).

Writing

The book explores the different genres through which extended reflective writing can be developed. Pupils' extended, reflective writing involves a specific genre. A genre consists of the authorial voice – the writer's choice of language in relation to the audience; the form or nature of the piece of writing; the genre's structure and its content. Extended reflective writing means pupils can explain what their writing is based upon, in relation to its arguments and the evidence upon which it is based. It develops from the pupil's involvement in an historical enquiry, finding and working upon sources and evidence and the resolution of the enquiry.

Reflective and discursive writing

A reflective composition is based upon a review of the historical evidence and the selection from it of relevant historical information, arguments, interpretations and imaginative and subjective, even emotional, reconstructions. Reflective writing can draw upon creative genres involving the informed historical imagination, for example genres used for writing fiction and poetry. As such, the writing is often from a particular, subjective personal point of view.

Discursive writing requires a more objective and balanced examination of an historical question that teases out the evidence, arguments and interpretations, usually in the generic form of accounts, narratives, expositions, arguments, interpretations and explanations. In all cases the reader must be able to identify the evidential basis of the writing and how the author has used this in the composition.

Both reflective and discursive writing can consider alternative interpretations and arguments in reaching a conclusion or conclusions. As such, reflective and discursive writing does not have to be neutral.

Part 1

Part 1 discusses the theoretical framework for understanding the role of spoken language and reading, in developing confident reflective writing, with reference to examples from practice. *History 5–11* was based on the premise, embedded in the National Curriculum for History, that children find out about the past in the same ways as historians do, but at levels appropriate to their knowledge and maturity.

In *Writing History 7–11*, chapter 1 considers the very varied aspects of the past that contemporary historians write about and the range of genres in which they write, which can be replicated by children. Chapter 2 explains what is meant by genres, shows readers how they can support children in writing in different genres and explains how children can learn to read and analyse texts, as models for structuring their own writing. Chapter 3 examines the role of oracy in teaching history and the many ways in which it can be planned for, with examples from practice. Chapter 4 examines what was meant, in the past, by narrative history, how this has changed over recent decades and the implications for planning both breadth and depth studies and the relationship between them, with reference to the Key Stage 2 Curriculum for History (DfE 2013). Chapter 5 links *History 5–11* with Part 2 of *Writing History 7–11,* by suggesting how activities described in the earlier book can be developed as extended writing.

Part 2

In part 2 case studies explore ways in which oracy and reading support extend writing in history, supported by examples of teachers' planning and pupils' spoken language, reading and writing, with references to the National Curriculum (DfE 2013) for English and for history at Key Stage 2. The case studies focus on different aspects of historical enquiry: discussion of the meaning of sources, aspects of chronology and of creating and evaluating interpretations.

Chapter 6 explores ways in which children can be supported in using historical sources to write narrative, in an attempt to narrow the gap between the quality of their speaking and listening and their writing in history. Chapter 7 discusses ways in which in-depth and over-view approaches to chronology can be planned for and suggests activities for learning time concepts. A broad chronological structure is seen as structure within which to place new knowledge but the case studies show how understanding concepts of time involves interrogating that framework. Chapter 8 consists of three case studies, in which many strategies are used to enable children to explore and write about different representations of the past. This is a long chapter because of the importance of understanding why people and events in the past may be represented in different ways, and seen from different perspectives. In chapter 9 children also create their own interpretations, based on evidence. Chapter 10 draws together five case studies introduced as examples of the use of genres in chapter 2 and in discussing oracy and reading in chapter 3. It shows how, through reading, speaking and listening, children's historical thinking and understanding is developed, enabling them to write accounts of the past in five different genres.

In all of the case studies in part 2 children between seven and eleven develop reflective and critical thinking, through reading and discussion, supported by a vast variety of strategies, to write with enthusiasm, in many different genres. In all of them historical enquiry is seen as dynamic. The case studies are seen as models, from which readers can develop their own strategies and apply them to their own content.

References

Cooper, H. (2012) (2/e) *History 5–11: A Guide for Teachers*, Abingdon: Routledge.

Department for Education (DfE) (2013) The National Curriculum in England (www.gov.uk/dfe/nationalcurriculum).

Theoretical framework for understanding the role of talk and reading in developing confident reflective writing

Historians' themes and genres

Hilary Cooper

> The present, backed by the past, is a thousand times deeper than the present when it presses so close that you can feel nothing else.
>
> Virginia Woolf 1976

Writing about objects

Neil McGregor, Director of the British Museum

In *A History of the World in 100 Objects* Neil McGregor (2010) describes objects representing a span of two million years and many civilisations. The text is based on scripts for twenty fifteen-minute-long radio broadcasts. McGregor is a great believer in the power of objects to get into the heads of people in the past, to get into someone else's life. He says that the point of a museum is to understand what the world looks like from 'somewhere else', not from the present. He explains that most of us learn history from books, but that physical objects give us much more immediate access to the ideas and concerns of the people who made them, how they lived and the things in which they believed. In his introduction (p.4) he says, 'It is of course only one history of the world, so we hope that you will enjoy finding and making your own connections, constructing your own history of the world'. Children would enjoy making their own illustrated history of the world, or of ancient civilisations, or of a particular time span, based on objects. They might begin by writing the radio scripts then combine these to write the book. And there are many ways this could be organised, at different levels.

The stories of objects

In *Shakespeare's Restless World* Neil McGregor (2012) explains the stories that objects can tell us. He explains, for example, that a beautifully made, little, wooden ship, about 20 inches long, which we may assume to be the toy of a proud sixteenth-century child, is in fact an offering of thanks to God for the safe delivery from witchcraft of James V1 of Scotland and his new wife, Anne of Denmark, who nearly drowned at sea in 1590. A woman called Agnes

Berwick had confessed, under torture, to being part of a coven of Scottish witches who raised the storm by sailing out to sea in a sieve and drowning a Christian cat. She was garrotted and burnt in front of Edinburgh Castle in 1591.

Sometimes, as with this wooden ship, we know the stories objects have to tell. Children might retell such a story in their own words. Or, with further research, in this case about James V1 and witchcraft, they might expand this story. Often no one can be sure how objects were used or what they may have meant to people at the time, or who might have made or owned them, especially if they are objects from prehistory. But it is possible, based on what we know of the time, and if there is no contradictory evidence, to write a possible story about it and the lives and beliefs of those who made and used it. Although it is always better to see objects rather than photographs a brilliant website for accessing images – or any information about the Anglo-Saxon period is http://projects.oucs.ox.ac.uk/woruldhord/education/daily_life.html.

Bee Wilson, historian and food writer

Another interesting example of writing about objects is Bee Wilson's book, *Consider the Fork: a history of invention in the kitchen* (2011), which focuses on kitchen tools. Wilson reflects on the fact that the tools that surround us in the kitchen have all been shaped by human inventiveness, and in turn have shaped our lives. And she reminds us that our kitchens are full of ghosts, not just those of the implement innovators but of the ancestors who used their inventions and in her fascinating book she lets us see these ghosts more clearly.

Wilson says that if you have no sense of the past you cannot place yourself within a context so that you will have no understanding of time or respect for memory.

Children might like to make a book about changes in kitchen utensils over a long period of time, or they might prefer to research and write about changes in other aspects of social history, from the Anglo-Saxons to the present, or the legacy of Greek or Roman architecture, art or literature on subsequent British history. Again there are many ways in which this could be organised, perhaps different children researching and writing about different objects related to the theme. Or they might compare objects, for example religious objects, from early civilisations.

This approach, similar to that of *A History of the World in 100 Objects*, would provide opportunities for making links within and between periods and civilisations over long periods of time, 'make connections, analyse trends, frame historically valid questions and create their own structured accounts' (DfE 2013:188 Aim 4).

Writing about sites

Tom Christenson, archaeologist

Recently a site has been excavated in Lejre, Denmark, which is very exciting indeed because Tom Christenson, the director of the archaeological project, thinks that it is the Mead Hall, described in great detail in the oldest English poem, *Beowulf*. It was this hall that was attacked by the monster Grendel, who was eventually defeated by Beowulf. The story takes place in the fifth or sixth century and was brought to England by the earliest Anglo-Saxon settlers. The story itself suggests many writing opportunities.

Christenson (1991) wrote about the early investigations of the site in an academic journal. His paper is illustrated with archaeological plans, photographs of the site, and artefacts found there and diagrams showing post holes where buildings stood. The paper explains why the site is important, what is already known about it, how it has been excavated, what has been found and what new understandings this might give us.

I am not suggesting that children should submit articles to academic journals. But they could write a paper in this style, about a site they have visited, for the information of other visitors (with an abstract, key words, subheadings, labelled figures and properly referenced to their reading). Some children may concentrate just on the abstract and key words, with some labelled illustrations. This would be a good opportunity to select key information and set it out logically and briefly. The longer paper would involve key aspects of information writing.

Or children might design and describe activities they would like to see developed at the sites, to help visitors to understand better who had lived there and how.

Writing based on diaries, letters and oral accounts

Peter Moffat, author of *The Village*

The BBC 1 drama *The Village* (2013) was constructed from diaries, letters and oral accounts, in order to tell the story of a village in the Peak District, over the whole of the last century. It illustrated the importance of such individual evidence, by translating it into small stories, to provide a counterpoint to the broad sweep of history. Peter Moffat, the author, wanted to use evidence of what life had been like, provided by ordinary people, to contest the broad general picture of the period, which often, through constant repetition, seems to have lost its subtlety and in which the truth becomes dulled. He wanted to make sure viewers put themselves from the present into the past. He became conscious of how small events, and also momentous events, such as the coming of war, were for ordinary people at the time. In this way he wanted to correct clichés, which have taken hold of the big picture, for example that the period before the Great War was a Golden Age. It was for a few . . .

It would be great fun, I think, for children to collect evidence from local people (and perhaps the local library archive), showing connections between local, national and world history and to use their data to construct small stories about real people, which could be written as a series of incidents in a narrative or play script, which could be performed. Like Moffat's BBC programme, this might show how ordinary people's daily life was and was not affected by the 'big events' and how generalisations about the period do not always reflect everybody's experiences. Dodwell (2013) gives very good ideas about how this can be done in practice.

Writing about churches

Bill Bryson: author of *Notes from a Small Island* – and much else

Bill Bryson (1996) has said that when he first entered St Paul's Cathedral tears stung his eyes and he wondered why. He concluded that when you stand in an ancient building you sense history in every stone and that this history was made not by kings and bishops but by ordinary people, who spent decades designing, planning and building it, out of a sense of shared purpose and belief. He reflects on how true this is for the 12,000 medieval churches and 600,000 sites of archaeological interest in this country. And he reminds us that because we have so many, such a wealth of old buildings and sites, many of them are taken for granted, forgotten or even razed over.

I know that children, visiting churches as historical sources, can share the sense of awe Bryson describes. And this can stimulate interesting stories. They could, for example, look at incomplete carvings and 'guess' the rest of the story (interpretations), or make up stories about how they had been damaged. They could make up stories to explain what someone in a carving or a stained glass window might be saying. Medieval carvings, statues and stained glass often depict different versions of the same story. (St George sometimes kills the dragon and sometimes captures it.) This is because folktales about saints were accepted by the Church as a device for explaining to people their lives and beliefs. These stories were part of the oral tradition and so different versions became frozen in statues. To find out where your nearest Anglo-Saxon church is and information about it, including photographs, visit this excellent website http://www.anglo-saxon-churches.co.uk.

Writing and historical fiction

Daisy Hildyard

I have selected Daisy Hildyard because she has recently written a fascinating and eccentric novel, *Hunters in the Snow* (2013). It is about exploring notes allegedly left by her grandfather, who was an historian. This led her to reflect, in a scholarly way, on the process of writing history. It is a novel about writing history. 'Suspend your belief', her fictional grandfather told her, meaning that you should ask the sources why they are telling what they tell, not to trust sources but to 'hold them against one another, to isolate inconsistencies, then work back to the truth' (p. 23). Some children particularly enjoy writing stories about the past. Some get hooked into history through historical novels. Novels by Rosemary Sutcliffe about the end of the Roman period in Britain and about the Anglo-Saxons are a good example: *Eagle of the Ninth, Dawn Wind, Beowulf Dragon Slayer, The King Arthur Trilogy*. And some children especially enjoy writing stories set in the past. This is fine as long as they make sure they are based on evidence and that what is imagined, to fill in the gaps, is likely, fits in with what we know about the period and there is no evidence to contradict it. Others may prefer writing reviews of the historical fiction they read. During a topic on the Bronze Age eight-year-old Natalie enjoyed Rosemary Sutcliff's *The Changeling* (figure 1.1)

Writing about food

Mark Grant and Rebecca Price

Most children are interested in food. And food history is the history of everything; economic and social history, trade and art history. It is also a way of connecting with the past through the senses, taste, smell, sight, touch. In cooking the recipes we are experiencing the processes, tastes and smells that people in the past experienced and neuroscience has found that smell is the most powerful way of making associations (http://faculty.washington.edu/chudler/

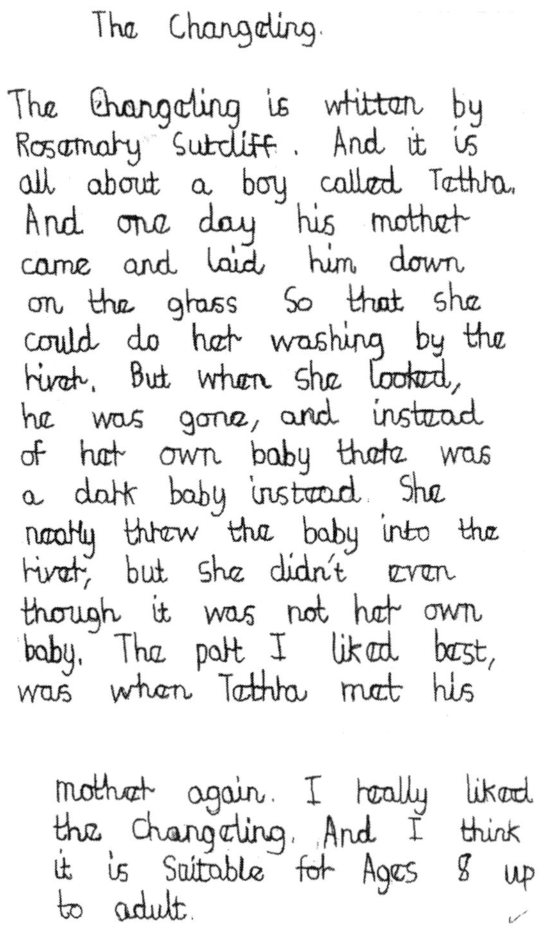

The Changeling.

The Changeling is writtan by Rosamary Sutcliff. And it is all about a boy called Tathra. And one day his mother came and laid him down on the grass So that she could do her washing by the river. But when she looked, he was gone, and instead of her own baby there was a dark baby instead. She nearly threw the baby into the river, but she didn't even though it was not her own baby. The part I liked best, was when Tathra met his mother again. I really liked the Changeling. And I think it is Suitable for Ages 8 up to adult.

FIGURE 1.1 Natalie's review of *The Changeling* (Sutcliffe 1974).

nosek.html). Cooking is not just a stimulus for writing recipes. It can be a stimulus for further research in order to explain the processes and utensils available for cooking them in the past, for finding out more about the lives of people who made and ate them, where the ingredients came from, how they were preserved, similarities and differences between 'now' and 'then', or between two periods.

In my school children took it in turns, in groups, once a week, to cook a recipe for their lunch, related to a period being studied. Parents were pleased to help work with them. In a topic on the Stone Age we deduced that people would have probably eaten fish and fruit. 'Oh, Mrs Cooper, I never could touch a wet fish', one parent cried. Similarly, we wrote receipts for Iron Age Stew, based on the knowledge that they had Soay sheep and root vegetables.

Mark Grant's *Roman Cookery: ancient recipes for modern kitchens* (1999) has the advantage of good written sources, which he quotes. School work on Roman food led one group of Year 6 girls to write a play about a Roman banquet, which, elegantly coiffed, dressed and bejewelled in Roman style, they presented to the class (who had been engaged in other Roman research) as a play.

Rebecca Price (1974) kept a book of the seventeenth century recipes she prepared for her friends and family. Children can cook many of them themselves. They may not like the boiled puddings cooked 'in guts', that is, cooked in the well cleansed stomach bag of a sheep, and could be excused for using a basin instead. But surely they would enjoy pippin jelly with cittorn, a cream of oranges . . . or the bacon and eggs made with marzipan, which was a great favourite when she was at school. As a child I would have loved to make 'A sweet water to wash with: my first cousin Clerkes' (p. 316), made from roses, lavender, marjoram, bay leaves and cloves.

Writing narrative accounts

The National Curriculum rightly stresses the importance of children at Key Stage 2, 'developing a chronologically secure knowledge and understanding of British, local and world history establishing clear narratives within and across periods of study' through breadth and depth studies (DfE 2013:189). How this may be done is discussed in chapters 2 and 5. The original claims that the new history curriculum would involve teaching British narrative history (Gove 2010) has not materialised. However, many historians do write narrative history, so if we are arguing that children's writing should reflect that of historians, it might be useful to look critically at, and so avoid, some of the difficulties they can encounter. One of the main decisions to be made in writing narrative history is what to include and what to omit; that is, what is significant?

Significance is discussed in chapter 5. But the following examples may cause further thought.

Political narratives

Simon Jenkins

Jenkins' *Short History of England* (2011) is a political narrative. It is about what many of us consider to be the central and most significant aspect of English history; what Jenkins describes as a nation forged between the hammer of kingship and the anvil of popular consent, the chain that holds the secret of how England comes to be where it is today. But he rushes through a history of kings and queens, to demonstrate his argument, ignoring all the complex changes in society that brought this about, as if this was an inevitable progression. The struggle has been more complex than kings versus parliaments. For example, only when workers organised into trade unions were they able to secure fair working conditions. Women were forced to challenge men in order to win the right to vote. And all were called traitors in their time.

Thomas Carlyle

Thomas Carlyle, the nineteenth-century historian, was critical of those who thought that everything in the past leads inevitably to the present. He wrote, in *Essays on History*, that actual events are not so simply related to each other as parent and offspring and every single event is the offspring of not one but of all other events (Strause 2002).

Norman Davies

In his recent book *Vanishing Kingdoms* (2011) Davies says that he thinks schools today are often guilty of telling tales of how states rise and of the glorious past that brought them to their particular peak of perfection. In his view school history is written by professional forgetters. He says that all children learn in school is the materialist orthodoxy of uninterrupted progress, in a cocoon of optimism, with no sense of the pitilessness of time, unlike their grandparents who survived wars. In Davies' world view it is now time, post World War II, to add Great Britain to the lost kingdoms of Alt Clud, the Dark Ages Kingdom on the River Clyde, the vast Vizigoth Kingdom of Tolosa and the Kingdom of Aragon. I'm not sure this was what Michael Gove has in mind. But we might less controversially cite the lost early civilisations of Bagdad, Maya and Benin.

False links do not create coherence

Peter Ackroyd

Ackroyd, in *Foundation: the history of England* (Vol. 1. 2011) also champions a coherent narrative. Yet his search for continuities between past and present leads to some surprising conclusions. For example, he claims that the discovery of fragments of 11,000-year-old deer skulls in the Vale of Pickering suggest that its inhabitants practised an early form of Morris dancing . . .

Different perspectives on a national narrative

The great tapestries of Scotland and Anglo-Saxon England

The recently completed Great Tapestry of Scotland and the Bayeux Tapestry describing the Battle of Hastings in 1066 provide visual narratives, which demonstrate that there are alternative perspectives of the story being told. The Great Tapestry of Scotland aims to commemorate the entire past of Scotland and, with a referendum looming, has an intense political symbolism. It is seen by Scottish Nationalists as illustrating a rich cultural past, in which Scotland was independent, as it should be again. But by Unionists it is seen as a Scotland that flourished in a rich political relationship with the south.

In this way it is similar to the Bayeux Tapestry, which to some is Norman propaganda, celebrating William I's victory at Hastings and a justification of his right to rule. But by others it is seen as a subversive British narrative, contesting the Norman claim to the English throne. No doubt the Scottish tapestry, like the Norman one, will be examined by historians for ideological meaning – and since the victor writes history, the result of the referendum will be significant in its interpretation.

Children writing narrative history

However, children can learn to question the accounts of others, in writing their own. Charles (Year 4) wrote this account, based on notes from class lessons. He uses vocabulary such as '*probably*', the Anglo-Saxon writers 'were *probably not very reliable*' contrasted with 'Archaeologists *know* that', and drawing together the '*similarity of some sources*', 'Gildas, Bede and Vortigern all say that . . . ' This class had been trained to distinguish between what is known and what is probable.

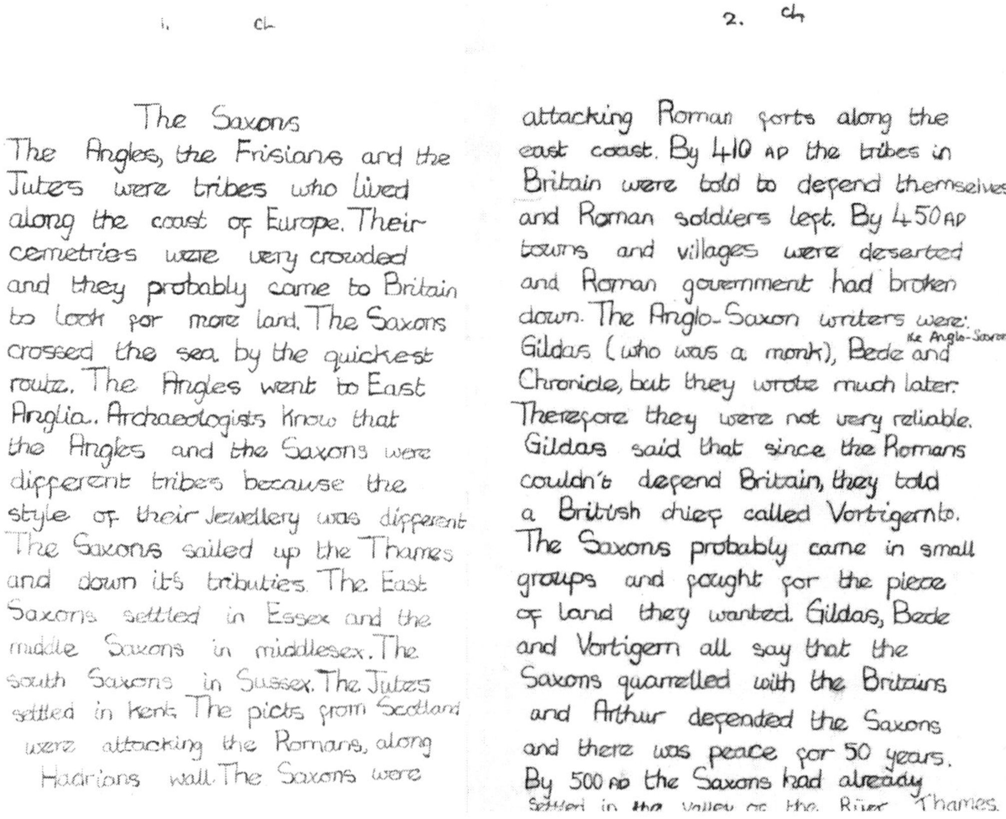

The Saxons

The Angles, the Frisians and the Jutes were tribes who lived along the coast of Europe. Their cemetries were very crowded and they probably came to Britain to look for more land. The Saxons crossed the sea by the quickest route. The Angles went to East Anglia. Archaeologists know that the Angles and the Saxons were different tribes because the style of their Jewellery was different. The Saxons sailed up the Thames and down its tributies. The East Saxons settled in Essex and the middle Saxons in middlesex. The south Saxons in Sussex. The Jutes settled in kent. The picts from Scotland were attacking the Romans, along Hadrians wall. The Saxons were attacking Roman ports along the east coast. By 410 AD the tribes in Britain were told to defend themselves, and Roman soldiers left. By 450 AD towns and villages were deserted and Roman government had broken down. The Anglo-Saxon writers were: Gildas (who was a monk), Bede and the Anglo-Saxon Chronicle, but they wrote much later. Therefore they were not very reliable. Gildas said that since the Romans couldn't defend Britain, they told a British chief called Vortigernto. The Saxons probably came in small groups and fought for the piece of land they wanted. Gildas, Bede and Vortigern all say that the Saxons quarrelled with the Britains and Arthur defended the Saxons and there was peace for 50 years. By 500 AD the Saxons had already settled in the valley of the River Thames.

FIGURE 1.2 Charles' account of the arrival of Angles, Frisians and Jutes.

A similar reinterpretation of a source to reinforce values is that of a wealthy young woman who was buried in the Roman city of York and whose remains were discovered in 1911. Her skeleton showed, on recent examination, traits that possibly indicate North African ancestry. Newspapers announced the discovery of York's 'African Queen'; so – we've always been multicultural!

Narrative interpretations may reflect the needs of our own times

Whether we see the Vikings as pillagers or settlers may reflect our own times

Christian monks in the Anglo-Saxon Chronicle described them from experience as rapists and pillagers. Yet at a conference in Cambridge in 2009 the Vikings were described as sharing technology and ideas and living alongside their Anglo-Saxon and Celtic contemporaries in relative harmony. Even Hillary Clinton has said that Viking society gave women considerable freedom to trade and participate in political and religious life (Fitzhugh and Ward 2000). Thus they were proto-feminists and early multiculturalists . . .

However, an exhibition at the British Museum (March – June 2014), the first major exhibition on the Vikings for over thirty years, returned to the traditional interpretation of violence, looting, raiding and slavery, rather than peaceful farmers who enjoyed travel . . . Exhibits included iron slave collars from Dublin, alarming spears, swords and battle axes.

Of course there was more to the Vikings than blood lust and they were eventually assimilated. But why do interpretations change with different times? Brink (2008:4) whose book contains the best contemporary scholarship on the Vikings, explains that 'every era uses history for its own purposes; every time shapes its own history. And especially during periods of strong political hegemony . . . it has been common to sanction the politics you pursue.' After the violence of World War II the focus on the peaceful side of the Vikings as traders was welcome. Indeed it has been suggested that this cosy notion of the Vikings might be ascribed to Swedish guilt about not participating in the war. But, as Brink points out, in the contemporary accounts, no one doubted that the Vikings were terrifying.

Seeing British history from the perspectives of others

Colin Firth, yes, he of the wet shirt in *Pride and Prejudice* (BBC), is the son of a history lecturer, who made him watch television and read newspapers sceptically, with a conscious awareness that he was seeing only one side of events and insisting that keeping doubt alive and never taking any one perspective is crucial. The book he wrote with Anthony Arnove, *The People Speak: voices that changed Britain* (2012) on the theme of justice, in the context of religion, democracy and freedoms, spans more than 1,000 years. It starts with the lamentations of a monk, Orderic Vitalis, complaining about life under Norman rule. Firth was influenced by Howard Zinn. Zinn attempted to tell history from the point of view of others, saying that we should not accept the memory of nations as our own memory. Firth was brought up in England, Nigeria, India and America. He says that if you travel frequently you are bound to be constantly subjected to the points of view of others.

Metacognition: understanding your thinking about history

It is important not just that we plan how to develop children's historical thinking in their enquiries and written accounts, but that they also understand what historical enquiry and account writing involves. Here is Mark's introduction to his history topic book (handmade) (figure 1.3). It was written in a class handwriting lesson. However, this allowed the opportunity to discuss with the class the work for the term and how and why it was planned in this way. This is also enlightening for their parents!

Conclusion

In this chapter we have considered different ways in which contemporary historians create accounts – interpretations of the past. Some as narrative histories (Jenkins, Ackroyd, Mortimer, Davies, Firth and Arnove), some as drama (*The Village*, Moffat), some as museum catalogues or stories, told in needlework (the Bayeux and Scotland tapestries), archaeological reports (Lejre Denmark), reflections on buildings as sources (Bryson) conference

Introduction.

This project has a Humanities focus. Time lines and Maps will show how ancient greek civilization developed during the 1600 years before Christ. We shall compare this with life in the Eastern Mediterranean today. In the British Museum we shall use the artefacts as clues to discover how Children in ancient Greece may have thought, felt and behaved. Then we shall use evidence from archaeology and from Greek stories, to see if they support our ideas. We shall use reference books to find out more about Greek thinking, thier beliefs, myths and legends, their discoveries in mathematics and science, their philosophy and political thought which still influence the way we live today. Investigations about the past will be displayed in a museam and information about the present will be collected in our "tourist information office"

FIGURE 1.3 Mark's introduction to a topic on Ancient Greece.

papers (Cambridge Conference, The Vikings 2009) or fiction based on historical scholarship (Hildyard).

Chapter 2 explains ways in which philosophers of history, over the past half century, have moved from seeing history as a linear narrative of simple cause and effect, how they gradually unpicked the more complex processes of historical, depth enquiry and how this is now understood to underpin the relationship between historical writing in both breadth and depth studies. This, as we shall see, is very relevant to planning work with children.

References

Ackroyd, P. (2012) *Foundation: the history of England*, Volume 1, London: Pan Macmillan.

Between the Islands: Interaction with Vikings in Ireland and Britain in the Early Medieval period, University of Cambridge Centre for Research in the Arts Social Sciences and Humanities, 13–15 March 2009.

Brink, S. (2008) *The Viking World*, London: Routledge.

Bryson, B. (1996) *Notes from a Small Island*, London: Harper Collins.

Carlyle, T. (2002) *Essays on History*, eds. N. and C. Strause, London: University of California Press.

Christenson, T. (1991) Lejre beyond legend – the archaeological evidence, *The Journal of Danish Archaeology*, Vol. 10: 163–185, available online at http://public.gettysburg.edu/~cfee/courses../English313/Complete%20Course%20Readings/Lejre%20Beyond%20Legend—the%20Archaeological%20Experience.pdf (accessed 09.02.2014).

An up-to-date account of this excavation can be found at http://ahgray.wordpress.com/2013/09/01/672/

Davies, N. (2011) *Vanished Kingdoms: the history of half forgotten Europe*, London: Penguin.

Department for Education (DfE) (2013) The National Curriculum in England: Key Stages 1 and 2 framework document, available online at www.gov.uk/dfe/nationalcurriculum/

Dodwell, C. (2013) Using creative drama approaches for the teaching of history, in H. Cooper (ed.) *Teaching History Creatively*, London: Routledge, pp.134–159.

Firth, C. and Arnove, A. (2012) *The People Speak: democracy is not a spectator sport*, Edinburgh: Canongate.

Fitzhugh, W.W. and Ward, E. (2000) *The Vikings: a North Atlantic saga*, Washington: National Museum of Natural History and Smithsonian Institution Press.

Gove, M. (2010) Michael Gove's speech at the Conservative Party Conference; section 'A new deal for teachers on the curriculum' (05.10.2010); 'The current approach we have to history denies children the opportunity to hear our island story . . . this trashing of our past has to stop.'

Grant, M. (1999) *Roman Cookery: ancient recipes for modern kitchens*, London: Serif.

Hildyard, D. (2013) *Hunters in the Snow*, London: Cape.

Jenkins, S. (2011) *A Short History of England*, London: Profile Books.

McGregor, N. (2010) *A History of the World in 100 Objects*, available online at BBC www.audiogo.co.uk.

McGregor, N. (2012) *Shakespeare's Restless World,* London: Allen Lane.

Moffat, P. (2013) *The Village*, drama, BBC1.

Price, R. (1974) *The Compleat Cook*, London: Routledge and Kegan Paul.

Sutcliff, R. (1954) (new edition 2012) *Eagle of the Ninth Trilogy*, Oxford: Oxford University Press.

Sutcliff, R. (1961) (new edition 2001) *Beowulf the Dragon Slayer*, London: Red Fox Classics.

Sutcliffe, R. (1961) (new edition 2013) *Dawn Wind*, Oxford: Oxford University Press.

Sutcliff, R. (1974) *The Changeling*, London: Hamish Hamilton.

Sutcliff, R. (1977) (new edition 2013) *The King Arthur Trilogy*, London: Vintage Books.

Wilson, B. (2011) *Consider the Fork: a history of invention in the kitchen*, London: Particular Books.

Genre and children writing history

Reflective and discursive learning and writing

Jon Nichol

Writing history and genre

Eight and nine-year-old pupils were answering questions about solving The History Mystery of Warley Woods; how a local man, Sam Whitehouse, had died one dark night in March 1822, while riding alone through Warley Woods, Birmingham. As history detectives, the pupils had undertaken an historical enquiry that involved them in 'Doing History'. The class investigated contemporary evidence, both written and visual sources, about Sam Whitehouse's death. Throughout their enquiry the children worked either as individuals, in pairs, teams or as a whole class to question, to investigate, discover and process evidence, to discuss, debate, consider and analyse clues and to develop ideas, hypotheses and conclusions. Their *reflective and discursive teaching and learning* enabled them to use their clues, information and understanding to write their *reflective and discursive accounts* of Sam's death, using the Harry Potter genre (see p. 19 for a definition of genre). The pupils' interviews illuminate how a genre can play an integral, central role in reflective and discursive writing.

Interviewer:	You did two pieces of writing?
Pupil:	*Yes, Warley Wood and the Harry Potter story.*
Interviewer:	How did you go about getting the ideas for your story?
Pupils:	*Who did it* [i.e. who killed Sam Whitehouse]
	Harry Potter people in the story.
	We thought two people [might have done it].
	Pictures – we looked at Warley Abbey.
	Couldn't sort out the mystery – so.

- *We did some interviews.*
- *We looked at them [the clues].*
- *Reading evidence, clues – might be you've found fingerprints.*
- *How can we trust the evidence – it sounds true?*
- *They could be telling the truth or lying.*
- *How likely these were true?*

The interviewer asked the pupils why they wrote the mystery as a Harry Potter story.

Pupils: *Harry Potter's a good story.*

- *Everybody reads it.*
- *Links up.*
- *Write how JK Rowling wrote it.*
- *Writing like you say you're JK Rowling.*

Interviewer: Who were you writing your stories for?

Pupil: *The teacher.*

History and reflective & discursive learning and writing

History provides an extremely rich context for reflective and discursive writing. As the interview shows, reflective and discursive writing is the final phase in a process in which pupils 'Do History' as apprentice historians. Children 'Doing History' is based upon *reflective and discursive teaching and learning* that treats history as a mentally challenging, problematic subject built around enquiry, discussion, debate, problem solving and interpretation. 'Doing History' requires children to:

- *ask questions;*
- *discover, select, organise [arrange/index/cross reference] and store primary and secondary sources;*
- *work on their primary and secondary sources* to extract, collate, organise and analyse relevant information and evidence that enables them to construct an overall chronology and narrative that is a context for their developing knowledge;
- *use and develop logical, imaginative, hypothetical and speculative thinking* based upon their sources to create ideas, hypotheses, interpretations, make judgments and reach and defend conclusions drawing upon their historical evidence;
- *choose a specific genre* to present their historical understanding that can involve reflective and discursive writing;
- *draft, revise and present* their discursive and reflective writing using that genre for a specific audience.

Reflective and discursive learning depends upon the teacher's orientation: i.e. beliefs about and understanding of history, its educational value and its overall curricular role. Central is an understanding of history as an academic discipline with its high-level thinking skills, disciplinary concepts, vocabulary/terminology and processes, procedures and protocols for 'Doing History' in its different forms and contexts, for example, local history, biography and historical fiction. Understanding of history as a discipline needs translation into pedagogic, teaching ideas and an understanding of what pupils' historical learning involves, i.e. pedagogic content knowledge. To develop pupils' knowledge of genres and how to use them for discursive and reflective writing our learning and teaching principles are those of the Nuffield Primary History Project and Cognitive Acceleration in History Education (CACHE) shown in figure 2.1.

Teaching principles: Nuffield history project

1 *Challenge* the pupils throughout.

2 *Questions and questioning* – make sure questions and questioning, including pupil questions, start and drive on an enquiry.

3 *Study in detail* so pupils can master the information, chronology, context, arguments and different interpretations that are essential for historical understanding.

4 *Use original historical material* that pupils can investigate and interrogate to understand both the topic and genres for writing: such sources can be both primary, i.e. first-hand historical sources and secondary, i.e. histories of the topic, including textbooks, topic books, biographies, film and video.

5 Provide support, mediation, *to make the historical material accessible* to the children.

Learning principles: cognitive acceleration

1 *Social learning* – pupils work socially usually *as pairs*, as *small teams* of from three to five, as larger teams or as a *whole class*. Social work is closely structured and supported with a focus upon historical enquiry, problem solving and resolution that draws and builds upon all members of a group. Pupils are forced to share knowledge, ideas, expertise through having different, inter-dependent roles in which oracy, see chapter 3, plays a central part.

2 *Cognitive conflict* – pupils have to accommodate different points of view through discussion, debate and disputation to reach an agreed new position, accept an existing one or, after full consideration, stick to their opening positions. Point 2 links closely to point 1.

3 *Psychological tools* – schemata – cognitive frameworks, schemata, for thinking. Schemata provide pupils with a mental toolkit. Examples for writing are concept maps, timelines, writing frames for genres. They support and enhance pupil understanding, providing structures, scaffolds that can support composition.

4 *Concrete preparation* – learning is based upon what the pupil already knows, can do and understand. Through analogy and metaphor the child moves from a confident known personal, social and cultural context, figure 2.2, to a linked, analogous historical context.

5 *Mediation* – the teacher as a coach and mentor supports the pupils' learning to ensure they can understand previously inaccessible material and ideas – see also point five of Nuffield Primary History Project principles.

6 *Mastery learning* gives pupils as long as they need to complete the task while working to the optimum. A simple, but very, very powerful idea.

FIGURE 2.1 Teaching and learning principles for reflection and discussion.

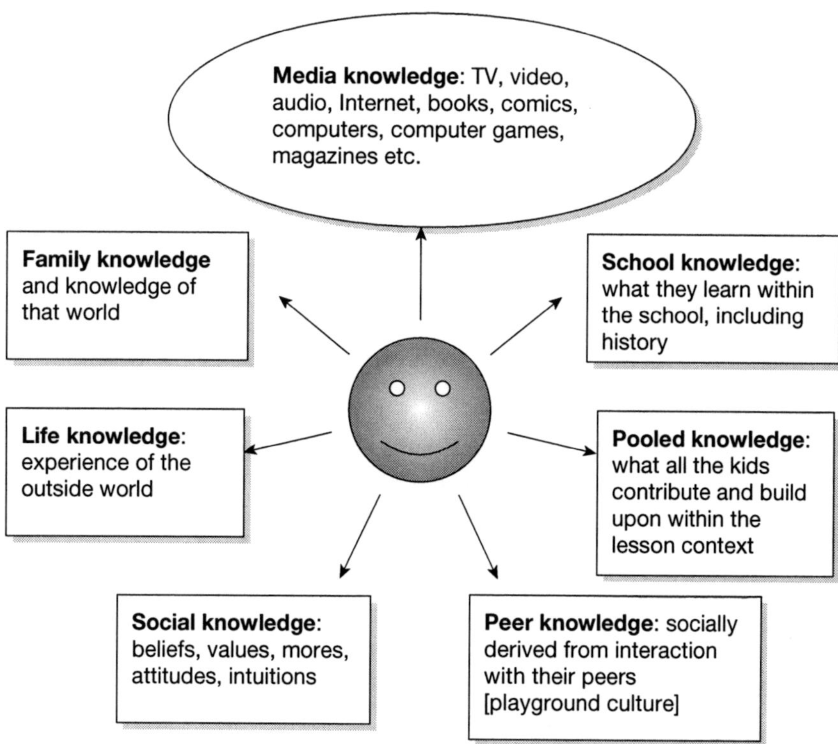

FIGURE 2.2 The pupil, culture and society: knowledge pupils can draw on.

Figure 2.2 shows the many kinds of knowledge that pupils can draw on in their writing.

Writing history, whole school policy and society

As such, *Writing History* is an element in a whole school policy that emphasises Language Across the Curriculum for all subjects and areas, something that is central to the National Curriculum for England (DfE 2013) (see page 18, figure 2.3).

The writing process

The writing process suggests that there are three phases, preparatory, expressive and formal, involved in pupils being able to write reflectively and discursively. In the preparatory and expressive phase the children build up a reservoir of information, evidence and related arguments, ideas, hypotheses and interpretations. They use a full range of linguistic modes, the iconic [visual], the symbolic [written and spoken language] and the enactive [dramatic/modelling/sculpting/physical activity]. This is shown in figure 2.3.

Pupils deepen their understanding through translating knowledge from one mode to another (Bruner 1966). This process is shown in figure 2.4.

Figure 2.5 shows the language children use in a range of contexts, when they translate knowledge from one mode to another.

Extending pupils' linguistic fluency and knowledge ranges from working on single words, phrases, sentences, notes and paragraphs to drafting compositions formally and informally.

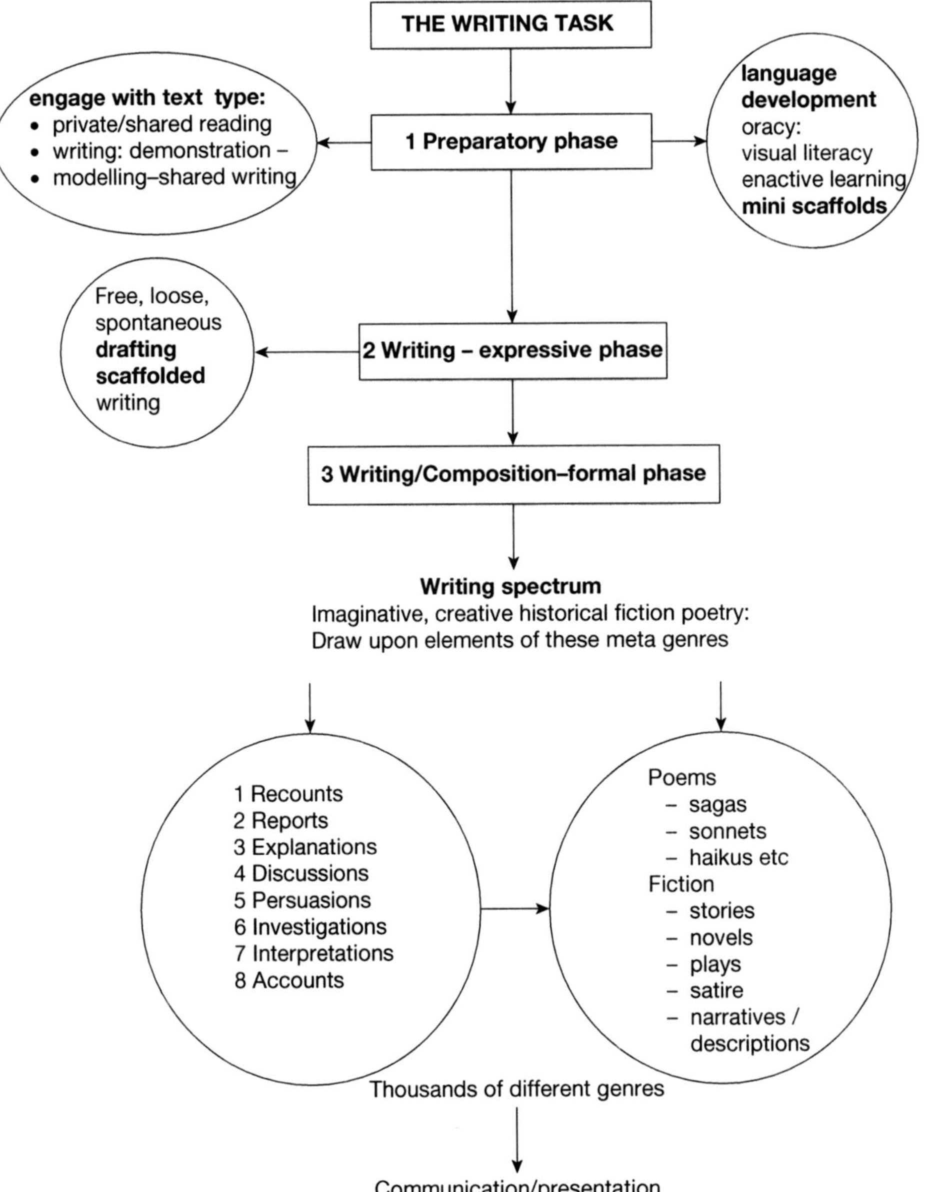

FIGURE 2.3 The writing process.

Reflective and discursive writing also depends upon the wider cultural context of the pupil, particularly in relation to their understanding of genres (see figure 2.3). For example, when we asked pupils to write in the style of J.K. Rowling, i.e. the Harry Potter genre, most of the class were reading or had read a Harry Potter novel. Likewise, we have used comics extensively for the pupils to use as a genre – drawing again upon pupils' own interest and knowledge of them. A third example is history mysteries – a common genre that pupils experience through their reading of children's fiction and watching TV programmes, film and video.

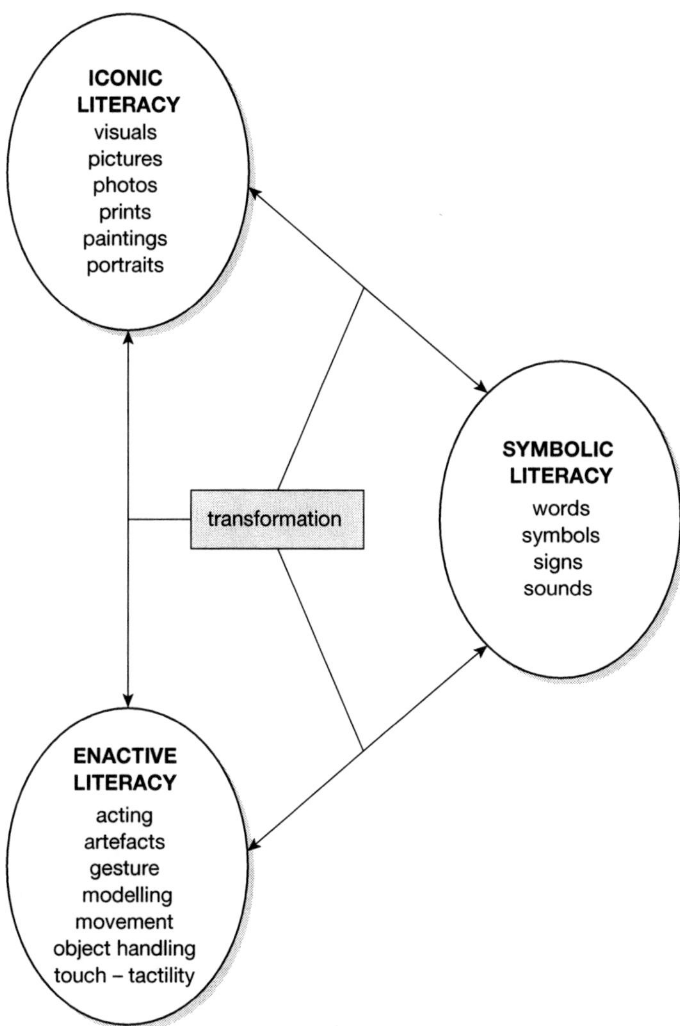

FIGURE 2.4 The links between iconic, symbolic and enactive literacy.

Understanding of genres

The interview at the start of this chapter suggests a key element in pupils' extended, reflective and discursive writing is their understanding and assimilation of the schema of specific genres to provide a framework, a structure for their own compositions. A genre is any composition, written or otherwise, with an audience in mind – from a bus ticket to the Department of Education's website. The genre's identity and unique voice, *register,* comes from a combination and interrelationship of its channel of communication, [*mode*], its authorial voice in relation to its audience, [*tenor*], and its content, [*field*], within its overall cultural context [*culture*].

The elements of the genre produce its distinctive, unique 'voice' or register (table 2.1). A twelve-year-old girl's reflective and discursive *The History of England* illuminates the meaning of genre:

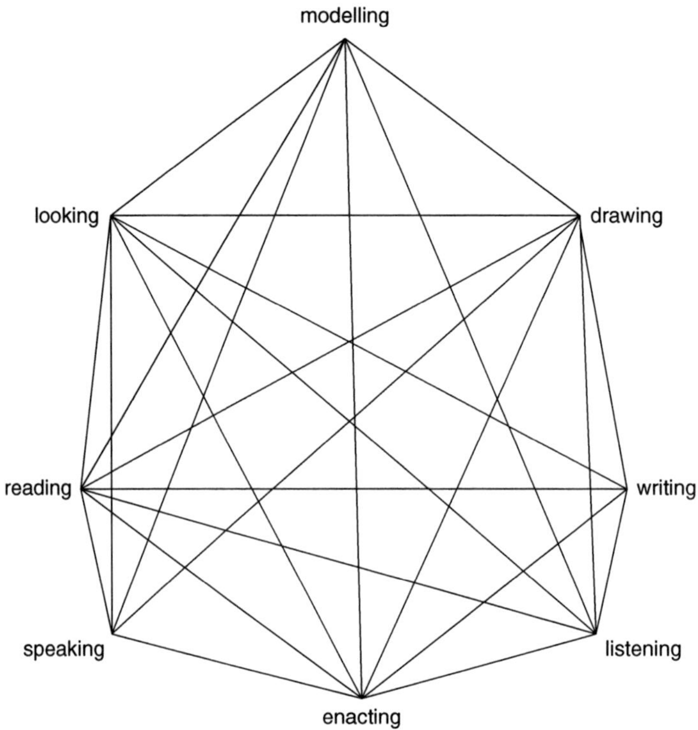

FIGURE 2.5 The literacy octangle.

TABLE 2.1 The five components of a genre; any composition written with an audience in mind.

tenor	The relationship between **the author** and **the audience** that gives the writing its force and direction. The author's purpose, i.e. pupils writing for a specific audience.
mode	The **channel of communication**, e.g. letter, news report, poem. ■ its specific vocabulary, phrasing, syntax, terminology, ■ its conventions – pattern, organisation, structure
field	**The content** of the writing: what the author is writing about – the historical information, ideas, details, knowledge and understanding.
register	The **voice** of the text/composition – the author in relation to the audience bearing in mind the purpose of the writing.
culture	The **cultural context** that frames and shapes the genre.

Henry the 4th ascended the throne of England much to his own satisfaction in the year 1399, after having prevailed on his cousin & predecessor Richard the 2nd to resign it to him, & to retire for the rest of his Life to Pomfret Castle, where he happened to be murdered. It is to be supposed that Henry was married, since he had certainly four sons, but it is not in my power to inform the Reader who was his wife. Be this as it may, he did not live for ever, but falling ill, his son the Prince of Wales came and took away the crown; whereupon, the King made a long speech, for which I must refer the Reader to Shakespeare's

Plays, & the Prince made a still longer. Things being thus settled between them the King died, & was succeeded by his son Henry who had previously beat Sir William Gascoigne.

(Jane Austen *The History of England*, 1787)

The *tenor* of the piece is satirical. Jane had a clear concept of her authorial role, 'By a partial, prejudiced, & ignorant Historian', in relation to her intended audience, her sister. The *mode* is equally clear: the history textbooks of the 1780s. The piece's *field*, its *historical content* is the reign of Henry IV, drawn from school textbooks. The *cultural context* is that of late Georgian England. The *register*, the text's overall voice, its style, combines *tenor, mode, content* and *culture* in an ironic parody of the traditional school textbook.

Jane's *The History of England* shows how a genre's schema is a cognitive tool that pupils can assimilate and adapt as a flexible framework for their writing.

The National Curriculum for English for 7–11 year olds includes genre in it prescription of the writing process. Pupil writing preparation should include:

1   *identifying the audience* for and *purpose of the writing;*

2   discussing *writing similar to that which they are planning to write* in order to understand and learn from its structure, vocabulary and grammar;

3   selecting *the appropriate form* and using other *similar writing as models* for their own;

4   noting and developing initial ideas, drawing on reading and research where necessary;

5   in writing narratives, considering how authors have developed characters and settings in what pupils have read, listened to or seen performed;

6   describing settings, characters and atmosphere and integrating dialogue to convey character and advance the action (National Curriculum for England – DfE 2013: 39, 47).

Pupils' understanding of a genre

Genres fall into a number of categories. These categories have separate identities but a common purpose. For reflective and discursive historical writing some examples are shown in table 2.2.

For history there are literally thousands of genres that pupils can use. For example the writing generator (table 2.3) shows sixteen possible genres in which pupils can write about a history mystery, The Body in the Bog. Each of these genres' distinctive register and structure reflects the different roles and purposes of the author vis-à-vis the audience.

Text, multi-modal and multi-media genres

Reflective and discursive writing can include genres that range from articles, textbooks, biographies, topic books, academic monographs, historical stories and accounts, newspaper and magazine articles to TV and radio programmes, film, video and digital age formats such as websites, interactive games, virtual reality recreations to drama, plays, poems, short stories, historical fiction, taped commentaries, animation, video, film and websites. In the digital age writing is as much multi-media and multi-modal as solely textual.

TABLE 2.2 Shows some of the genres children can use to write history reflectively and discurssively

Type of genre	*Purpose*	
	'Transactional writing'	
1 Account	To tell a historical story, a narrative . . .	that informs the reader of what happened.
2 Counter factual	To provide a realistic alternative . . .	to what actually happened as the basis for deepening understanding.
3 Debate	To report on an historical debate or controversy . . .	presenting the different arguments with supporting evidence and conclusions.
4 Explanation	To explain why something happened . . .	in a historical situation or scenario.
5 Interpretation	To interpret . . .	what happened and why.
6 Investigation – process	To explain what an enquiry involved, i.e. . . .	how an historical enquiry or investigation was carried out from the initial questioning to reaching a conclusion.
7 Persuasion	To persuade . . .	the reader to accept the viewpoint of the writer, with supporting arguments and evidence.
8 Report	To report . . .	on what the author has discovered.
9 Solution	To present a solution to . . .	a historical problem, including history mysteries.
	'Poetic writing'	
10 Fiction	To use the historical imagination to write a fictitious historical story . . .	grounded in the historical evidence.
11 Poetry	To use the poetic medium to present understanding of a scenario . . .	such as a Saxon scene using a Saxon poetic genre.
12 Recreation	To recreate and describe . . .	imaginatively what an historical scene or situation might have been like based upon the historical evidence.

Analysing genres using Textbreaker

How can pupils develop a detailed understanding of a genre? We created a tool, Textbreaker, which is shown in table 2.4, can help pupils socially, as members of a class, with their teacher's support, to break into a text and understand the features of the genre.

How do Textbreaker's sections, A–F, help children to understand a genre, and on that basis, use it to structure their own reflective and discursive writing?

TABLE 2.3 Shows the different genres in which pupils might write about the mystery of The Body in the Bog.

Writing generator: The Body in the Bog		
Content/field: The mystery of the body found in the bog and evidence relating to it		
Choose ONE **relevant** category from each column to provide the unique writing genre		
Author	*Mode*	*Audience*
Archaeologist	Advertisement	Bank manager
Detective	Confession	Best friend
Enemy	Debate	Boyfriend
Examiner	Imaginative reconstruction	Employer
Friend	Instructions	Enemy
Ghost	Interview	Girlfriend
Grauballe man	Leaflet	Grandma
Journalist	Letter	Local person [choose from list]
Judge	Newspaper story	TV audience
Local person [choose from list]	Notes – aide memoire	Policeman
Newspaper reporter	Poem	Self
The Devil	Poster	Teacher as examiner
Writing team	Report	The class
You personally	Script of play	Bank manager
Historian	Historical account	Historian
TV programme maker	Obituary	Public

Section A: textbreaker – modes/style

A mental frame or schema is important in reading difficult and challenging texts. This is a 'model' that links into the world of the child. Such schemas are analogical frameworks for understanding the text. We move from the world of the pupil to the world of the text. Pupils often bring to the text extensive experience and knowledge of the genre. For example, when our class of 10/11-year-olds was asked if it could read a letter from Anne Frank's diary, its members all reacted positively. But, when they turned over the page they were faced with the challenge of reading it in Dutch. The form, features and conventions of a 'letter' text-form immediately came to their help – they identified and translated the address, the date and the opening and concluding phrases and then moved on to words and phrases. The children's

TABLE 2.4 Textbreaker can help pupils to work with the teacher to break into a text and understand the features of the genre.

Textbreaker	Elements in the text
A Mode/style	OUTLINE FEATURES CONVENTIONS: structure: layout: patterns PATTERNS/STRUCTURES OF THE GENRE – ITS FORM ■ Main ideas ■ Hierarchy of ideas and information ■ Sequence of ideas ■ Logical structure
B Register / voice	VOICE OR TENOR AUTHOR AUDIENCE PURPOSE of the author in relation to the audience
C Vocabulary: **-WORDS** **- PHRASES** **- SENTENCES** **[MODE]**	ABSTRACT NOUNS *SOCIAL ORGANISATIONS, e.g.* government, police, tribe ■ *THOUGHTS* ■ *BEHAVIOURS* ■ *FEELINGS* CONCRETE NOUNS ■ *PEOPLE* ■ *FAUNA, e.g.* animals, birds, butterflies, insects. ■ *FLORA, e.g.* flowers, trees, weeds, vegetables ■ *TOPOGRAPHY. e.g.* hills, rivers, lakes, buildings ■ *WEATHER, e.g.* clouds, mist, rain, wind ADJECTIVES e.g. colours, sounds, size ADVERBS e.g. quickly, squarely CONCEPTS – substantive, e.g. Roman, Tudor, Middle Ages
D Historical **disciplinary** **concepts** **[Field]**	TIME ■ dates ■ periods ■ sequence ■ terminology CAUSE ■ reasons ■ results EVIDENCE ■ clues, sources ■ nature, reliability, perspective INTERPRETATIONS
E Field	THE CONTENT Substantive factual ideas, information, concepts, descriptions
F Culture	**The overall cultural context of the general**

knowledge of the field, i.e. the 'D' Day invasion of Europe in 1944, enabled them to translate the passages. Likewise, when looking at an 1857 trade directory our Year 3 pupils first created their own trade directory for buying presents for a birthday. When asking pupils to read the 1605 Monteagle letter, that warned James I of the Gunpowder Plot, they began by writing a coded message to their partners warning them indirectly of some terrible thing that might happen to them.

The conventions also serve as a 'model' of the genre that pupils can use to create their own analogical text using the genre's form. In our teaching of Saxon England with two classes we produced 'models' of two poems, *The Ruin* and *Beowulf* that the class used to produce their own poems, describing respectively the destruction of a Roman town (table 2.6) and the Sutton Hoo burial.

Pupil decoding of a text enables them to understand the 'structure and main ideas in the text' (Oakhill 1996: 77). The content of every text has a structure, pattern and sequence to its ideas. The identification of these, the working upon individual elements, the re-assembly of the parts into a coherent whole, are central elements in learning from difficult and challenging texts:

> . . . the reader needs to identify the structure and main ideas in the text. In the case of stories, they need to identify the main character(s) and their motives, follow the plot, etc. In the case of expository texts they need to ascertain the topic of the text, distinguish important from less important information, follow a line of argument, etc . . . the reader needs to go beyond what is stated explicitly, both by linking up ideas in the text to form a coherent overall model, and by bringing their general knowledge to bear on their understanding of it. Authors necessarily leave some of the links and expansions in a text implicit.
>
> (Oakhill 1996: 77)

Strategies for using Textbreaker include identifying the meaning of the text through a one-word phrase or sentence summary. We introduced our Year 3 pupils to Ibn Fadlan's tenth-century account of a Viking burial by playing a tape recording of the text. Then we asked pairs of pupils for a single sentence summary of what the tape was about. In another class of seven and eight-year-olds we read four Saxon riddles to the class, gave them out to the pupils and asked them in groups of three or four to decide on titles for the riddles. We pooled suggestions on the board and discussed which was the most likely. Another approach is to label sections of a text, and match the label with the appropriate section. Once ideas are identified the children might sort them into order of significance or into an appropriate sequence. Flow charts and logic trees enable them to identify the logical structure of a text. In handling ideas we extensively use expressive movement and drama, giving pupils a scene that they have to mime, act out or produce as a 'freeze-frame' for the rest of the class.

Section B: textbreaker – patterns/structures within the mode: its purpose

At a deeper level, what is the purpose of the genre, for example, is it a business or love letter, a saga or sonnet, a political account or bill for a meal, a medieval land grant or a town charter or a boys' or girls' teenage magazine? The reader has to identify the perspective of the author[s] and linked intention, the nature of the selected subject matter and the intended audience (Kress 1990). The contextualisation of the author, the content of the message and the intended audience, i.e. purpose, is reflected in the conventions of a specific type of genre, be it a love letter from Henry VIII to Anne Boleyn, begging letter or a cartoon. The text's conventions organise and sequence the ideas, information and messages. Thus sequentially a love letter like Henry VIII's draws from a specific set of words, phrases, connectors and their relationships to express most effectively the range of thoughts, feelings and emotions of the writer (http://www.gutenberg.org/files/32155/32155-h/32155-h.htm).

Section C: textbreaker – Vocabulary: words – phrases – sentences

While labelling allows an understanding of the overall pattern, detailed understanding relies upon decoding individual words and phrases and understanding their syntax. Categories provide another layer of understanding. Within a text the teacher has to select categories that help the pupils fill in and flesh out their mental model, for an example, see table 2.5, *The Ruin*. Categories cover abstract and concrete nouns, verbs and adjectives and their semantic and syntactic relationships. Textbreaker provides an entry to word level work, through identifying different categories of words and phrases, according to whether they are abstract or concrete nouns, adjective or adverbs or substantive concepts. Thus we asked our eight and nine-year-old pupils to decode one of Henry VIII's love letters to Anne Boleyn through finding words that express his feelings towards her. The pupils wrote them down inside a love heart that they had drawn. Similarly, in reading Pliny's description of the eruption of Vesuvius two classes had to find words and phrases that dealt with colours and sounds.

The extent and nature of the pupil's knowledge at the word and phrase level draws upon a semantic network of lexical understanding. Individual words and phrases are the network's nodes; its filaments are the associations that connect the nodes. In going beyond making initial sense of a word or phrase in a text, the reader's inferences draw upon both the pupil's existing semantic network and what can be added to it during the reading process. The richer and more extensive the network, the greater the range and depth of the reader's understanding, based upon elaborative inferencing. In relation to semantic understanding, contextualised, subject-based knowledge is significant. Subject-based linguistic knowledge adds new words and phrases to, and extends the meaning of those, already in the pupil's everyday mental lexicon. Thus, a class working on Juvenal's description of a Roman city were able to explain the meaning of the phrase 'clattering over greasy flesh scrapers' as they had already covered this aspect of Roman life in their history lessons. The pupils' inferential knowledge included knowledge of the Roman system of bathing, involving as it did rubbing with oil and the use of strigils as body scrapers. In our public reading of the text, the teacher pooled the detailed knowledge individual pupils had of Roman toiletry and built upon it through discussion, explanation and exposition.

Section D: textbreaker – historical disciplinary concepts

Historical concepts are similar to categories, but relate to the nature of history as a discipline, both the process of enquiry and its conceptual foundations, i.e. chronology, causation and evidence.

Section E: textbreaker – field

The field is the historical and related knowledge that enables the reader to make sense of the text. The Saxon poem illustrates this perfectly. To understand the poem the pupils first worked upon what a British Roman town was like at the end of the Roman period.

Section F: textbreaker – culture

The overall cultural context was, in the case of the Saxon poem, the outline history of England that saw the invasion and settlement of Saxon tribes from the fifth to seventh centuries AD.

Genres in the classroom: what does it mean in reality?

Genres are embedded in our schemes of work. Because genres are central to literacy we can either introduce a new genre through analogy, demonstration and modelling, as in the case of the 1851 trade directory, Saxon poem, Juvenal's satire, or drawing upon pupils' existing generic knowledge, as in the cases of Henry VIII's love letters and Anne Frank's diary entry. In each case we carefully choose the genre to fit the overall teaching context and the specific topic the children are studying – for example, getting the class to carry out a census of their pets as an introduction to reading an 1851 census of the area around the school, in the original school as I had left the transcripts at home!

We consciously use Textbreaker so that pupils can assimilate and use a genre's schema in their own composition. The Saxon Poem, below, is one such example, where the pupil's reading of an original poem, *The Ruin*, provided the 'model' for writing their own poems.

Theory into practice: The Saxon Poem

How, in a typical lesson, do we engage our pupils in the reading of texts that previously we might have considered either too difficult or challenging for them to be able to write recursively and discursively, using that genre? The eight and nine-year-old pupils were studying Saxon England; a central element in the teaching was their reading the Saxon poem *The Ruin*. The poem was integrated into the class's literacy work on poetic genres.

The teaching took place with a normal mixed-ability class in a state school. We introduced the Saxon poem text through an introductory lesson that explored an artist's reconstruction of the forum of the Roman town of St Albans. The lesson opened with the class in two teams playing an I Spy game, through which they built up an understanding of what an artist's reconstruction of the forum showed. Then we asked the pupils in pairs to imagine that they were guides to different places in the city marked on a plan of it, for a rural child visiting St Albans for the first time.

The pairs then reported back to the class what they had found on their visit to their part of the town, such as the circus, the baths and the temple. The lesson ended with the arrival of a message, saying that the child who had been the guide would be leaving the town and returning to Rome – for the year was 410 AD and his father was the commander of the garrison. The troops were going back to Rome for good.

Reading the poem

This provided the context for introducing the Saxon poem, *The Ruin*. We told the class that the children had kept in touch during the early period of Saxon invasion. After fifty years the child who remained in Britain, now an old person, sends a translated Saxon poem, *The Ruin*, to Rome to tell people what had happened to the city. We gave each pair a copy of the poem, prepared for them to use Textbreaker to read it. Interestingly, in the previous year's teaching

TABLE 2.5 The Saxon poem, *The Ruin* – pupil copy.

<table>
<tr><td colspan="3">Title:</td></tr>
<tr><td>Splendid this rampart is, though fate destroyed it.</td><td>WORD LIST</td><td>What it means</td></tr>
<tr><td>The city buildings fell down, the work of giants crumble.</td><td>ceilings</td><td>part of a room - at the top</td></tr>
<tr><td rowspan="2">Tumbled are the towers, ruined the roofs and broken the gate with its bars.</td><td>collapsed</td><td>fall down</td></tr>
<tr><td>crumble</td><td>break into small bits, like a biscuit</td></tr>
<tr><td rowspan="2">Frost breaks up the plaster and all the ceilings gape wide open.</td><td>decay</td><td>rot</td></tr>
<tr><td>destroyed</td><td>wreck, ruin, break</td></tr>
<tr><td rowspan="2">For they are torn and collapsed, age has eaten them up.</td><td>disease</td><td>illness - germs cause this. You are sick</td></tr>
<tr><td>fate</td><td>what the gods say will happen to you</td></tr>
<tr><td rowspan="2">In the hard earth lie the dead long gone builders, a hundred generations of people have passed by. [A]</td><td rowspan="2">fountains</td><td rowspan="2">water sprays out of them, like in a garden</td></tr>
<tr></tr>
<tr><td rowspan="2">The moss has stained this wall red and grey while it stood through storms as kingdoms rose and fell.</td><td>frost</td><td>cold weather that makes water freeze</td></tr>
<tr><td>gape</td><td>wide open</td></tr>
<tr><td>Now the high curved wall itself has fallen down.</td><td>generations</td><td>time a person lives</td></tr>
<tr><td rowspan="2">The builders put up their round arch buildings, the public halls were bright with high chimneys.</td><td>glorious</td><td>great, famous</td></tr>
<tr><td>heroes</td><td>a famous person you look up to.</td></tr>
<tr><td rowspan="2">Many were the bathhouses ringing with happy noise, many the beer houses full of human joy. [B]</td><td>kingdoms</td><td>lands a king rules</td></tr>
<tr><td>loaded</td><td>weighed down with</td></tr>
<tr><td>Mighty fate brought change to it all.</td><td>plaster</td><td>a kind of cement you put on walls</td></tr>
<tr><td>Slaughter was widespread and disease spread,</td><td>public</td><td>all the people</td></tr>
<tr><td rowspan="2">Death took away those brave men, the halls of warriors became empty places. [C]</td><td>rampart</td><td>walls of a city</td></tr>
<tr><td>rubble</td><td>broken bits of brick, plaster, stone etc.</td></tr>
<tr><td rowspan="2">The city crumbled, its builders fell and its armies are in the earth.</td><td>sheds</td><td>throws down</td></tr>
<tr><td>slaughter</td><td>kill</td></tr>
<tr><td rowspan="2">And so these halls are empty and this red curved roof now sheds its tiles.</td><td>splendid</td><td>great, wonderful</td></tr>
<tr><td rowspan="2">tile</td><td rowspan="2">small, thin square flat piece of stone to put on a roof</td></tr>
<tr><td rowspan="2">Decay has brought it to the ground, smashed it to piles of rubble.</td></tr>
<tr><td>towers</td><td>forts on the walls you fight from</td></tr>
<tr><td rowspan="2">Long since gone an army of heroes, glorious, loaded with gold</td><td>tumbled</td><td>fall down</td></tr>
<tr><td>warriors</td><td>fighters, soldiers</td></tr>
<tr><td>shone in their armour, gazed on jewels and treasure.</td><td>widespread</td><td>all over</td></tr>
<tr><td>Stone buildings stood, hot streams threw out fountains of water</td><td></td><td></td></tr>
<tr><td>inside the city walls. [D]</td><td></td><td></td></tr>
</table>

TABLE 2.5 *(continued)*

The Ruin				
Buildings		Colours		Action – Doing Words
Thoughts and Feelings		Sounds		People
What does paragraph A tell us?			What does paragraph B tell us?	
What does paragraph C tell us?			What does paragraph D tell us?	
Who might have written the poem?			Who might he or she have written it for?	
Can we believe what it tells us?			How can we check the truth of what the poem tells us?	

of *The Ruin*, before we had created Textbreaker, we had prepared a simplified version, thinking the original text was far too difficult.

Working on the poem

- Introducing the poem

  The class sat on the carpet. We said that we were going to read them the poem that the child who had returned to Rome received from his or her friend in England. The poem tells about changes that had happened to the town since the Saxons invaded.

- Eyes shut – mental imaging, the first reading

  To get the class to concentrate we asked them to shut their eyes. We asked them to think of mental pictures, images as they listened to our reading of the poem. Then Jo [the class teacher] and I read the poem out, paragraph by paragraph. This was presenting the poem **orally**, i.e., acquainting them with the words and phrases, getting them to build up in their minds an overall impression and understanding of what was involved.

- Brainstorm: → ideas about the poem
  I asked each pupil to think of a title for the poem. They discussed their ideas with their partners and then wrote their title down on the poem sheet (table 2.6). We wanted to build up a collective impression of what the pupils thought the poem was about. So our next step was to produce a class brainstorm of these ideas, using the device of the face at the centre of a spider diagram, with ideas coming out from the head.

Second and third readings: underlining and circling of words that they did not understand

- Individual words and phrases
  We now moved on to work on individual words and phrases. We asked the class to underline or ring words that they did not understand, as we read out the poem for a second time.

  In our third reading of the text we stopped after each phrase or sentence to explore the meaning of words that pupils did not know. They used the word list to help them write in the meaning of the text on their copy (table 2.4).

  We had decided on buildings, doing words and feelings as the categories we wanted them to extract from the text. The first job was to ask them to write down in the boxes words that they found that fell into these categories. Again they worked together in pairs.

- Scaffolding – board work: word game
  Now we went around the pairs, pooling words that they had come up with for the various categories and historical concepts. These we put on the board in columns, under their headings.

- Making sense of paragraphs through mime / freeze-frame
  Working in groups of four or five, the pupils had to plan a tableau or freeze-frame of a scene in a paragraph we allocated to them. Then one of the group had to read out the paragraph to the rest of the class while the group produced the tableau. The rest of the class had to guess what scene it showed.

- Annotated picture: how things might have changed
  We then annotated the picture of the Roman town, referred to in chapter 3 on p. x (http://www.stalbansmuseums.org.uk/content/view/full/14438) showing how things had changed from the time that it represents to that of the Saxon poem.

- Writing a poem
  We now returned to the form of the poem, working with the pupils on how the poet had expressed his ideas. As a class we discussed:

  a   The division of the lines into two balanced elements.

  b   The use of alliteration to stress ideas.

On the board we demonstrated how the poem had been created, and asked the children to create their own poems of up to six lines, using this model.

Pupils wrote their poems

The pupils were then told that they would write their own short, six-line Saxon poems, about what had happened to St Alban, to their friend in Rome. We discussed four things they should think about when writing:

a   The author – what would their reaction be as a visitor to St Albans during the time when the poem had been written?

b   The audience – they were writing the poem for their friend in Rome – but knew that other members of the class would read it.

c   Content – what content would they select to convey the message that they wanted their poem to have?

d   Genre – we would work within the Saxon poem genre.

TABLE 2.6 Some examples of pupils' poems.

Pupil's name	*Title*	*Saxon poem*
Alice	Gone to Rubble	Tumbled are the towers, ruined are the roofs, Flattened are the floors, crushed are the ceilings, Smashed are the statues, mashed are the market stalls, Dead are the dancing men, piled are the pillars Burning are the buildings. The whole city gone to rubble.
Andrew	All Destroyed	The city is crumbling down, then a crash, There was a smash, tiles off the roof, going down, down, down. Crying of the people, screaming of the children, Dogs barking loudly, while blood was flowing by. Stone wall tumbling down, down like the rain. City is crumbling down, then a crash, There was a smash, tiles off the roof, going down, down, down.
Ben	Boom Goes the City	Long ago, before I was born My father used to blow a horn, To tell the town of fears ahead Archer, swordsmen, ballistae and all As they were marching forward to us, We got frightened, as we prepared But soon enough they started attacking, As we had no choice, Boom goes the city

Pupils' poems

The pupils' poems were the outcome of a process that, from the start, had forced them to think, to speculate, to master the linguistic discourse of the Saxon poem and use what they had learned to write their own six-line poems, using the genre of the Saxon poem. The examples from this mixed ability class (table 2.6) suggest that such writing is perfectly feasible with seven and eight-year-olds. Given considered support, we should not underestimate the writing primary school children are capable of.

References

Austin, J. (1787) *The History of England*, available online at http://www.janeausten.co.uk/the-history-of-england/ (accessed 11.02.2014).

Bruner, J.E. (1966) *Towards a Theory of Instruction*, Cambridge, Mass.: Harvard University Press.

Department for Education (DfE) (2013) *National Curriculum in England*, London: DfE.

Kress, G. (1990) Foundations of discourse: critical discourse analysis, *Annual Review of Applied Linguistics*, Vol. 11, Cambridge: Cambridge University Press.

Oakhill, J. (1996) Mental models in children's text comprehension in J. Oakhill and A. Garnham (eds.) *Mental Models in Cognitive Science*, London: Routledge, p. 77.

Oracy: speaking and listening

Jon Nichol

Oracy in the classroom: what does oracy look like in the history classroom?

Elaine had been on a ten-day in-service course on teaching the National Curriculum for History to 5–11 year olds. A researcher interviewed her on the course's overall impact, including the role of oracy. Elaine and the interviewer discussed her teaching of a mixed-ability class of nine and ten-year-old children about the Tudors.

Interviewer   So presumably, with the portraits for example, earlier Tudor portraits are different in style to the later ones.

Elaine   Absolutely.

We had the Henry VII – the classic – and then what we compared him with was things like gender. So it was a Henry, and an Elizabeth or a Mary. I did things like Henry VII and Elizabeth of York, Henry VIII with his son Edward. They were specifically meant to make them think . . .

The Terry Deary book (1998) is wonderful – he's so good. I did an overhead and it's the one right at the beginning . . .

I put it on an overhead and asked the children, 'What does it tell you about the Tudors?' And the talking I got back was amazing. The things the children came back with – they thought of things I hadn't even thought of. We'd have to go and find my flipchart, which is down by the computers, because I wrote down exactly their responses to it. And they were saying things like, 'They tell us this, that and the other, etc.', you know, but it was stuff like that, it was really good literal stuff. There was some inputting which was very clever, and talking on the questioning level and the understanding level. And that actually went on longer that I thought it would do. It was so good.

What is oracy?

This example of children's enthusiasm to talk spontaneously about Tudor portraits helps answer the question: what is oracy? As a concept oracy is a relatively new phenomenon.

- Andrew Wilkinson (1970) coined the term oracy and defined it as an holistic area with its own, discrete, sophisticated pedagogy (Wilkinson 1965).

- Oracy was implicitly at the heart of the the government's 1975 Bullock Report *A Language for Life* (DES 1975) on the teaching of literacy across the whole curriculum that helped shape the teaching of literacy in England for the next twenty-five years.

- England's original National Curriculum (DES 1991) embedded oracy in its English requirements.

- From 1997 the government, educationalists and teachers increasingly recognised the importance of oracy (Alexander 2012).

- Oracy's steadily increasing role in the teaching of literacy culminated in England's 2013 National Curriculum (DfE 2013), which emphasised its cross-curricular importance (see figure 3.1).

Oracy and the National Curriculum in England, 2014

Language and literacy

Teachers should develop pupils' spoken language, reading, writing and vocabulary as integral aspects of the teaching of every subject. English is both a subject in its own right and the medium for teaching; for pupils, understanding the language provides access to the whole curriculum. Fluency in the English language is an essential foundation for success in all subjects.

Spoken language

Pupils should be taught to speak clearly and convey ideas confidently using Standard English. They should learn to justify ideas with reasons; ask questions to check understanding; develop vocabulary and build knowledge; negotiate; evaluate and build on the ideas of others; and select the appropriate register for effective communication. They should be taught to give well-structured descriptions and explanations and develop their understanding through speculating, hypothesising and exploring ideas. This will enable them to clarify their thinking as well as organise their ideas for writing.

The national curriculum for English reflects the importance of spoken language in pupils' development across the whole curriculum – cognitively, socially and linguistically. Spoken language underpins the development of reading and writing. The quality and variety of language that pupils hear and speak are vital for developing their vocabulary and grammar and their understanding for reading and writing. Teachers should therefore ensure the continual development of pupils' confidence and competence in spoken language and listening skills.

Pupils should develop a capacity to explain their understanding of books and other reading, and to prepare their ideas before they write. They must be assisted in making their thinking clear to themselves as well as to others and teachers should ensure that pupils build secure foundations by using discussion to probe and remedy their misconceptions. Pupils should also be taught to understand and use the conventions for discussion and debate.

Statutory requirements that underpin all aspects of speaking and listening across the six years of primary education form part of the national curriculum. These are reflected and contextualised within the reading and writing domains that follow.

FIGURE 3.1 Shows the oracy skills required by the National Curriculum across the curriculum (DfE 2013).

Department for Education (July 2013) The National Curriculum in England Framework document

Figure 3.1 shows the oracy skills required by the National Curriculum across the curriculum (DfE 2013).

Oracy is the collective term for discourse: 'language in its social context, as it is used to carry out the social and intellectual life of a community' (Mercer 1995: 79), that is, what we say and hear when communicating with others. In schools the social context of oracy is the relationship both between pupils and pupils and between pupils and teachers and others, including classroom assistants, parents and carers.

The example of oracy (p. 33) on children's willingness to talk about Tudor portraits, suggests that it can play a central role in the teaching of history as enquiry, that is, 'Doing History': an evidentially based subject that develops a range of high-quality thinking, enquiry, speaking, listening and social skills and processes.

> Speaking and listening are crucial for practising and embedding new vocabulary and concepts, and as such form the bedrock on which literacy is built. They also form the basis of social interaction, and are skills to be taught, as listening and turn-taking do not come naturally to children. Harassed teachers, too, do not always give children enough time to develop confidence in speaking.
>
> (Dean 2013)

Speaking, hearing, responding and exploratory discourse

The four vertebrae of the backbone of oracy are speaking, hearing/listening, responding and exploratory language.

Speaking

Speaking takes individual, social and personal forms.

Individual speech is where the individual treats his or her audience as being passive and not actively involved. Elements can also occur in social speech episodes of a discourse. Individual speech includes:

bullying, commanding, controlling, declaiming, decision making and taking;

describing, dogmatism, explaining, exposition, instructing, monologue, narrating, ordering, organising, recounting, reporting.

Social speech involves interaction between participants as in the introductory description of Elaine's classroom (p. 33). Social speech:

- involves two or more participants working together in pairs, groups of up to four, larger groups or as a whole class (see table 3.1);

- is an element in the full range of organising a classroom, from interactive, whole class teaching to individualised and group learning programmes where pupils work on different tasks and activities as in the integrated day;

- can include argument, cooperating, debating, describing, discussing, explaining, listening, presenting, reporting, reviewing and summarising;

■ is based upon a positive interaction between participants, that requires listening, hearing, accommodating and accepting different opinions and points of views to either reach agreed or different but defensible/evidenced conclusions.

Personal speech is both personal, internal private speech or self-talk and 'thinking aloud' talk that can occur in a social context.

Hearing/listening

Hearing/listening involves the acts of listening, assimilation of what is being said, reflecting on it and reviewing thoughts to develop full understanding of what was said.

Responding

Responding can be both verbal and non-verbal, including enaction, (e.g. drama, role play, making artefacts and models, sculpting, building, iconic or visual understanding), filming, ICT authoring packagers, drawing, engraving, painting, photography and sketching.

Exploratory discourse or talk

The speaking/hearing/responding dimensions of oracy underpin exploratory discourse or talk. Exploratory talk involving pairs, small groups and the whole class, is central to writing in all its shapes and form, including extended or discursive writing. It enables pupils

■ to reflect upon ideas, thoughts and information;

■ to monitor, re-organise, structure and shape their thinking;

■ to relate 'new' knowledge to the old;

■ to record such talk through exploratory writing that can help inform and shape extended and discursive writing.

Exploratory talk and writing underpins pupils' initial writing phase in which they record words, phrases and sentences that can help shape both 'expressive' and extended and discursive writing. Expressive writing is rough work that gives full rein to pupil thinking without the constraints of being grammatically accurate in terms of spelling and syntax. Expressive writing is personal, private – it enables the pupil to express fully what he or she knows and understands.

Classroom culture

Speaking, hearing/listening, responding and *exploratory discourse* do not occur in a vacuum: they depend upon the classroom culture that reflects the beliefs, values, attitudes and expectations of the teacher and the school; the teacher and the school's orientation. Culture shapes teaching styles and the relationships between teachers and pupils.

REFLECTION

Review your last full day's teaching. Reflect upon what role oracy played in it in relation to:

- individual, social and personal speech – what was its role, how much of it occurred;
- hearing and responding;
- exploratory talk: when did it occur, what form did it take, what was its value;
- the classroom culture that you have in relation to oracy;
- the classroom culture you would like to develop involving oracy.

What is the role of oracy in history classrooms?

In history classrooms we develop children's oracy through asking children to:

- question, predict, raise doubts, speculate, hypothesise;

- problem-solve;

- defend conclusions reached;

- explain their thinking processes, ideas and conclusions and upon what they are based;

- evaluate their own learning;

- discuss in pairs;

- pose questions;

- set the agenda;

- enquire;

- reach agreement on meaning;

- develop and and refine ideas;

- work as teams usually of four pupils on an historical task;

- debate in a large group or whole class setting;

- participate in simulation, role play and drama.

What does oracy involve?

Oracy is an integral element of teaching in which teacher and pupil interaction involves individual, pair, small group, large group and the whole class interactions (see table 3.1).

The rest of this chapter explores oracy in the context of individual, pair, small group and whole class teaching. We have left out large group oracy as it is relatively uncommon.

TABLE 3.1 Interactive whole class teaching

Interactive whole class teaching: classroom interaction and oracy.

Mode of working			*Teacher active*	*Teacher inactive*	*No. of pupils involved*
O1a	SINGLE	Pupil private study from reading to writing without teacher support. Can involve individual speech		√	1
O1b		Pupil private study from reading to writing with teacher support	√		1
O1c		Teacher-pupil coaching/mentoring	√		1
O1d		Pupil to whole class	√	√	1
O2a	PAIR	Pair work – pupils work in pairs independently		√	2
O2b		Teacher works with a pair	√		2
O2c		Pairs report to small groups, large groups or the whole class	√	√	2
O3a	SMALL TEAMS	Small team work: pupils work independently as small groups		√	3–4
O3b		Small team work: teacher works with the group	√		3–4
O3c		Small teams report to large groups or to the whole class	√	√	2
O4a	LARGE TEAMS	Large team work: pupils work independently as large groups		√	5–17
O4b		Large team work: teacher works with the group	√		5–17
O4c		Large teams report to small groups or to the whole class	√	√	2
O5a	WHOLE CLASS	Whole class – whole class runs the activity independently of the teacher		√	20–35
O5b		Whole class – teacher in charge of the whole class's teaching that can involve individual, small, large group and whole class feedback and involvement.	√		20–35

Oracy in the classroom [1]: individual pupil participation

An example from the opening episodes of a lesson on The Roman Town reveals how a class of Year 3 and 4 pupils were able to develop writing at word, phrase and sentence level, from individual oral contributions to a teacher-led whole class activity as shown in figure 3.2. The lesson was on The Roman Town. The resource the pupils used was a painting by Alan Sorrel, a detailed reconstruction of the forum at Verulamium. The original is in St Albans Museum. (http://www.stalbansmuseums.org.uk/content/view/full/14438). Of course this strategy could be used with any painting. A lesson objective was to build up pupil vocabulary and develop understanding of Roman town life.

The lesson ran as follows:

The Roman Town

EPISODE 1 – VOCABULARY

Focus: Reading a picture – teasing out the picture's meaning using an 'I spy with my little eye' game to build up vocabulary and insights into the scene.

I gave out copies of the picture of Roman St Albans, one per pair/trio of pupils, telling the class we were going to play the game 'I spy with my little eye'. After making sure all of the class understood the rules, I split the class into two teams, teams A and B.

One member of team A had to ask Team B to find an object in the picture beginning with a letter of the alphabet. 'I spy with my little eye something beginning with [a letter of the alphabet].'

The members of Team B had three attempts to answer the question correctly. If they got the right answer they received one mark, if they failed, team A got the mark.

Sinead began with: 'I spy with my little eye, something beginning with L.' Annika from Team B gave the correct answer: lady. Team B got a mark.

The person who had answered correctly then asked Team A a question. We kept the score on the whiteboard. Great excitement and pleasure from the pupils during the playing of the game. We listed the words on the board. Among them were:

building, castle, city, cloud, dog, food, people, roof, stall, statue, temple, tent, wall.

EPISODE 2 – PHRASES

Focus: Holistic impression of picture: title of the picture for a children's book.
I told the children that they had been given the picture to put in their books.
They had to think of a title and put it on top – this they did in pairs.
We listed the titles on the board, and talked about them. Titles included:

Roman History, Roman Picture, Roman Feature, A Town Called Robeeta, Roman City Centre, Romans in History.

I liked Adam's best: 'Cracking City Centre.'

EPISODE 3 – SENTENCES

Focus: Getting deeper into the picture and bringing it to life.

I asked the children to put their fingers on two dogs in the picture and to look for the lady with a cloak and two children.

Then I said, 'Imagine that you are one of the two children with the lady, watching the dancer.'

One of the children lives in the town, the other is a friend who has come from the country. You will be the guide to that child.

Working in pairs, in their drafting books they had to put down what they would see, hear, smell, taste, feel.

Pairs then reported back to the whole class: Josh and Kieran smelt *the Roman baths, felt a cake, saw people dancing and watched a show, while Adam and Helena smelt drinks, fish and air, saw dancing, saw statues, buildings, and people watching.*

For the rest of the teaching, see the case study in chapter 10, p. 159–62.

REFLECTION

Consider the relationship in the teaching account of pupil-teacher interaction of oracy to pupil development of word, sentence and phrase level knowledge.

How might you take the ideas in the 'I spy with my little eye' account and the pedagogy involved into your own teaching?

Oracy in the classroom [2]: pupils working in pairs

The oracy that pupil pair work makes possible underpinned a lesson with a class of thirty Year 5, mixed-ability pupils, in an inner-city Birmingham school. The pupils had to solve a history mystery as history detectives investigating a murder mystery, the death of a body found on the edge of a peat bog.

The lesson opened with a brief recap of the previous week's work in which the class had listened to an oral retelling of part of the story of Beowulf and Grendel, then found out about myths and legends. The lesson began with a whole class question and answer episode. It then moved on to pupils working in pairs. The account is an extract from the teacher's reflective diary.

EPISODE 1 – STARTING WITH THE WORLD OF THE PUPIL

The opening episode began with me asking the class if, 'at the weekend or during your last school holidays have you been on any walks or taken part in any other outdoor activities?' Numerous hands shot up. In turn I asked individual pupils to tell us their answer. As a class we discussed each response in turn. One girl said that she and her mum and dad had taken their dog for a walk in the country. This was the perfect opportunity for me to introduce on the whiteboard a country scene, for the pupils to study and work upon in pairs. The photograph was of Nebelgard Fen, in Jutland, Denmark (see Images for Nebelgard Fen Jutland, www.google.co).

EPISODE 2 – CHALLENGE AND PROBLEM SOLVING

I divided the pupils into pairs giving each pair a copy of the photograph with space around its perimeter to write upon/annotate and each pupil a sheet of blank paper for drawing. The pupils discussed the picture and drew a quick outline sketch of the main features of the picture showed – this was a technique they were used to. Each pair had to discuss and agree upon a title for their picture and what main colours the picture might have had, i.e. blue sky, green trees, brown or light green grass. They wrote their colours on the features their outline sketches showed.

EPISODE 3 – TEACHER QUESTIONS AND PUPIL RESPONSES

I then helped the children bring the picture to life with a series of questions:

- *What could they see?*

- *What animals and birds might live there?*

- *What sounds might they hear?*

- *What smells might they smell?*

- *Walking through the meadow, woods and swamp land what feelings, sensations might they have?*

The pupil pairs discussed the questions. On the flip chart I listed what they could

see: *hills, woods, forest, pond, sky, field, lake, reeds, tree – branches, twigs, bushes, grass, forest*

possible colours: *green grass, dark green forest, yellow, dark brown?; light blue sky*

animals, which might be there: *rabbits, bears, deer, foxes, badgers, farm animals, red squirrels*

sounds they might hear: *rustling of the grass / trees; water rippling; splashing; birds* twittering. NB – more thoughtful and imaginative responses here rather than just simple nouns

possible smells: *damp earth*

EPISODE 4 – TIME TRAVEL: HARRY POTTER AND HERMIONE

I told the class that we were travelling back in time with Harry Potter and Hermione – they were the children on a walk when Hermione had taken the photograph of Nebegard Fen, which we had studied in chapter 2. In the distance, close to the lake, the children could see a group of men standing around leaning on their shovels. The workers were looking at something in the soil that one of them had just uncovered. Again I prompted the children's thinking, through asking them quickly to discuss, in pairs, ideas of what they might be looking at. I fielded replies that ranged from:

Beowulf, body, coffin, dead rabbit, Grendel, Grendel's arm, kidnapped person, knife to *bones from the children the troll may have been feasting on.* [NB the children had just been studying Beowulf in English.]

EPISODE 5 – SOURCE WORK: CHALLENGE

At this point I put on the whiteboard an image of what the peat cutters were looking at – the head of Grauballe Man. (Many images of Grauballe Man can be found on Google, but again cannot be downloaded, so must be looked at online.) There was an expectant atmosphere and muted gasps. We asked for immediate single word or phrase reactions. These included:

> *feel sick; gross; shock; disgusting; 'What do I do?' shout – 'Help!' 'run off screaming to police.*

In their pairs the pupils then discussed what they thought the photograph showed. I listed pairs' comments on the board:

- *Body trying to get out of ground*
- *Dead body*
- *Grendel's hostage buried*
- *Human tissue*
- *Looks like voodoo in 'King Kong'*
- *Man or a lady's head and arm*
- *Murderer had killed a man and covered him in – buried (the body) [two comments]*
- *Grendel because we can't see both arms [one had been left in Beowulf's grasp]*
- *Person sunk*
- *Person trapped in swamp*
- *Sunk person in a bog*
- *What the troll had been feasting on*
- *Person attacked*
- *Old peat cutter had fallen in hole*

A pair of pupils began speculating aloud:

- *Might not be old, but could be*
- *Looks as if it's been there quite a while – rotting*

EPISODE 6 – PUPIL QUESTIONS AND QUESTIONING

I asked the class: what questions would they ask about the photograph of the head? A hand shot up. One child pre-empted the next part of the lesson by saying we should ask questions using the trigger words:

Who? What? Where? When? How? Why?

The pupils discussed what questions they would ask in pairs. We wrote up the pairs' responses on a flip chart:

- *Who do you think it is?*
- *Did you see anyone acting suspiciously?*
- *What is on its face?*
- *When did it (the event?) happen*
- *How did he die?*
- *When did he die?*
- *How did he get there?*
- *Did anyone recognise him?*
- *What are the curious scratches on his face?*
- *Who did this?*
- *What did this?*
- *Who killed him or her?*
- *Has anyone been missing?*
- *Who might have done something like this?*
- *Who or what went missing, and when?*
- *Where did he live?*
- *How old is he?*
- *How long do you think he was down there?*
- *What's it doing down there?*

(continued)

(continued)

- *Did anyone see anyone or anything wandering around?*

- *Did he want to die?*

- *Is there anyone (locally) in the village who might do this?*

- *Where was he going?*

- *How deep did the peat cutters dig?*

- *What was the exact position*

- *Did a peat cutter look suspicious?*

The lesson then moved on to the pupils investigating the mystery in teams of four.

REFLECTION

Read through the lesson account. Use table 3.2 to annotate the kinds of classroom interaction that resulted in pupils writing at word, phrase and sentence levels.

Consider how oracy enhanced the pupils' learning and how it might support their subsequent extended and discursive writing.

Relate the teaching and related learning to the Nuffield Primary History Project's teaching principles, table 3.3 and the learning principles of Cognitive Acceleration in History Education (CACHE) table 3.4, upon which the lesson was based.

TABLE 3.2 Note the kinds of classroom interaction that resulted in pupils writing at word, phrase and sentence levels.

Oracy element: pupils	Extensively	Much	Some	None
Question				
Predict				
Raise doubts				
Speculate				
Hypothesise				
Evaluate their own learning				

Oracy element: pupils	Extensively	Much	Some	None
Explain their thinking processes, ideas and conclusions and upon what they are based				
Problem solve				
Defend conclusions reached				
Discuss in pairs and small group to:				
Pose questions				
Set the agenda				
Enquire				
Reach agreement on meaning				
Develop and refine ideas				
Debate in a large group or whole class setting				
Participate in simulation, role play and drama				

TABLE 3.3 Nuffield Primary Project's teaching principles.

Nuffield Primary History Project – Principles

1 Challenge
Challenge the pupils throughout facing them with problems to solve.

2 Questioning
Pupil and teacher questioning drive on genuine historical learning.

3 Study in depth
Study in detail/depth is the only way to achieve genuine understanding.

4 Authenticity
Where possible use real, authentic sources.

5 Economy of resources
Use the minimum amount of resources needed.

6 Accessibility – mediation
The teacher mediates the learning: he or she makes the past accessible to the pupils and provides guidance and support as needed.

7 Communication
The pupils should communicate what they have learnt to an audience using an appropriate mode and genre.

TABLE 3.4 Nuffield Principles for acceleration in history education.

Cognitive Acceleration in History Education [CACHE]

Cognitive Acceleration argues that we have a single, general cognitive processor that underpins our overall cognitive development. Factors that affect the development of the general cognitive processor are:

1 Schemata – thinking tools
Cognitive development involves the production of schemata that develop in response to environmental stimuli. Schemata are 'thinking 'tools' that provide pupils with a mental toolkit. For example, a concept map is a schema, as is a writing frame. They develop from the schemata pupils already have, linked to element 2, concrete preparation.

2 Concrete preparation
The pupils need to have assimilated the context in which their learning develops, including understanding the situation/information involved, mastery of the vocabulary they need to think and discuss it: the procedures they can follow: the processes, skills and concepts that they will use and develop in their schema. Learning has to build upon secure, established foundations. It grows out of the world of the child, the immediate, the known, the concrete.

3 Cognitive conflict
The mind develops in response to challenge – so continuously face the children with a challenge[s] or problem to solve. Ideally the pupil cannot solve the challenge or problem on his or her own: it has to be done cooperatively, shared through shared learning based upon oracy (see point 4).

4 Social learning
Pupils have to solve problems through working with other pupils. Social learning depends upon a socially cohesive, non-threatening, supportive co-operative environment. Here there is freedom to argue, to discuss, to debate, to hypothesise, to imagine and even fantasise, i.e. oracy, and to work together as a pair, group or team with or without teacher support. But, such teamwork has to have clear goals, rules and regulations. Central to co-operative learning is the idea that children have complementary roles needed to solve the problem. In this way they can move towards a common solution beyond their individual capacities and thus solve the problem[s] they are working upon.

5 Metacognition
Pupils should develop the ability to think-about-thinking so as to rationalise the thinking involved. To be metacognitive the children need to have both the vocabulary, the phraseology, the discourse [oracy] and the training to think metacognitively. It is what, we call 'reflection', the ability to rationalise and analyse what problem solving involves, and to see how the problem solving process – its protocols / heuristics – can be applied to solve analogous problems in the future (see point 6).

6 Bridging
Pupils should be able to transfer and apply the newly developed problem solving skills both within history and across a range of other subjects / situations. This means transferability, the 'new thought processes must be made available across a wide range of contexts' (Shayer and Adey 2002).

TABLE 3.4 *(continued)*

> **7 Teacher mediation**
> The teacher provides information, suggestions, structures, scaffolds and supports at each stage of the problem solving. The teacher works closely and continuously with the pupil to support learning, providing training in skills and procedures as and when necessary. This is guided learning. The teacher's role is central and continuous.
>
> **8 Mastery learning**
> Pupil engagement on any task must be individualised, taking into account baseline assessment of needs, aptitudes, context and situation. Crucially, learning should last as long as it takes for the pupil to master that task. While this idea at one level is laughably obvious and simple, at another level it has very, very profound implications for practice (Block 1971).

Oracy in the classroom [3]: pupils working as teams of four or five

Oracy plays a major role in pupils working as teams, usually as groups of four. Discourse is the medium through which the team solves problems and reaches fully argued and evidenced conclusions, probably beyond them as individuals. Working as a team of historical investigators involves:

a   team members having separate team tasks: team leader, reporter, note taker, manager of resources and observer;

b   taking roles as investigators such as archaeologist, detective, historian, newspaper reporter, policeman, pupil, spy and TV programme maker;

c   as a team agreeing upon a plan for their investigation, including initial questions;

d   oracy as the working medium for teamwork from the initial setting of an agenda and related questioning through discussing and sharing information, ideas and solutions to reaching conclusions and reporting findings. The exploratory talk involves results in:

e   writing in a number of modes from jottings, notes, speculative-expressive thoughts, completing scaffolds, concept webs, mini-writing frames and writing frames to help produce extended and discursive writing.

History investigations involve pupils working in teams with three or four members, usually four. The example of oracy below is taken from the investigation of the contents of a suitcase.

Investigating a suitcase

The activity draws upon and develops the skills and processes of historical enquiry – 'Doing History'. The lesson is based upon both the teaching principles of the Nuffield Primary History Project (table 3.5) and the learning principles of Cognitive Acceleration in History Education (table 3.4). The suitcase contained a collection of clues that enables the pupils to find out about its owner. We have used the suitcase exercise dozens of times both in Britain and abroad: it always fully engages the children. The account below is typical of the teaching. It indicates the scale and nature of the oracy involved.

TABLE 3.5 Pupil's responses to the suitcase clues.

REPORT FORM		
Your name:		**Date:**
Whose suitcase was it?		
Surname:		
Forename[s]:		
Where she lived – address:		
List of things in the suitcase:		
You can draw a picture of the person, showing what she was like [with title, label, captions, colours] on a *separate piece* of **paper**		
What I think she was like? Brainstorm ideas about her. Jot them down below:		
1 2 3 4 5 6 7 8 9 10 11		

The teaching

The suitcase: the teaching activity

EPISODE 1

Focus – the dramatic opening: the policeman. Involving the pupils immediately in a gripping drama, that links straight into their own lives.

The policeman. I walked in and took on the role of a policeman. 'Hallo, hallo, hallo, what have we got here?' A suitcase. etc. etc. As the policeman I accused the teacher, Linda, of having stolen it. She vehemently denied the accusation.

The history detectives. We now posed the problem to the class of what we should do with the suitcase. They were now cast in the role of history detectives helping us in the investigation of the suitcase.

EPISODE 2

Focus – the initial questions: Involving the pupils in creating and pooling the initial questions

Jotters. We wanted the pupils to come up with questions about the suitcase. In pairs the children had to think of questions they would ask about the suitcase and its contents, as if policemen, then write them down in their rough jotters.

On the whiteboard I fielded answers from the class – they included:

1   *What is in the suitcase?*

2   *How and why is it here?*

3   *How old is it?*

4   *Who put it here?*

5   *Do you think it is safe?*

6   *Have you found out what is inside?*

EPISODE 3

Focus – opening the suitcase: investigating the contents

Group work. We divided the class into seven groups of four to five pupils. These were organised deliberately so that there was a fluent, confident reader in each group.

We organised the groups according to a Canadian scheme for pupils working as a group, a team, and not as individuals in a group. Each group member took one of these roles:

(continued)

(continued)

1   A recorder of what happened.

2   A reporter of what the group had discovered to the rest of the class.

3   A resources manager.

4   An observer of how well the group worked.

Volunteers. We asked for volunteers to open the suitcase. Despite fears of a bomb, there was a rush of children willing to open the suitcase. Maria gingerly unlocked it, revealing the contents. She returned to her group. Next . . . .

The lucky dip. I took the suitcase around the groups, the resource manager in each case picking out two objects. We circulated the class twice, until the suitcase was empty. The pupils eagerly examined and discussed their clues as we moved from table to table.

EPISODE 4

Focus – working on the clues. Building up a mental picture of the owner

The Report Form. We gave the pupils a *Report Form* each. They had to fill this in using the clues.

Circulating. So, with seven sets of clues on seven tables, we got the pupils to circulate in an orderly, clockwise manner. On the word change, each group moved to the next table. Lots and lots of animated, focused discussion. This part of the lesson continued until the seven groups had visited all seven tables, worked through all the clues and completed their sheets in terms of name, address and contents.

EPISODE 5

Focus – developing questions

The lesson now took an interesting, and rewarding turn. The brainstorm list of points on the *Report Sheet* turned into a list of new questions. So we went round the class. Each table produced one question, and the responder then asked another pupil from another table [different gender] to come up with another question. The list of questions read:

- *Did she have any hobbies?*

- *What is she like?*

- *Who did she look like?*

- *What school did she go to?*

- *What was her school like?*

- *Did she have pets?*

- *Did she travel?*

■ *Has she got brothers and sisters?*

■ *Did she like toys?*

■ *Did she go on holiday?*

■ *Did she go to the Isle of Scillies?*

EPISODE 6

Focus– the information network – answering the questions

The information network. I realised that we could use the questions as the basis for a information network, a concept web, using the information already on their Report Sheets and the questions. This we built up on the whiteboard.

Answering the questions. On the board we listed feedback about each heading, for example, for *toys*:

'liked barbies', school, 'learnt French, good school report, Year 1 pupil, Stoke Hill First School', hobbies 'liked skipping, played, read, liked drawing, music', looked like 'short brown hair, pale skin'.

The first six episodes of the lesson had laid the foundations for the pupil's extended and discursive writing – see chapter 10 on pages 153–156 – the final element in the investigation was a classroom discussion and debate.

Pupils analyse ways in which team members work together

An interview of pupils solving The Body in the Bog mystery (chapter 2, p. 23) shows the oracy process at work with team members dividing the work up between them before pooling ideas and findings:

Pupil 9: What we would do is look for clues; ask questions; and sort out the clues . . . ask villagers; find out what would happen at the end . . . and the questions: we would ask what happened? Why did it happen? When did it happen? How did it happen? (We need) to find out the reason of death; the location of (the) death.

REFLECTION

Read through the account, noting how oracy helped the pupils develop their investigation and the language they used.

The Report Form, (table 3.5) is typical of the scaffolds / frames we use to support pupil preparatory writing.

What benefits do you think a scaffold / frame like this has for helping pupils' extended and discursive writing?

Oracy in the classroom [4]: whole class discussion and debate

When pupils work in teams, solving the same problem, the final element in the teaching is a classroom discussion or debate to decide which interpretation is the most convincing.

A class of nine to ten-year-olds investigating The Body in the Bog mystery in eight groups of three or four worked upon a set of clues about the body and came up with a range of interpretations. These the class debated, in a session in which, taking turns, each group's reporters gave the group's conclusion and upon what it was based, followed by a whole class discussion:

- two groups decided a local farmer had killed Red Christian in a row over a girl friend;

- two groups decided that a local old man was responsible for Red Christian's death;

- two groups thought that Red Christian had fallen into the bog when going home drunk;

- one group could not decide and gave three possible scenarios;

- the final group to report argued, 'We don't think it's Red Christian. The cauldron's from the Iron Age. It could have been a Roman because Tacitus wrote about them.'

The class then talked about how the body could be scientifically dated. Two pupils mentioned forensic tests on bones or mummies. We told the groups that there were problems with dating the body using Carbon 14 when it was found, due to radioactive material in the atmosphere from 1952 USSR and USA atomic bomb tests. However, when Carbon 14 tests resumed, they revealed that the body was c.1,500 years old: it was from the Iron Age and not the recent past. The investigative phase of the lesson was over. The pupils were now able to use what they had learned and their exploratory written work to help produce their extended and discursive writing.

Conclusion

There is widespread recognition of the value of oracy in developing pupil knowledge and understanding: in this chapter we have tried to present a framework where a pattern of teaching incorporates oracy as a permanent, pervasive, ever present element. It reflects the argument that pupil learning should draw upon social learning as much as independent study. Social learning provides an additional dimension to pedagogy – its benefits are already widely recognised through role-play, drama and simulation. Here we have extended the argument to all phases of pupils 'Doing History' which have oracy at their heart, i.e. using the high level thinking, organisational, procedural and linguistic skills of history as an academic discipline. Oracy, through its exploratory language, lays the foundations for pupils extended and discursive writing, a theme we explore in chapters 2 and 10.

References

Alexander, R. (2012) Extended and referenced version of a presentation given at the DfE seminar on Oracy, the National Curriculum and Educational Standards, 20 February 2012.
Block, J. (1971) *Mastery Learning: theory and practice*, Austin, Texas: Holt, Rinehart & Winston.
Dean, J. (2013) Nuffield Primary History Project, available online at www.history.org.

Deary, T. (1998) *Terrifying Tudors*, London: Scholastic.

Department for Education (DfE) (July 2013) The National Curriculum in England Framework document available online at www.gov.uk/dfe/nationalcurriculum (accessed 11.02.2014).

Department of Education and Science (DES) (1975) The Bullock Report, A Language for Life, London: HMSO, available online at http://www.educationengland.org.uk/documents/bullock/bullock1975.html (accessed 11.02.2014).

Department for Education and Science (DES) (1991) The National Curriculum, London: HMSO.

Mercer, N. (1995) *The Guided Construction of Knowledge: talk amongst teachers and learners*, Clevedon, UK: Multilingual Matters Ltd.

Shayer, M. and Adey, P. (2002) *Learning Intelligence*, Maidenhead: The Open University Press.

Wilkinson, A. (1965) The concept of oracy, *English in Education*, Vol. 2, issue A2: 3–5.

Wilkinson, A. (1970) The role of literature, *English in Education*, Vol. 4, issue 2: 4.

Talk, reading and writing in breadth and depth studies

Hilary Cooper

History is an unending search for truth with the only certainty . . . that there will always be more to be said and before long others will say it.

(G. R. Elton 1967)

For analysis, especially in depth, you need to study selected topics, even if it has to be within a broader chronological context.

(Richard J. Evans 2012)

The National Curriculum 2013

The new National Curriculum for History (DfE 2013) requires Key Stage 2 children, to 'develop a chronologically secure knowledge and understanding of British, local and world history, establishing clear narratives within and across the periods they study. However, through a combination of overview and depth studies they should also learn to engage with the processes of *historical enquiry*: to note connections, contrasts and trends over time, use *proper historical terms*, *address* and *devise valid questions* about change, cause, similarity and difference and significance. They should *select and organise relevant historical information*, understand how knowledge of the past is *constructed from sources*.

Children at Key Stage 2 then, are expected to have a broad chronological overview, (taking into account local studies and themes beyond 1066), from ancient civilisations until recent times, but also to learn the processes by which we find out about the past.

To explore the relationship between breadth studies and depth studies, which this requires, it is helpful to trace the thinking of philosophers of history over the past fifty years, as they moved from seeing history as essentially a narrative, constructed by linking causes with effects, but gradually analysed the reasons why this approach is far too simplistic and that the ways in which finding out about and understanding the past is complex and controversial and depends on discussion and dialogue.

Structuralist theory: history as an overarching narrative

'Structuralism' originated in the 1900s, in the linguistic theory of Saussure (recent translation 2006). This emphasised that the elements of a culture must be understood by their relationship to a larger, overarching structure. Hayden White (1973) and Danto (1965) argued that historical narratives consist of tracing and explaining the causes of a series of past events in a linear sequence. Gallie (1964: 66) claimed that history is a type of story, a narrative of action and that it is the human content of these narratives that makes them comprehensible. Mink (1966) claimed that the *structure* of narrative history is what gives history a claim to be a contribution to knowledge, a means to seeing and understanding things, that narrative represents the structure of the reality of the past and is not a construct made by historians. Olafson (1970) added that the historical process consists of the reconstruction of a series of human actions, each one leading to the next, because human beings are purposeful and goal-directed. Lemon (1995) continued the argument, saying that human reality is a world of 'story-objects', sequences of occurrences, which constitute a unity, and that it is the job of the historian to 'uncover' these stories. Historians, he says, *must* concentrate on the actions of individuals, in order to locate 'intelligible continuity' in the real world (pp. 81–3).

Structuralist theory and the grand narrative

By the 1960s the discipline of history had expanded to include, for example, economic, social and cultural, local, global and national history. So philosophers of history, trying to counteract expansion of the discipline into new areas, tried to define exactly what was meant by 'history'. Influenced by structuralist theories of the 'big picture', they defined history as a 'grand narrative of the past'. Narrative knowledge is knowledge in the form of storytelling. In tribal times grand narrative was disseminated as myth, for example in the *Iliad, Odyssey* and *Beowulf*. Later, in the worlds of Christianity and Islam, values and beliefs were embedded in the narrative, for example, in Bede's *Ecclesiatical History of the English People* and in *The Koran*.

Initially structuralism resulted in a revival of the idea of history as a 'grand narrative' of the past. In terms of English schooling in the 1960s the British 'grand narrative' was the dominant, even the only, history, that was taught (Cannadine et al. 2012: 44–5). This grand narrative, known as *The Whig Interpretation of History* (Butterfield 1965), was central to the continuing debates about the form that history education should take (Evans 2011). It was argued that what is distinctive about the discipline of history is its story-telling character, tracing the causes and explanations of sequences of human actions and events.

This not only explained but also legitimised knowledge conveyed by the grand narrative. A grand narrative or metanarrative is an abstract idea, supposed to be a comprehensive explanation of historical experience or knowledge, which encompasses and explains other smaller stories.

Structuralists, mostly American and French philosophers, had a significant impact on historians and history educationists, with their arguments about narrative history emphasising the major importance of pupils' historical composition. As such, history was at the centre of pupils' overall development of literacy and their ability to communicate their knowledge and understanding of the past.

A grand narrative consists of a sequence of stories with a beginning, a plot and an end, which might convey significant meaning, usually about a society's emerging sense of identity and its subsequent development. It often reflects unexamined cultural values (for example the importance of technological progress) and political ideology (for example the assumed inevitable benefits of democracy for any society). It may reinforce our existing actions and beliefs. Grand narratives that trace sequences of human actions generally focus upon the actions of 'great men' who impact upon, shape and determine what occurs, ignoring those who oppose their decisions. Grand narrative history, which assumes that actions are sequential, because human beings are 'goal oriented' and act to achieve outcomes, tends to be political history.

Post structuralist theory

But in the late 1960s and 1970s many of the basic claims of structuralism were challenged, mainly by French intellectuals and in particular by the philosopher and historian Foucault and the literary critic Roland Barthes. By the 1970s and 80s philosophers reacted to structuralism with alternative 'post structuralist' theories. They criticised structuralism for its rigidity and for its historicism (the notion that there are inexorable laws of idealistic human destiny). Post structuralists argued that there can be no stable human sciences because human beings are such complex creatures.

Derrida's Theory of Difference (1978) claimed that meaning is inherently uncertain and contestable; for example FISH conveys an image of a fish, but not an image of any particular kind of fish. Therefore the reader of a text is involved in the process of interpreting the text. The reader has to deconstruct the text and this indicates a new kind of reading. Deconstruction does not mean destruction, but analysis and understanding of the text, so that the reader creates a personal meaning. So what did post structuralism mean for the grand historical narrative?

Post structuralism and history

'History is . . . what has happened, what is thought to have happened, what some claim to have happened . . . There is no received truth, just a tenuous thread of events amongst a whirlpool of dispute and conflicting interpretation . . . but the past is real' (Lively 2013: 138).

As analysis of what is meant by narrative history deepened, some philosophers became critical of the claims made for it. In history intentions almost never lead to the intended outcomes. (Did Luther set out to break up the Catholic Church?) And many events in grand narratives are not the result of 'great men' but of the actions of groups or economic, cultural or social processes and movements.

Mandelbaum (1967) said that, even in the most favourable examples, when the specific events are traced (from 'a' to 'b' to 'c' and so on) they are overwhelmingly assumed to be the decisions and actions of one individual; a simple narrative view is unconvincing because it ignores the complexity of causation. As an example he says that an account of an election campaign, in which each event is assumed to be causally connected to a previous and later event, would be a gross distortion, because it would ignore the interests, disaffections and needs of different economic, geographic and ethnic groups.

Similarly a biography, which is a linear sequence of causal events, is an oversimplification, because events must be seen in the context of the person's personality and of the society in which s/he lived, if the person's activities are to be understood. Historiography examines connections between parts to the whole, not linear sequences of events.

Mink (1966) had originally defended narrative history but later argued (1978) that it is an imaginative construction, which cannot defend its claim to truth by any accepted procedure of argument or authentication. He concluded that stories are told but not lived. Life does not have beginnings, middles and ends, and so narrative qualities should not be transferred from art to life.

According to Lyotard (1979), in the postmodern period belief in grand narratives disappeared, in the face of personal interpretations and subjective narratives from a range of positions and perspectives. As such, each person's 'history' was as truthful as anyone else's. Grand narratives are homogenous and ignore heterogeneity, i.e. competing and alternative narratives. Grand narratives have the status of a transcendent and universal truth, a 'truth' that ruling elites and their governance create, implement and enforce. As such, they are specious interpretations that are untrustworthy. Grand narratives created to legitimise the ruling elite's version of the truth have no legitimacy, being tendentious, partial, subjective and inaccurate.

Indeed, the leading theorist on postmodernism and history, Hayden White (1981), concluded that the value of narrative to represent reality is nil. Lyotard suggested that grand narratives should give way to modest, localised narratives, focusing on the diversity of human experience and on a multiplicity of standpoints.

Post structuralist history and history education

The next section of this chapter aims to demonstrate a synthesis between the post structuralists' claims about the nature of history and the processes of historical enquiry identified in the extensive discourse on history education since the 1970s, exemplified in the National Curriculum for History (DfE 2013). It will show how children's engagement in each stage of the processes of historical enquiry is consistent with the post structuralists' analysis of the writing of narrative history.

The statutory curriculum for history

Readers will recognise that the following processes constitute the Purpose of Study and Aims of the English National Curriculum for History 2013. They are outlined below in slightly different groupings:

- Equip pupils to ask perceptive questions; to frame historically valid questions.

- Understand methods of historical enquiry, including how evidence is used rigorously to make historical claims.

- Understand the history of these islands in a coherent historical narrative.

- Understand concepts such as continuity and change, similarity, difference and significance and use them to make connections, contrast and analyse trends.

- Discern how and why contrasting arguments and interpretations of the past are constructed.

- Create structured accounts, including written narratives and analyses.

As the philosophers of history challenged and contested each other's arguments the post structuralist position deepened to eventually encompass each of these processes, within a theory of narrative history. The following section will analyse how this came about, considering each process in turn and its implications for the teaching of history.

Asking questions

Theory

It is significant that history is seen as beginning with a question (rather than an account, told for political, moral or other reasons). Mandelbaum (1967) argued that if it *is* the aim of an historian to recount a sequence of events this is not represented by the model of telling a story, because s/he is engaged in an *enquiry* to establish what actually occurred. R.G. Collingwood (1939, 1946), whose analysis of history as a discipline underpinned the development of radical new approaches to teaching history in Britain from the 1970s, identified the asking of questions as central to history as an academic discipline. Without questions there is no history: questions and questioning drive historical enquiry forward, triggering off the process that ends in the construction of an answer or answers to the original and subsequent questions. Resolution can take many forms, including a story, narrative, account or analysis.

Hobsbawm (1980: 4) refuted the claim made by Stone (1979) that there had been a revival of 'the grand narrative'. Hobsbawm (1984: 4) said that, 'The Event, the individual, even the recapture of some mood or way of thinking of the past are not ends in themselves, but the means of illuminating some wider question, which goes far beyond the particular story and its characters.'

Olafson (1979) points out that questions are not necessarily about the actions of individuals. The Irish famine (1846–9) was the result of a natural event, crop failure, not of an individual action. Historians of the famine, like Woodham-Smith (1962), have therefore asked what could have been done in the circumstances, to prevent the starvation. Was the famine controllable or unpreventable? If it might have been prevented what was done to prevent it? Why was this not successful? If nothing was attempted, why not? Were things considered and rejected? If so, why?

Asking questions

Practice

Intellectually children benefit little from being passively told about a person's actions or an event. They need to engage with it, so that it becomes part of what constructivists call their own 'mental map' (Cooper 2012: 21–3; 99, 161, 24, 69, 151, 158). They need either to ask and research their own or others' questions about a topic, or having heard an account, discuss questions it raises for them, and research them further, in order to construct their own accounts, based on what they discover. These questions may involve finding out more about the time in which the event occurred. In our teaching we should encourage children to ask a full range of questions, which historians and philosophers argue, are the backbone of history.

Making inferences from sources

Theory

Mandelbaum (1967) argued that we expect historians to engage in research, to weigh alternative possibilities and to *marshal evidence* that leads them to support one of the possibilities. Olafson (1970) concluded that it is not sufficient to record human actions. An historian must attempt to interpret them; to consider the person's perceptions, motivations and calculations. In 1979 he said that the historian does not focus on the sequential, but on analysis of evidence and arguments, which embed narrative in the wider patterns of culture. He stressed the importance of the role of evidence in limiting and validating narrative structure, which depends on non-narrative description and analysis. For example, the execution of Charles 1 depended on human actions, but these were embedded in social and economic issues, involving different social groups.

Although Elton (1970) defended the idea of accounts of the past based on the causes of human action, reason and thought, he claimed that what distinguishes history as a discipline is the role of evidence in generating and limiting, as well as validating the statements of historians. He said that the historical method consists of the critical examination of evidence. Interpretations of the past must arise from the evidence. The veracity of an account should be judged against all known evidence. But Elton (1967) was clear that inferences have to be made from evidence, because of the fragmented nature of surviving evidence. Hexter (1971) like Elton, a practising historian, who recognised the primacy of explanatory narrative accounts, formulated what he called the Reality Rule, that is, that accounts must be rooted in and adhering to, the historical evidence. Hexter argued strongly that historical accounts, analyses, reconstruction and interpretations draw upon what the historian brought to the record of the past – his or her 'second record'.

Making inferences from sources

Practice

The academic debate on the nature and role of history since the 1960s has reinforced the role, in history education, of teaching children how to write history that is evidentially based and fully argued, in a full range of macro-genres, including recounts, reports, persuasions, debates, analytical narratives, biographies, short stories and historical fiction. In turn, these genres can be multi-modal, drawing upon the opportunities that digital communication provides to produce history in a multiplicity of micro-genres that can incorporate text, pictures, sound, moving images and a full range of text, fonts and design features. Pupils' writing in history is a social process, involving the overview, guidance and support of the teacher – who provides for the pupil a scaffold to support, sustain and validate the histories the pupils construct.

Children can now research major national events using a wealth of digital sources, a significant, epochal change of the past ten years – something that was previously impossible (Cooper 2012: 180–2). They can also engage with local evidence, relating to a national event or change and consider ways it relates to the bigger picture. The historical association's *Primary History* journal has produced several examples of this occurring, including a History Club in which pupils researched a wide range of topics from Celtic and Roman Britain onward. Such evidence may be local census returns, directories or maps, a statue, memorial, photograph, building, railway station, canal, factory, oral account. What is it? Who had it made? Why is it here? Is there other local evidence? Why was it important? Does it still matter? Why did the person represented in the statue or photograph or newspaper account act as they did? Were they significant? If so why? (Cooper 2012:17–32, 58–9, 62–3, 70, 94, 98). And of course, in finding out more about a period, as suggested above (asking questions), it is possible to make inferences from any traces of the past which remain, from buttons to buildings, a key element of any historical enquiry (Collingwood 1939, 1946).

The scope of historical enquiry

Theory

Gallie (1964) asked whether an element of story or narrative is essential to history. He concluded that, although in his view every genuine work of history features story, history contests the simple rules of narrative and romance because of the complexity of historical situations. Accordingly, works of history may be abstract and complicated, and explore massive and impersonal causes: disintegration of empire, unification, flowering of a great, artistic style, achievement of a moral reform.

The scope of enquiry

Practice

The National Curriculum (DfE 2013) requires us to consider, in breadth overviews, some abstract and complicated themes and to explore massive and impersonal dimensions (for example cultural, economic, military, political, religious and social, local, regional and international history, the expansion and dissolution of empires) and concepts such as civilisation. Depth studies will be drawn from within some of these overviews.

Causes and effects

Theory

Post structuralist philosophers addressed each of the following concepts of time, which Key Stage 2 children are expected to address (DfE 2013). They recognised that links between causes and effects are not simple and linear, for three main reasons. First, historians describe and analyse the context and circumstances in which events, actions and behaviour are embedded. Mandelbaum (1977) pointed out that historians present their research as explanatory accounts, identifying the factors responsible for past occurrences, and interpretive accounts, which focus on portraying the background to subsequent developments. Olafson (1979) considered that historians do not concentrate on the sequential, but on the complex embedding of each episode of a narrative in wider patterns of culture and institutional life. Narrative, he said, depends on non-narrative description and analysis. Historians inform us about the uniform patterns of life against which events are happening. Narrative passages exist within these detailed descriptions. He cites Braudel (1995) whose two volumes on *The Mediterranean and the Mediterranean World in the Reign of Philip II* described events in the context of the agriculture, economy and geography of the Mediterranean at the time.

Second, as Carr (1986) pointed out, historians have the advantage of knowing what happened next and this is not always the result of a person's intended actions. There are often surprises and fortuitous events. Ankersmit (1983) argued that because historians deal with both intended and unintended consequences historians who interpret them create their own meanings; there is inevitably a difference between the historian's perspective and that of the person whose actions s/he is explaining. Olafson (1979) made the same point. In order to understand people's actions it is necessary to understand how they perceived things; why they wanted to achieve a particular goal.

And third, Carr (1991) added the observation that narrative historians relate the activities, not just of individuals but also of groups, organisations, communities and nations. Similarly Dray (1964) says that significant narrative offers explanations of developments and declines in social movements, institutions, reigns, wars, revolutions and climates of opinion. He gives, as an example, Huizinga's *The Waning of the Middle Ages* (1924), which is a portrait, a cross-section of an age, not a narrative.

First, an attempt must be made to understand causes and effects in the wider context of the time in which they happened. As Mandelbaum (1977) and Olafson (1979) state, causes and effects of events are explained and interpreted against an understanding of the background of the circumstances at the time.

Causes and effects

Practice

Bage (1999) said that, to develop an understanding of cause and effect, children should be encouraged to criticise, rather than copy stories. He suggests, for example, that the storyteller should suspend the story at certain points, in order to discuss motives and causes of decisions and to discuss moral issues. Children need to understand the background, values and attitudes of the times in which individuals and groups made decisions. As Dray (1964) above, points out, this may involve understanding the societal background to the decisions. Lee *et al.* (2000) show how children's ideas about explanation in history depend on them understanding the situation the person was in, on background, contextual historical knowledge and the use of the informed 'historical imagination' (in Cooper 2012: 47). In terms of pedagogy, these factors shaped and informed the development of drama and simulation as powerful tools for developing pupils' historical understanding through the 'modelling' of historical situations.

Similarities and differences between periods

Theory

Chronological understanding and concepts of time also involves comparing the similarities and differences between different periods and the reasons for the changes between them. Lemon (1995: 47–80) cites as an example a description of Birmingham at two different periods, noting the differences. He says that this is not a narrative but two states of affairs, connected by changing states of affairs. This requires explaining the reasons for the changes and this involves explaining the actions of people in the process.

Similarities, differences between periods

Practice

Again, this has major resonance in pedagogy where a standard approach is comparing the same scene at two different times and setting pupils the task of explaining how and why the changes occurred. Ofsted (2011) found that most pupils were not able to compare and explain similarities and differences between periods, because it was not built into the English National Curriculum for History with associated pedagogy. One solution is to focus upon similarity and difference between periods by collecting, comparing and explaining images related to key themes, or key protagonists in each period.

Interpretations

Theory

The debate about causation led philosophers to identify the reasons why accounts must be interpretations, that accounts are constructed by historians and why they differ, due to the difference between individual historians and the personal and cultural contexts in which they are writing their histories.

The structuralists had claimed that historical accounts are inevitably narratives, with a plot that has a beginning, an elaboration of the argument (a plot), and a conclusion. However, they came to accept that the historian, in response to the question or questions posed, must create a 'plot' with chronological boundaries, i.e. a starting point and end point. Different stories on the same historical topic will start and end in different places, depending on the historian's 'plot' to make sense of the selected evidence from the body of historical data. Hayden White (1992) called this 'emplotment' and said that the historian develops the structure of the plot according to the answering of the question or questions and the structure of the genre he or she adopts (comedy, play, monograph, historical novel, short story, satire or television series), selecting the events from the multiplicity embedded in the historical data.

Interpretations

Practice

Discern how and why different arguments and interpretations of the past have been constructed.

(DfE 2013: 188)

Hayden White's (1992) meaning becomes clear when we think of children writing historical accounts as plays, historical fiction, newspaper or television interviews. Inevitably these genres address questions and so evidence is selected to answer that question, and having adequately done so, the piece of writing comes to an end. Nevertheless, it has been answered in the context of broader background knowledge.

Conclusion

Because on any topic there are multiple accounts of the past that reflect the academic discourses upon it, it is important that children develop their understanding of the topic through engaging in the processes of historical enquiry, from the initial question to its resolution, i.e. they 'Do History'. To 'Do History' pupils work with teacher guidance and support throughout. Each child must identify and consider questions to investigate, work upon the sources and possible interpretations of them, extract from them evidence germane to the question, organise, analyse, consider, speculate, imagine, create views and hypotheses, test them and reach conclusions creatively, in order to plan and draft their own historical accounts, i.e. 'histories'. The final stage involves the formal writing/composition of these histories in a chosen genre. Each pupil's 'history' is particular, even unique. The children can then compare them through classroom exposition, discussion and debate and display. This process enables them to fully consider other alternative interpretations and the evidence on which they are based, something that illuminates and deepens their own understanding of the topic.

Accordingly, the three premises of this book are that:

1   Children should engage fully in the range and varied processes that 'Doing History' can involve, ranging, for example, from archaeology, local history, biography and family history to historical fiction. 'Doing History' enables pupils to both know what they are writing about and upon what it is based, i.e. its provenance and reliability. It empowers them to compose their own histories or interpretations that depend and draw upon story and narrative of the past, and to evaluate other pupils' histories and understand why they may be radically different.

2   From the start of an historical enquiry children are actively and fully engaged in writing from initial jottings, notes, planning and recording; writing with a range of purpose and foci. Pupils' writing culminates in the composition of their own 'history' that responds to and answers the historical question(s) that initiated their historical enquiry.

3   The 'histories' that schoolchildren plan, compose and present/communicate can take the form of any appropriate genre, each of which has writing as a major, if not its major element.

In this chapter perhaps Elton (1991: 73) should have the final word.

A knowledge of the past should arm a man against surrendering to the panaceas surrendered by too many myth-makers. This is known as growing up . . . By enormously enlarging personal experience history can help us to grow up, to resist those who, with good will or ill, would force us all into the straightjackets of their supposed answers to the problems of existence.

References

Ankersmit, F.R. (1983) *Narrative Logic: a semantic analysis of the historian's language*, Leiden: Brill Publishers.
Bage, G. (1999) *Narrative Matters: teaching and learning history through story*, London: Falmer.

Braudel, F. (1995) (first published 1949) *The Mediterranean and the Mediterranean World in the Age of Philip II*, London: University of California Press Ltd.

Butterfield, H. (1965) *The Whig Interpretation of History*, London: Norton.

Cannadine, D., Keating, J. and Sheldon, N. (2012) *The Right Kind of History: teaching the past in twentieth century England*, London: Palgrave Macmillan.

Carr, D. (1986) Narrative and the real world: an argument for continuity, *History and Theory*, Vol. 25: 117–31.

Carr, D. (1991) *Time, Narrative and History*, Bloomington: Indiana University Press.

Collingwood, R.G. (1939) *An Autobiography*, Oxford: Oxford University Press.

Collingwood, R.G. (1946) *The Idea of History*, Oxford: Clarendon.

Cooper, H. (2012) (2/e) *History 5–11*, Abingdon: Routledge.

Danto, A.C. (1965) Analytical philosophy of history, in A.C. Danto (2007) *Narration and Knowledge*, New York: Columbia University Press, pp. 1–16.

Department for Education (DfE) (2013) The National Curriculum in England: Key Stages 1 and 2 framework document, available online at www.gov.uk/dfe/nationalcurriculum (accessed 11.02.2014).

Derrida, J. (1978) *Writing and Difference* (trans. A Bass) Chicago: Chicago University Press.

Dray, W.H. (1964) *Philosophy of History*, New Jersey: Prentice Hall.

Elton, G.R. (1967) *The Practice of History*, Oxford: Blackwell.

Elton, G.R. (1970) *Political History: principles and practice*, London: Penguin.

Elton, G.R. (2002) *Return to Essentials: some reflections on the present state of historical study*, Cambridge: Cambridge University Press.

Evans, R.J. (2011) The wonderfulness of us (the Tory interpretation of history) *London Review of Books*, Vol. 33, No. 6: 9–12.

Evans, R.J. (2012) 1066 and all that, *The New Statesman* (23.01.2012).

Gallie, W.B. (1964) The historical understanding, *History and Theory* 3: 1549–202.

Hayden White, M. (1973) *Metahistory*, Baltimore: Johns Hopkins University Press.

Hayden White, M. (1981) The value of narrativity in the representation of reality, in *On Narrative* W.J.T. Mitchell (ed.) Chicago: University Press of Chicago, pp. 1–23.

Hexter, J.H. (1971) *The History Primer*, New York: Basic Books.

Hobsbawm, E.J. (1980) The revival of narrative; some comments, *Past and Present*, 86: 3–8.

Huizinga, J.H. (1924) *The Waning of the Middle Ages; a study of the life, thought and art of France and the Netherlands in the fourteenth and fifteenth centuries*, London: Fritz Hopman.

Lee, P., Dickinson, A. and Ashby. R. (2000) 'Just another emperor': understanding action in the past, *International Journal of Educational Research*, 27 (3): 233–44.

Lemon, M.C. (1995) *The Discipline of History and the History of Thought*, London: Routledge.

Lively, P. (2013) *Ammonites and Leaping Fish: a life in time*, London: Penguin.

Lyotard, J.F. (1979) *Post Modern Condition: a report on knowledge* (trans. 1984 by G. Bennington and G. Massumi), Minnesota: University of Minnesota Press.

Mandelbaum, M. (1967) A note on history as narrative, *History and Theory*, 6, no.3: 411–19.

Mandelbaum, M. (1977) *The Anatomy of Historical Knowledge*, Baltimore: John Hopkins University Press.

Marshall, H.E. (1905) *Our Island Story*, reprinted (2005) Bath: Bath Press.

Mink, L.O (1966) The autonomy of historical understanding, *History and Theory* Vol. 5 no.1.

Mink, L.O. (1978) Narrative form as a cognitive instrument, in R.H. Canary and H. Kozicki (eds.) *The Writing of History*, Madison: University of Wisconsin Press, pp. 127–144.

Ofsted (Office for Standards in Education) (2011) *History for All: History in English Schools 2007–2011*, available online at www.ofsted.gov.uk/publications/090223.

Olafson F.A. (1970) Narrative history and the concept of action, *History and Theory* Vol. 9, no. 3.

Olafson, F.A. (1979) Narrative history, in *The Dialectic of Action*, chapter 4, Chicago: Chicago University Press.

Saussure, F. de (2006) *Ferdinand de Saussure: writings in general linguistics*, Oxford: Oxford University Press.

Stone, L. (1979) The revival narrative, *Past and Present*, 85, Issue 1: 3–24.

White, H. (1992) Historical emplotment and the problems of truth in probing the limits of representations, in *Probing the Limits of Representation*, S. Friedlander (ed.), Cambridge: Cambridge University Press, pp. 37–53.

Woodham-Smith, C. (1962) *The Great Hunger: Ireland 1845–49*, 2/e (1999) London: Penguin.

Theory into practice

Hilary Cooper

Synopsis

This chapter is a link between *History 5–11* (Cooper 2012) the companion book of *History 7–11*, and also between theoretical rationale for this book and the case studies which illustrate this in Part 2. The chapter suggests how activities in *History 5–11* could be developed into enjoyable extended writing, with references to speaking and listening, reading and writing in the National Curriculum for History and for English (DfE 2013). It is not intended that specific activities described in *History 5–11* are necessarily replicated but the scaffolding strategies suggested can be applied to any similar activities. This should precede Site Visits.

Site visits

Penelope Lively, a wonderful novelist, who is also a history graduate, and whose books are imbued with a curiosity about time, insists that all children should learn as much history as possible. She says that without a sense of the past or of historical narrative you 'cannot see yourself as part of the narrative, you cannot place yourself within a context. You will not have an understanding of time, a respect for memory' (Lively 2013: 137).

Site visits discussed in *History 5–11* (Cooper 2012) are: sites related to significant local or national events or changes (p. 61); a local industrial site (p. 70) and an archaeological site (p. 178).

Local sites relevant to the 2013 curriculum can be found in the *Historical Map and Guide to Roman Britain* (OS 2001), which gives an overview of and information about Roman sites in Britain over 400 years, in the *Stone Age to the Early Middle Ages*, with each period identified, in the *Ancient Britain* (OS 2005) and in *Viking and Medieval York* (OS 1988). Ordnance Survey Maps of counties and town plans in England, Wales and Scotland, from the mid nineteenth century onwards, showing step by step changes in land use, can be viewed and purchased at www.old-maps.co.uk

Planning for oracy, reading and writing

Table 5.1 identifies the opportunities for oracy, reading and writing related to a site visit, with references to the National Curriculum for History and for English at Key Stage 2 (DfE 2013).

TABLE 5.1 Opportunities for oracy, reading and writing, in designing a site enquiry, with references to the National Curriculum for English.

Activity	*Spoken language*	*Reading*	*Writing*
Teacher and pupils design an enquiry to investigate on site. Make links between the site and the national/international picture.	*NC: Spoken language Y1–6* *Listen* to pre-visit information *Discuss* questions to investigate in groups and how to gather and record findings on site. Listen and respond to adults and peers. Ask relevant questions to extend vocabulary, understanding, knowledge. Articulate and justify answers, judgements, opinions. Participate in collaborative conversations. Speculate, hypothesise, imagine and explore ideas. Speak audibly and fluently. Participate in discussions. Consider and evaluate viewpoints.	*Comprehension Y3–6* After visit read in order to *research* links between site and its significance in the 'bigger picture'. *Write notes* (*with references*). *Discuss* reference books to explain words and meaning, discuss words or phrases that capture imagination. Ask questions, draw inferences.	**Writing Y3–6** Before visit complete proforma showing how group question will be investigated on site (Table 5.2). *Make notes* on site of findings. *Write* accounts of findings from visit and research, with references to evidence and sources. Plan writing modelled on a reference book. Evaluate, proof read, read aloud.

The table reflects Aim 5 of the history curriculum, to understand the methods of historical enquiry and how knowledge is collected from sources. Table 5.2 shows a proforma for collecting evidence on site.

Comparing interpretations in books

History 5–11 (pp. 34–35) considers criteria for comparing interpretations in history information books; pp. 156–158 consider the history and literacy objectives involved in the process, in the context of Egyptian houses. *Writing History 7–11* suggests a writing scaffold to support children's writing when comparing different textbook accounts of the same thing.

TABLE 5.2 Scaffolding headings for collecting evidence on site, related to agreed question.

Question to investigate	Possible evidence on site	Method of recording: notes, diagrams, sketches, photographs, interviews

National Curriculum for History and for English

This reflects the National Curriculum (DfE 2013) for history and for English:

Spoken language: ask relevant questions, justify answers, explore ideas, evaluate different viewpoints.

Reading: read non-fiction and reference books, discuss understandings and ask questions, identify main ideas from more than one paragraph and summarise, organise paragraphs around a theme, evaluate own and each other's writing, provide reasoned justification for views. Table 5.3 suggests a proforma for comparing different accounts.

Writing: draft, discuss writing similar to that which they are planning, to learn from its structure, vocabulary and grammar, retrieve, record and present information from non-fiction, justify views, select and use appropriate vocabulary.

TABLE 5.3 Proforma for comparing different accounts in reference books.

Differences	Notes	Possible reasons for differences
Review Title Author, date of publication, place of publication, publisher Names of reviewers		
How does the information differ?		
Is the focus on a particular group of people?		
Are there inferences about values, beliefs, thoughts or feelings?		
Are statements supported by evidence?		
Is it written from a particular point of view?		
Are men, women and children represented?		
Are illustrations artists' impressions or photographs?		
Do you think the books are accurate? Why/ why not?		
Which account do you prefer and why?		

Activity: to analyse and explain why accounts in history books may be different

Read 2 (or more) accounts of a person or event. *Discuss* ways in which they are different and suggest why. (Differentiation is inbuilt, as the selection of books can be adjusted for each group.) Discuss the two accounts in pairs, in order to complete (an appropriate adaptation of) the scaffold below, in order to identify and explain reasons for the differences.

In pairs *discuss* this analysis.

Using a word processor, each write a review of one of the books for the school library, based on your notes.

Visit to an historical reconstruction

History 5–11 (pp. 35–36) refers to a number of sites where re-enactments take place and to children's accounts through re-enactments, and on p. 178 to digital re-enactments.

Activity

To understand what is meant by a reconstruction; to find out more about the period being studied and lives of people at the time. (Check when reconstructions are taking place on the site!) Well known reconstructions include:

Vicus and Roman Britains (www.vicus.org.uk) aimed at KS2;

LEGIO V111 Augusta MGV Roman Living History Society (www.roman.org.uk);

LEG 11 AVG (www.legiiavg.org.uk);

The Antonine Guard (TAG) Legio V1 Scotland (www.theantonineguard.org.uk);

The Ermine Street Guard (www.erminestreetguard.co.uk);

Regia Anglorum (www.regia.org), a group that presents living images of Anglo-Saxon, Viking, Welsh and Norman people, has many branches in the British Isles and says that teachers are the 'very people they need to give depth to their lesson plan';

Bede's World (www.bedesworld.co.uk);

West Stow Anglo-Saxon Village (www.weststow.org);

Jorvik Viking Centre (www.jorvik-viking-centre.co.uk);

The Vikings: Celtic, Norman and Saxon re-enactments (www.vikingsonline.org.uk);

Vikings of Middle England (www.vikingsofmiddleengland.co.uk);

Viking and Dark Age Re-enactment (www.clash-of-steel.com) lists Viking re-enactment groups in Hampshire (Jutes), South Wales, Manchester, West Yorkshire, Leeds, Peterborough, West Midlands and East Anglia.

This activity reflects the National Curriculum for History (DfE 2013) and for English in the following ways:

Spoken language

Listen and respond appropriately to adults and peers, ask relevant questions, participate in lively, relevant conversations, imagine, speculate, explore ideas, speak audibly and fluently, maintain interest of listener, build on comments of others, select proper register.

Reading

From non-fiction text, make sense of and ask questions, draw inferences, such as inferring feelings, thoughts, motives for actions, identify and summarise main ideas.

Composition

Discuss and record ideas, evaluate and develop ideas, drawing on reading and research, consider characters and settings, write for an audience, read out loud using appropriate intonation.

National Curriculum for History

Understand what is meant by a reconstruction, understand how and why contrasting interpretations of the past may be constructed.

This activity suggests interviewing characters in a reconstruction, which would have to be previously negotiated with the re-enactment group, who are usually enthusiastic volunteers. They will need to know something of the age and abilities of the children, the work they have done on the topic, the kind of questions they may ask and the expected length of the interview. They should also understand the kinds of historical thinking and oral skills the teacher is trying to develop.

Activity

Read the information leaflets and online information related to the site. *Research* the period and event being reconstructed. (The teacher organises interviews in advance of visit.) *Draft* interview questions. Table 5.4 suggests how interviews may be planned. (Use audio or video to record interviews on site, if this is preferred to note-taking.) *Listen* to recordings or read notes. In small groups *discuss* a possible plot line for a short scene involving your characters. Table 5.5 shows how a play based on evidence can be constructed. *Write* dialogue in groups and in role. Each group *presents* their scene as of a series of *reconstructions* of life during this period, or the event reconstructed.

TABLE 5.4 Notes for interview preparation.

Interviewer Interviewee (in role)	Summary of answers
Three closed questions e.g. What is your name? Where is this? Why are you here?	
Number of open-ended questions to obtain more information based on previous reading.	
Closing question to bring person back to present.	

TABLE 5.5 Writing frame for drafting a play: a reconstruction, based on evidence.

Characters: names, ages, personalities Motives for being here.	Setting	Scene: beginning middle, end

Learning complex concepts

History 5–11 (pp. 42–50) discusses the way in which new concepts can be learned, by sorting pictures or artefacts into categories, by trial and error and by discussing the common characteristics of each category or analysing a picture typical of a period. It goes on to discuss the importance of chronology and time concepts in order to understand 'the big picture' and the language and numeracy skills involved.

The National Curriculum (DfE 2013) emphasises the importance of understanding a chronological narrative in 'understanding how people's lives have shaped the nation and how Britain has shaped and been shaped by the world; the importance of understanding abstract terms, such as 'empire', 'civilisation', 'parliament', and 'peasantry' and of understanding the 'historical concepts of change'. This might fit in with a breadth study, extending children's knowledge of British history beyond 1066, for example, the changing power of monarchs.

The following model could be used to tease out the meaning of any of the above concepts – or many others, for example: conflict/cooperation; movement and settlement or the concept of the British Isles; the changing relationship between England, Ireland, Scotland and Wales.

This exemplar activity investigates the abstract concepts of 'power' and 'democracy' (Dawson 2009). But this will not provide a coherent picture if there is nothing to hold the concepts together apart from the chronological thread; the story also needs to involve different viewpoints, to suggest that themes that are constructed can be challenged. Differentiation depends on the different levels of reference sources children are given, or select themselves.

Activity 1

Aim: To investigate power struggles between subjects and monarchs (DfE 2013) and construct them into narratives for a sequence of television presentations.

Discuss the role, powers and constraints of the British monarchy today. Select subjects who had a significant clash with their monarchs. These might be linked to depth studies and will certainly be linked to a time line.

In four groups, each divided into two, children research their character keeping notes and references to sources on the scaffold shown in table 5.6. Table 5.7 shows how children could research groups involved in power struggles with the Crown. This would allow individuals to create backgrounds for themselves and decide on their personal motives and involve women and children in completing a similar writing scaffold. The end product might be to write small role plays in groups, drawing on their research.

Alternatively children could write individual narratives and compare their similarities and differences. They use this, after discussion with the teacher, to construct the story script for a 'Simon Shama' type narrative history programme for 'television'. After further discussion each story can be video recorded and the programme seen and discussed by the whole class or a wider audience. This activity relates to the National Curriculum for English Year 3–6 in the following ways:

Reading and comprehension:

Non-fiction and reference books: comparisons across books.

Distinguish between fact and opinion.

Check makes sense; make notes where necessary.

Draw inferences such as inferring characters' feelings, thoughts and motives from their actions.

Read aloud for an audience.

Composition:

Identify the audience and select appropriate form using model

Draw on reading and research

Draft, evaluate, proofread, perform

These activities would provide good information for a hot-seating session as described in *History 5–11* (pp. 59, 70).

TABLE 5.6 Shows how children research their characters, to investigate power struggles between subjects and monarchs keeping notes and references to sources. This could support 'a theme from British history, for example the changing power of monarchs'. (DfE 2013: 191).

Date	Causes	Power struggles		Outcomes
1170		Thomas Becket	King Henry II	
1215		The Barons	King John	
1381		Watt Tyler	King Richard II	
1649		Oliver Cromwell	King Charles I	

TABLE 5.7 Shows how children could research groups involved in power struggles with the crown.

Date	Group	Causes	Power struggles	Outcomes
1381	Peasants' Revolt			
1642–51	Levellers			
1838–48	Chartists			
1897–1918	Suffragettes			

TABLE 5.8 Shows how children could research individual characters involved in a power struggle, and their motives.

Paragraphs	Notes	Source
What is your name? How old are you? Where do you live? What is your family like? What is your daily life like?		
Why did you join this group? What do they hope to achieve?		
What have you done as part of the group?		
What happened?		
What was achieved?		

Activity 2

This researches, compares and contrasts three ancient of civilisations, Sumer; Indus Valley; Ancient Egypt and Shang dynasty of China (DfE 2013: 191). It compares the overarching concept, civilisation, and its subordinate concepts, as evidenced in these civilisations (beliefs, social customs, art, architecture and music), prior to an in-depth study of one of them.

In six groups children could research *three* aspects of *one* of these civilisations, making notes for each concept, discuss and collate their findings as spidergrams, find supporting images and present their findings as three sets of Powerpoint presentations, which the whole class discuss. Table 5.9 suggests a framework for comparing three ancient civilisations.

TABLE 5.9 A framework for comparing three non-European societies.

Civilisation	*Dates*	*Beliefs and religious practices*	*Social customs*	*Art*	*Architecture*	*Music*	*Links with other countries*
Islam							
Mayan							
Benin							

Understanding paintings as historical sources and as interpretations

In *History 5–11* (pp. 182–186) the ways in which children can learn the methods of historical enquiry, in enjoyable and powerful ways through art, is discussed: visual sources as statements about human existence across cultures (Arnheim 1970), to convey the strong feelings of people in the past (Gombrich 1982), questioning images, stories and symbols in art and so on. I should like to continue, in *Writing History 7–11*, with some inspiring insights, by quoting Jeanette Winterson, then pick up the idea of constructing tableaux based on an image or event and questioning the characters (*History 5–11*: 59; 164–5).

The power of paintings to connect us with people across the centuries.

Jeanette Winterson (1996: 1–19), who had previously said that art didn't talk to her, came to believe that pictures, poetry and music connect people across time, that they are both marks in time but marks through time, of their own time and ours, not antique or historical but exuberantly living. 'The true artist', Winterson says, 'is connected, and has much to give us because it is connections we seek, connections to the past, to one another, to the physical world.' She explains that if you look and look at a painting there is a triangular dialogue between the painter and you, the viewer. The painting becomes part of you. Winterton sees art objects as many voices, affirming life over time: the Lascaux Cave paintings, the Sistine Chapel ceiling, the quiet paintings of Vanessa Bell (http://www.bbc.co.uk/arts/yourpaintings/paintings/search/painted_by/vanessa-bell). It is possible for pupils who have never been introduced to art, or seen it as relevant to them, through learning to look, to connect with other times and places in transforming ways.

Constructing tableaux

Decoding a visual source

All the aspects of historical enquiry are involved in the process of decoding a painting before the tableaux can be created. These questions can be discussed by the whole class and children can make notes as the discussion develops, or they might make notes in groups afterwards. The discussion might be recorded using the scaffold in table 5.10. Table 5.11 suggests how roles and conversations can be developed based on this discussion of the image.

The criteria decoding a visual source (table 5.10) could be applied to any visual source. The Bayeux Tapestry would be an excellent example to explore in this way. The website at www.bayeuxtapestry.org.uk tells the history of the tapestry and the story of the tapestry, scene by scene, with information about the people in each scene and what is happening.

Planning a class museum

History 5–11 (pp. 147–150) links literacy objectives in the National Literacy Strategy (1998) with Knowledge Skills and Understanding in the National Curriculum for history (1999). *Writing History 7–11* updates these to links between the 2013 National Curriculum for English and for history.

Activity

Understand that inferences about sources may differ, to *form and express opinions*. Create labels with headings for a display of artefacts related to a period. Each group examines a source, an artefact (or image of an artefact). Individually members of each group *record their opinions* about what the source is, how it may have been made and what it may have meant to people who used and made it. *Compare opinions. Write a label* inviting visitors to the exhibition to record the opinions they think most likely on a checklist.

Conclusion. *Write* reviews of the exhibition and design advertising posters.

Analyse text to explore the relationship between fact and historical imagination

History 5–11 (pp. 162–164) considers how historical fiction can help children to develop historical understanding. The history curriculum (DfE 2013) does not explicitly refer to imagination, presumably because the concept of historical imagination may be misunderstood. An analysis of the relationship between evidence, historical imagination and empathy is given in *History 5–11* (p. 219). In *Writing History 7–11* we shall first consider how children can be supported in analysing the relationship between fact and historical imagination in fiction, then how an imaginative description of a place or old building can be analysed, to trace the way in which apparently mundane objects can be used to inspire historical imagination, which can lead to further questions and research, and finally how oral or bibliographical writing can be used to model children's imaginative writing about a locality. It can then be used as a model for writing similar descriptions.

TABLE 5.10 Decoding a painting using observation, inference and deductions.

1 Engaging with the picture	
What is it about?	
Principle features?	
What people can you see?	
Who do you think they are?	
Where are they? Why?	
What do their gestures suggest?	
Are there any letters, numbers? What do they tell us?	
2 Details: deductions	
What are people wearing? So . . .	
What buildings can you see? Therefore . . .	
What transport? Therefore . . .	
3 What can we infer?	
About peoples' thoughts, feelings, what might they be talking about?	
What sounds might you hear?	
4 What would you like to know?	
5 Engaging with historical imagination	
What happens next?	
6 Time concepts	
Compare with contemporary images of such a scene today. How valid do you think it is? Now/then; continuity/ change; cause/effect	
7 Interpretation	
Who created the image? When? why?	
How valid is it as an historical source? Are there contradictory images?	

TABLE 5.11 Suggests how discussion of an image can lead to creating roles and conversation.

Name? Occupation? Age?	
A bit about your family/history	
How do you come to be there?	
What are you saying in the image?	
Relationship with group?	

Activity

Read an extract, perhaps from two or more novels on the same theme, for example stories about the Second World War (e.g. Westall 1975, McEwen 1985, Foreman 1995). Extracts might also be from Rosemary Sutcliff's novels about the end of Roman Britain and the coming of the Saxons (see pp. 27–32, 39–44, 162–166). Or an Anglo-Saxon poem could be analysed in terms of what is probably based on fact and what is imaginative. *The Anglo-Saxon World: an anthology* (Crossley Holland 1982/2009) contains excerpts from Bede and the *Anglo-Saxon Chronicle* and Seamus Heaney (2008) provided an evocatively illustrated translation of *Beowulf.* They really connect us with Saxon life, feelings, beliefs, hopes and fears. An eight-year-old in my class, after we had read and discussed parts of *Beowulf* and written our own poems based on this, told me that, her parents having left for work, she read her version to the milkman!

In groups *discuss* and *write* notes, under headings, analysing each extract, using the headings in table 5.12 or a modified version, depending on the extracts read. Groups share and compare their analyses.

The class could debate the motion: Much can be learned about the past from historical fiction.

TABLE 5.12 Analysis of historical fiction.

Novel, author, date	
How are characters presented, in dialogue and descriptions? Implications of their gender, race, nationality, class	
Narrator's viewpoint and influence on reader's view of events	
Fact or opinion or fiction?	

Conclusion

In this chapter we have considered a variety of writing frames, which were designed to support and help teachers and children in developing the kinds of activities and discussions introduced in *History 5–11* into extended writing at Key Stage 2. Part 2 describes recent case studies that analyse the process of developing extended writing from activities, talk and research in greater detail. Chapter 6 focuses on writing developed from time concepts, chapter 7 on sources, chapters 8 and 9 on interpretations and the final chapter on writing, which combines all of these aspects of historical enquiry.

References

Arnheim, R. (1970) *Visual Thinking*, London: Faber & Faber.

Cooper, H. (2012) *History 5–11*, Abingdon: Routledge.

Crossley Holland, K. (1982) (reissued 2009) *The Anglo-Saxon World: an anthology*, Oxford: Oxford University Press.

Dawson, I. (2009) What time does the tune start? *Teaching History*, 135: 50–6.

Department for Education (DfE) (2013) The National Curriculum in England, available online at www.gov.uk/dfe/nationalcurriculum.

Foreman, M. (1995) *After the War is Over*, London: Pallion.

Gombrich, E.H. (1982) *The Image and the Eye: studies in the psychology of pictorial representation*, Oxford: Phaidon.

Heaney, S. (2008) *Beowulf: an illustrated edition*, New York: W.W. Norton and Co.

Lively, P. (2013) *Ammonites & Leaping Fish: a life in time*, London: Penguin.

McEwen, I. (1985) *Rose Blanche*, London: Jonathan Cape.

Ordnance Survey (OS) (1988) *Viking and Medieval York*, Southampton, UK: Ordnance Survey.

Ordnance Survey (OS) (2001) *Historical Map and Guide to Roman Britain*, Southampton, UK: Ordnance Survey.

Ordnance Survey (OS) (2005) *Ancient Britain*, Southampton, UK: Ordnance Survey.

Westall, R. (1975) *The Machine Gunners*, London: Macmillan.

Winterson, J. (1966) *Art Objects: essays on ecstasy and effrontery*, London: Vintage Books.

Case studies: models for practice

Using sources to create narrative

Hugh Moore

Exploring chronology

Sequencing artefacts

In class-based discussions of museum artefacts sourced from the 'Timeline Museum' I was impressed by the children's ability to make links with their own prior knowledge and to make logical guesses in an attempt to understand a complex artefact. Moments that stand out have reflected Hodkinson's (2004) work on children's developing sense of historical time; children remember more of what they are taught in history if they have an efficient chronological framework within which to place, store and retrieve what they have learned.

Building a chronological framework

One of the 'Timeline Museum' timelines was a series of axes, the oldest being Acheulean and some 350,000 old, whilst the youngest was Viking and a mere 1,000 years old. During my discussions with Year 3/4 children it emerged that many of them were comfortable with the terms 'Stone Age' and 'Bronze Age'. The discussion was also interesting in that many were able to sequence the different 'Ages' and also in that they questioned me about the very short 'Copper Age'.

A good example was a twelve-year-old boy with severe Autistic Spectrum Disorder (ASD) who inspected a timeline that runs from the first coins issued in Lydia more than 2,500 years ago to a silver Victorian crown. He quickly commented: 'You need a Viking coin.' He was right, and it was indeed the most significant gap in the collection. His prediction about a chronology (which went: Greek/Lydian, Egyptian/Ptolomaic, early Roman, tribal British, Emperor Hadrian, Medieval, Elizabeth I and Victoria), showed a grasp not only of historical time but a clear ability to make links across time periods in different parts of the world.

Misconceptions?

At a recent primary history conference in Manchester the keynote speaker, Tim Lomas, told us that children viewed people who lived in the past as being less clever than we are. I wonder, however, if is possible to deconstruct such a response and to follow a logic that goes something along the lines of – 'there was less knowledge about the world in the past and, therefore, if people had less knowledge could they be construed as being less intelligent?' It is often tempting to relate mistakes as evidence of similar misconceptions and immature thinking in history.

Learning about materials aids identification

A twelve-year-old recorded this note about a timeline of mobile phones.

> *Me and George predict what (age) the Motorola 8500X and Motorola razor are. I predicted 1912 and he predicted 1919. It was actually 1987.*

He and George had used the Internet to date the phone, a particularly successful activity where makes and model numbers are available as search terms. This can work equally well through using descriptions of objects which are hard to identify, such as Roman artefacts. Describing for the purposes of identification is a skill learned by archaeologists and museum curators alike. Where a Roman artefact such as a Samian ware bowl or a fibular broach is to be identified, terms such as 'red ware' pottery and 'bronze brooch' are helpful and can often lead us to an image of a similar artefact. We as teachers, therefore, need to give careful thought to the key words and aid the identification of different metals and materials, before presenting them to pupils as possible search terms.

Misconception or experimentation?

As a follow-up to the timeline project the boys from the ASD school engaged in imaginative letter writing about Victorian schooling. The letter below is quoted in full and although it roundly condemns the Victorians' teaching approaches, it makes links to Victorian morals and attitudes ' . . . these ideas will land you in hell'. The writer, when questioned, did not feel that the Victorians were stupid, merely that their educational ideas were 'cruel'. The letter appears to demonstrate this:

> *Dear Sir,*
>
> *The event of Victorian was not very pleasing, as methods from the past were not very discreet. The use of embarrassment and violence is a dangerous path to follow. The new social services system has restrained this method. ★★(writing obscured)★★ I feel that these methods will land you in hell. I have evidence that 92% of parents will indeed phone the local police and the school will suffer. A further 5% will deal with this themselves. But only 3% agree with the rules. Please take me seriously, sir.*
>
> *Yours sincerely, the boy next to the boy, next to the math teacher, next to the dunce cap in the bin.*

Misconceptions, I would argue are a natural part of learning and they often occur in situations where a child is experimenting with thoughts and ideas. I love this boy's fusion of modern ideas about social services and percentages with thoughts about Victorian educationalists using embarrassment and violence.

Testing a theory?

Similar experimentation in a child's response to the artefacts was demonstrated when a Year 4 girl asked if she could still spend a denarius of the Emperor Hadrian in the shops. Had I taken her question at face value it might have been possible to use it as evidence of a misconception but her face told a different story. Her look suggested that she doubted it very much and indeed many of the children around her said, 'no' almost instantly, although a few waited for the answer with some expectation. In a subsequent discussion with the class teacher who had noted the same incident we both came to the conclusion that the girl was simply testing a theory and was not surprised by the answer that 'you can't'.

Or deliberately engendered confusion?

It is of course possible that a creative and engaging approach may actually increase a child's confusion about the past. The 'denarius' child's misconception may also have been fostered by a previous visitor to the class, a Viking re-enactor.

The following Year 3 recount of the day demonstrated a deliberately engendered and obviously enjoyed confusion between past and present:

> *The activity was led by awesome Thor. The place was XXXXXXXX school in (our) humongous echoey hall. What they did was told us about the Vikings.*

> *First of all Thor came and taught us how to speak Viking and Anglo-Saxon. Thor taught us how to spell and say woman and Viking in the Viking language. How you say women in Viking is wimen for Viking it is Vikin.*

None of the recounts raised questions about who Thor was and the only mention of role-play was in comments about their own part in the proceedings. Many of the children indeed faithfully reported his stories about dragons, gods and monsters − although in some of the recounts these were identified as legends. Their teacher was reluctant for me to ask children who Thor was or where he had come from and wanted the children to retain their sense of wonder and mystery about the whole event.

Children need opportunities to think creatively

Opportunities for creative thinking allowing children to test theories and experiment with ideas, are often situations where the fear of being wrong is removed and a child can 'follow the logic'. Examining the writing that one class of children had previously produced was, however, a disappointment and not − as Fines (2013) suggests it should be − at the heart of 'Doing History'. Much of it was formulaic and clearly sometimes driven by the need for the texts to pass the head teacher's next 'book inspection'. The following piece of writing is short, highly structured and clearly driven by the requirement to demonstrate good use of grammar and to provide answers that can be marked easily. The children were asked to write sentences speculating about the uses of various artefacts which were presented in the form of drawings. In this Year 4 work it seemed that the need for logic, problem-solving skills, enquiry learning and creativity was lost in favour of a mantra that went something like, 'the children must write'. Even the class teacher confessed that it was a 'bit boring'.

I can use artefacts to find out about Roman schools.

(Drawing of abacus). I think it is used for counting.

I think it is made out of wood.

It is actually used for counting.

(Drawing of pot) I think it is made of pot.

It is used for holding water.

It is actually used for storing equipment.

The best writing I saw during the earlier part of the project was often written when pupils were free to express their own thoughts and it would sometimes contain half formed ideas, which I as a teacher would love to have seen developed more fully. This ASD pupil is commenting on a timeline, which featured a series of weapons dating from the Palaeolithic period to World War II:

This timeline is important because it is how our weapons have been evolving from something as simple as an axe to something as deadly as a Bren gun.

The reason we have evolved our weapons is because we are always at war and people have made weapons because the(y) decided to make weapons that mean people don't die as easily.

This is un-engineered, unstructured and leaves a burning question; what does he mean when he says 'people don't die as easily'? Most of the writing, like this one, was based on little prior or logical reasoning, but they expressed embryonic ideas and feelings.

Trying different approaches

In an attempt to counter the lack of creativity in these responses further approaches were designed and tested with groups. A significant constraint in designing these approaches was the notion of prior knowledge and historical understanding – we needed to move away from guesswork and move towards writing that incorporated prior knowledge, research and creative and novel ideas.

The 'Saying Goodbye' project

The 'Saying Goodbye' project was conceived as an attempt to fire historical imaginations, understand behaviour and motivation (Heathcote 2013), and to offer an opportunity to write short scripts: mindful of the impending 100th anniversary it was centred on World War I and built around a collection of battlefield artefacts. World War I of course is easily covered in curriculum 2014 as *'a study of an aspect or theme in British history that extends pupils' chronological knowledge beyond 1066'* (DfE 2013) and is a significant turning point in British history, but the principles below could be as easily applied, for instance, to the departure of a Roman soldier.

Never having been a fan of the idea that a child might be able 'to write a diary entry as if they were a World War I soldier' I considered that children might be able to use the opportunity to 'occupy the space' of another person by focussing on a very small aspect of their experience, a space where the child would have a chance of being able to identify with the soldier's feelings.

Working with three pilot groups I explored the idea of an experienced World War I soldier returning to the front (see Richard Jack's York-based painting 'Return to the Front', which inspired the original thoughts) and saying goodbye to his loved ones. This can be viewed on the BBC website at http://www.bbc.co.uk/arts/yourpaintings/artists/richard-jack/paintingsslideshow.

This simple process would give an opportunity for groups to write and perform a short drama of two to three minutes about those moments of leaving and saying goodbye.

It is practically impossible to place ourselves in the mind of a person who lived in the past because we don't have the same social mores, morality, religious views, knowledge of the world, expectations, material wealth and the same possibilities for moving out of or staying in our own sphere. It is also impossible for us to un-know what we know and to us the world is a smaller and less mysterious place than it was for them. It is, however, possible to, based on our common humanity, and what we know of the situation of people in the past, to suggest what those past people might have been feeling and to imagine what we might do if we were in their place (Collingwood 1939).

In order to allow participants to empathise with the World War I soldier and those he was leaving we discussed how goodbye is said in differing circumstances and participants were encouraged to perform their goodbyes:

- after a transaction in a shop;

- when they were leaving for school;

- leaving friends or siblings for a short time;

- when they were leaving grandma or granddad;

- leaving a pet behind;

- when they were leaving their parents for a long period of time.

We discussed what might occur if somebody is leaving for a long time and may face some danger. We looked at why people might hug, cry or simply be silent and again volunteers gave small performances to demonstrate their thinking.

We also considered that:

- Those staying behind might be sad but not wanting to show their feelings.

- The person leaving might be excited and nervous at the same time.

- Those staying might not be able to hide their feelings.

- The person leaving might be putting on a brave face.

- Children, grown-ups, girl/boyfriends, grandparents may all have different reactions.

- People might be saying one thing and thinking another.

Developing knowledge and understanding of the historical period is an essential part of this process and to do this we looked at a video to see images of soldiers and we listened to people talking about the events and poetry from the trenches in order to hear how they spoke. We also considered facts and figures such as the 19,000+ British soldiers who died on the first day of the Somme battle.

- We watched *Battle of the Somme* (1916) which is available on DVD from the Imperial War Museum. This is a contemporary silent film and, therefore, we discussed our expectations of a black and white film shot in the trenches at the time. We also were aware of what British soldier would look like and how the trenches would appear before we watched the film.

- We listened to carefully (not all are suitable) selected excerpts of poems by G.A. Studdert Kennedy, which are written in 'soldier speak', notably 'The Stretcher Bearers', 'The Spirit' and carefully selected lines from 'What's the Good?' accessed via http://www.poemhunter.com/geoffrey-anketell-studdert-kennedy. This was so that they could hear the language of the period and begin to understand some experiences of the soldiers.

- We looked at 'Timeline Museum' artefacts excavated from the Somme and Ypres battlefields, including shrapnel, shells and bullets and considered the amount of these lethal materials that were flying around the soldiers. We considered diary entries from 2nd Lt Kenneth Macardle:

The German shells littered the battlefield with dead and wounded: all around us and in front, men dropped or staggered about. A yellow mass of Lydite shrapnel would burst high up and a section in two formation would crumple up and be gone. 'A' Coy was in front of us, advancing in sections, with about 20 paces between blobs, in perfect order at a slow walk.

These are available via http://www.hellfirecorner.co.uk/hartley/jh.htm.

- We looked again at the faces on the Richard Jack painting and considered what those soldiers might be feeling and considered the the that fact that they were returning to the front.

We discussed what a soldier might be feeling.

- Does he feel sad for the friends he has lost?

- Does he feel that he might be the one to die this time?

- Is he putting on a brave face?

- It was possible that he hasn't told his family how bad life on the battlefield really was. We contextualised this part of the discussion by discussing the way that information reaches us now and how rapidly it is available. We discussed the fact that during World War I many people in Britain were simply unaware of what was really happening on the Western Front.

- He might feel proud of serving 'King and Country' and we looked at posters including Kitchener's famous 'Your Country Needs You' image.

We asked: What kinds of things he might be saying to encourage his family and 'keep their chins up' and discussed what different members of the family might be saying in return.

After re-visiting the conventions of play writing the groups were asked to write a short script, based on that very act of saying goodbye. The script had to incorporate things they had learned about being on the battlefield but the groups also had to use enquiry learning to find out the kinds of names the characters might have had and how they might have spoken. Each group was asked to include as many of the group as they wished in the performance, with the proviso that any not acting would be involved as directors or researchers. The groups were shown the available costume. This included a soldier's hat (this was a 1990s Belgian officer's hat, purchased very cheaply from a local military surplus shop and looked very similar to those depicted in the videos. It was re-badged for the 'King's Own' – our local regiment). The participants were also offered a greatcoat and a de-activated Lee-Enfield rifle. The groups were then asked to select other simple costumes, such as shawls and hats, which could be worn by the remaining performers. They did this through looking at the 'Jack' painting and other contemporary photographs that had been placed in the room.

The groups were asked to rehearse, and make improvements to their script as required, before it was performed. The following excerpt incorporated many of the elements we discussed as a group, particularly in terms of the participants thinking one thing but saying another. It also reflected information they had discovered during their research. Here is an extract from one script.

Soldier. 'No Mum don't you be worrying I'll be fine. The lads are good, we watch each other's backs.' Thinks to himself. 'I'm not going to make it am I? Not this time.'

Mother. 'Well just you remember, I'm proud of you, we all are, the whole country is.'

The actual performances were largely well done and thoughtful, knowledgeable and often quite emotional. I was pleased that a project so centred on war, and with the possible distraction of being able to hold a real World War I weapon, had turned into a performance piece of real quality and depth. There were problems; it took time to develop the pupils' knowledge of World War I and they needed to understand the conventions of script writing, as well as to make sufficient time for rehearsals. There was also a small cohort of children who did not or were not able to engage with the process. This work also took time and was fitted into the curriculum across two weeks.

Making predictions and researching stories about sources

An adult's experience

During the summer I visited a number of World War I battlefields including Cambrai, where I was fortunate enough to see the wreck of a World War I Mark IV Tank 'Deborah', D51, which stands in a barn in the French village of Flesquières, very close to the cemetery where my partner's grandfather is buried. The story of its discovery was amazing, because for six years Philippe Gorczuynski (see http://www.tank-cambrai.com/english/tank/discovery.php), a local hotel owner, searched for the tank, which an elderly lady had remembered being pushed into a huge hole in 1917. Philippe, however, did not end his search and once the tank had been excavated began to look into the lives of those who died in the tank during the important Battle of Cambrai, which took place on 20 November 1917. Philippe's dedication in finding the tank and researching the lives of those who were involved in the battle was inspiring, and quite humbling, and made me think about one of the great tools of the historical researcher; the ability to make predictions.

Philippe did not discover the deeply buried tank by chance but spent many hours looking through archives both in Britain and France and he also enlisted the help of many specialists in detecting buried structures.

I use Philippe's story as an example when talking to groups about archaeology. It is useful in countering misconceptions that archaeology is the preserve of buccaneers such as Indiana Jones. It allows us to see that discoveries are often the product of predictions, lengthy research and a great deal of skill and expertise.

Children's predictions

Predictions

A child's ability to predict accurately is also based upon a combination of skills and knowledge and, as suggested earlier, I was interested to see whether children in Years 3 and 4 would be able to make suggestions about timelines of archaeological artefacts. Their skills in doing this would be indicative of their historical understanding and reasoning. These Year 3 children were making predictions about what might be contained in an archaeological timeline case.

A: 'You might get metal.'

Me: 'Do you know what sort of metal?'

A: 'Bronze.'

B: 'And copper.'

C: 'And bones.'

D: 'Not wood, you don't get wood.'

Just like Philippe Gorczuynski most children appear fascinated by the idea that archaeological artefacts come from under the ground and are curious about what they tell us of lives lived in the past. Having experienced the 'digging and brushing away sand' approach taken at the Archaeological Resource Centre in York, and feeling uncomfortable about what children were learning, I decided to investigate whether I could test children's thinking about archaeology more deeply while at the same time enabling them to produce writing of real depth and quality. To do this I took more Timeline Museum artefact timelines into school and explored them with groups of Year 3 and 4 children. Once again I wrapped and placed the objects in my 1930s suitcases (because they look interesting) and gave the children museum cotton gloves to wear whilst handling the precious artefacts.

We explored four of the timelines:

- mobile phones;

- axes and weapons;

- decorative artefacts and jewellery;

- coins.

Children researching sources

Establishing the date

As Cooper (2012: 11–30) points out sources are complicated and don't yield their secrets easily. Thus the first activity was not about archaeology but based upon the process of enquiry and beforehand the children had been asked to find out what kinds of mobile phones their parents (or another adult) remembered having and in what year they thought they had used them. The most common answers were the Nokia 3310, which was made from around the year 2000, the Motorola Razr c.2004 and the Motorola 8000 series ('the brick') made during the 1980s. When one of these mobiles was mentioned I would remove an example of one from the case and give it to the group, which then would be asked to use the internet to find the correct date of first issue. This allowed the children to experience the idea of cross referencing sources – did their parents' ideas of when they bought a particular mobile tie up with the actual dates the phones were sold?

Researching the period

Once they had dated the phone the groups were asked to identify events that occurred at the same time as the phones were made. They were to look for events in the news (preferably centred on Britain), what the weather was like and aspects of popular culture, such as music, films, TV shows and fashion. Then the groups were asked (in a similar manner to that outlined above), to script a phone call between themselves and their parents at the time when they first owned the phone. Obviously some of the later phones in the collection were made around the time that the children were born. Some of the scripts were amusing as children tried to explain about, for example, an iPad, and one truly wonderful example was written in text speak. The following excerpt from a child's writing contains a reference to what an historian might call contemporary culture. I loved 'Robot Wars' (and so did my boys when they were young).

Me: 'Wot u doin' now?'

Mum: 'Watchin' telly.'

Me: 'Wot u watchin'?'

Mum: 'Robot Wars.'

For primary children of course mobiles are often an aspiration rather than a reality (although this child was clearly familiar with some of the conventions of text writing). These mobiles also provided an excellent opportunity to discuss artefacts and some fond memories with their parents.

This activity was successful because the children were clearly interested in the mobiles and they had an understanding of their purpose and meaning. With the archaeology there was a chance that this relationship would be more challenging, both because there would be little understanding of what the child was seeing and because they were essentially looking at 'rubbish' that had been deposited in the deep past.

Stories of archaeological sources

Therefore timelines were chosen which had a similar link to our present lives. Coins are part of the experience of even the youngest child and even the earliest hammered and punched silver Lydian disc has a recognisable form with a head (in this case a lion), on one side and an abstract form on the other. Coins are also (sometimes) cheap to buy (I have purchased a genuine Roman coin of Constantine the Great for a mere £1.50) and through using various numismatic books and websites, often easy to identify.

Archaeological decorative artefacts and jewellery have similar qualities, are easily available and, whilst not quite as cheap as coins, I have purchased a pretty and wearable Roman ring from the Timeline Museum for less than £30. Such artefacts, therefore, can often be worn and provoke great interest amongst the viewers.

Axes are a more challenging but equally recognisable artefact and have the merit of forming the longest timeline, which is over 350,000 years.

This time the children were told that the suitcases contained timelines of archaeology and if they could predict what was in them then they would be able to see and handle the artefacts, often using the gloves.

Predictions

I was surprised that no child predicted that there would be gold and treasure in the cases (possibly the Indiana Jones era has passed) and nor did they mention skulls – just as well because I had no gold and only one bone. Instead they predicted that there would be arrow heads, axes made of iron, stone and copper (in one case prompting was needed to elicit bronze) and after discussion, coins. They also predicted bracelets and brooches, which led us to discuss jewellery and decorative artefacts. In two of the discussions I was asked what my favourite artefact was, which enabled me to share a mammoth vertebrae (not really my favourite) and a cuniform writing tablet (probably my favourite). With one of the groups I asked them to predict the ages of the oldest artefacts and the answers predictably ranged between 1,000 and 12,000 years old.

As I said at the beginning of this chapter the children's predictions demonstrated an often very good grasp of archaeological concepts and vocabulary (thought not chronology) and this prompted me to test the children's understanding still further.

Similarities and differences through time travel

The last writing task was arrived at very late in the research process and to date it has only been possible to test it in a limited manner. During this last task pupils were asked to apply their knowledge to a novel situation and choose one of the artefacts that they felt inspired by. They could use me as an 'expert archaeologist' to answer questions or if they preferred engage in other forms of enquiry learning to build up their understanding of the people who used the artefact.

We then recalled such time-travel books as the classic *Tom's Midnight Garden* (Pearce 1958) or the more modern, *TimeRiders* book series by Alex Scarrow. A list of time-travel books for children can be found on the Book Trust website: http://www.booktrust.org.uk.

Once the children understood the artefact, its place on the timeline and who used it they were then asked to try and locate an image using books or the internet that would be a good example of such a person. They were also asked to give them (if possible) a period name and understand what they did to survive. This would then constitute the 'back-story' of a character that they were going to involve in a piece of fiction. They were encouraged to make the character one that they liked and understand what qualities made them likable (Browne 2001). Finally we discussed the notion that 'back story' is the life of a fictional character, which is known about by the author but not necessarily communicated in the story. It is important, however, because this 'back story' will inform the character's reactions in novel situations.

Time-travel writing

In this limited case we used Roman characters who had time-travelled forwards in time and were now staying in the child's own house. The children were asked to carefully and gently (so as not to frighten them too much), go about introducing the Roman to, and instructing them on, life in the modern world. In this 'story' the children were asked to concentrate on aspects of daily life in the home, because as yet the Roman was too 'scared' to be taken outside. We also asked them to predict some of the funny situations that might arise and what some of the risks might be.

The stories were very interesting, (especially for those who are familiar with the social learning theories of Bandura (1977)), as the children sometimes adopted the role of an adult taking responsibility for a new child. There was considerable concentration on the 'telly' and computers, which would need to be explained quickly, in order to reassure the person that there weren't small people inside a box. There was an acknowledged need for the character to understand how to operate an electric light but also that they would need to know how to flush a toilet and use toilet paper (because they used a sponge on a stick). There was also a discussion of whether they would know about taps, washing machines, brightly coloured and painted walls and fitted carpets. One child pointed out that it would be very difficult to explain about satellite dishes. Some of them were looking forward to showing them how to play with electronic toys. An interesting response was a child who wanted to show them a plasma ball because they are 'cool'. The most memorable phrase used was that they would have to explain the 'wireless radio', which I thought was a very interesting and careful choice of words.

> *Mum shouted up that somebody had forgotten to flush the toilet so I pretended it was me and look(ed) at Claudia. I hoped she had used toilet paper this time and not the sponge. When I got down for breakfast I saw that she was looking behind the telly again.*

This was an activity with real creative potential, where children had to understand and empathise with a Roman character.

Interpretations based on sources

A final activity, which has been useful for considering the notion of interpretation. For some strange reason I have a collection of different newspapers, dated Wednesday 11 September 1974. These are: *The Guardian, The Mail, The Mirror, The Sun, The Times, The Express* and *The Telegraph*. The main headlines were about the wreck of Prime Minister Heath's yacht – the *Morning Cloud*, the possibility of President Ford pardoning those involved in Watergate and the leaking of the Tory election manifesto. *The Mirror* and *The Sun* also ran headlines about a parrot. The pupils were asked to read two or three versions of the same story and decide which was the most accurate. They were then asked to re-write the story in their own words whilst trying to be as accurate as possible.

In this case Emily had chosen the story of the *Morning Cloud*, which was covered in most of the papers but was by then an old story. She commented that:

> *Most of the papers had a picture of it because it was very damaged but some didn't even mention when it had happened or that two people were killed.*

She decided to research the story still further using the internet and was fascinated to learn that Edward Heath was the Prime Minister and he had five yachts called *Morning Cloud* during his lifetime. She was amazed that yachts no. 1 and no. 3 had been wrecked within three days of each other. She then looked up further details about the Prime Minister's life and included facts about his life and love of music. During this work Emily worked as both a historian and journalist as she tried to make her story, as informative and as accurate as possible. In terms of reading and further research it was excellent preparation for study at a higher level.

Conclusion

Whilst researching for this chapter it was noted that some teachers had a real desire to re-embed creativity within their teaching while others felt guilty about the formulaic nature of their work, worries that are echoed by Lomas (2013).

Rebecca Sanders a Key Stage 1 teacher commented that it was a real struggle to find the time to allow the children to be creative and take risks. She said, you had to actually make time that was not just about grammar and spelling. The best approaches were, she said, cross curricular, and ones that the children come back to again and again. They were, she said, often something of real value, which was built up over a week.

Writing in history can be demanding whilst at the same time creative and engaging. It was also noted that good teaching, such as the use of artefacts and drama, play a crucial part in this process. It is also, however, often good to use strategies such as script writing or journalistic articles where the narrative has a strong and replicable structure.

References

Bandura, A. (1977) *Social Learning Theory*, New Jersey: Prentice Hall.

Battle of the Somme (1916), Published and produced as a DVD by the Imperial War Museum.

Browne, A. (2001) *Developing Language and Literacy 3–8*, London: Paul Chapman Publishing.

Collingwood, R.G. (1939) *An Autobiography*, Oxford: Oxford University Press.

Cooper, H. (2012) *History 5-11*, Abingdon: Routledge.

Cooper, H. (2013) *Teaching History Creatively*, Abingdon: Routledge.

Department for Education (DFE) (2013) National Curriculum in England, Subject Content for Key Stages 1 and 2, available online at www.gov.uk/dfe/nationalcurriculum.

Fines, J. (2013) Children writing history paper published on the Historical Association website available online at http://www.history.org.uk/resources/primary (accessed 12.02.2014).

Heathcote, D. (2013) History, drama and education for life, first published in *Primary History 48* and available as a paper on the HA website: http://www.history.org.uk/resources/primary (accessed 12.02.2014).

Hodkinson, A. (2004) The social context and the assimilation of historical concepts: an indicator of academic performance or an unreliable metric? *Research in Education*,71: 50–66.

Lomas, T. (2013) OFSTED, Primary history and creativity, published on the Historical Association website, available at http://www.history.org.uk/resources/primary.

Macardle, Kenneth (1916) War diary entries, available online at http://www.hellfirecorner.co.uk/hartley/jh.htm (accessed 12.02.2014).

Pearce, P. (1958) *Tom's Midnight Garden*, re-issued London: Puffin Books.

Richard, Jack, Return to the Front. York Museums and Galleries. Image accessed Oct 2013 via http://www.bbc.co.uk/arts/yourpaintings/artists/richard-jack/paintings/slideshow.

Scarrow, A, (series) *TimeRiders*, London: Puffin Books.

Studdert Kennedy, G.A., poems available online at http://www.poemhunter.com/geoffrey-anketell-studdert-kennedy (accessed 12.02.2014).

Writing about time

Hilary Cooper

Concepts of time

Concepts of time are at the heart of history. A broad chronological framework provides a structure within which to place new knowledge, in relation to existing knowledge and so to develop a coherent understanding. But understanding concepts of time also involves interrogating that framework (Cooper 2012: 41–51). What changed when, why and what was the effect on people's lives? Why did some things change very slowly and others rapidly? What did different periods in the past have in common? How was life in one period different from another; how did people live and think differently? What people and events were most significant? What are the connections between different aspects of change (economic, political, social, cultural), or between different countries or civilisations. Above all, how are we connected with the past; why is it relevant to us?

The National Curriculum framework is dynamic

The National Curriculum (DfE 2013) is intended to develop children's coherent understanding of the past. This involves more than memorising of the dates of kings and queens. Constructing this coherence is a dynamic process. Children need to constantly revisit these questions in the light of their increasing historical knowledge and maturity. For these can be answered in different ways, even by historians. There is little chance of building up a coherent picture of the past when there is nothing but a chronological thread to hold it together (Howson 2007).

Planning for overviews and depth studies

Why is an overview important?

There has been justified criticism that young people do not have a coherent picture of the past. (This is inevitable, given that the primary National Curriculum for History (DEE 1999) moved from Saxons and Vikings to Tudors, jumped to Victorians, then to Britain since 1930. Children knew a lot about the periods they had studied but were not able to make connections or see a 'big picture'. Dawson (2008) claims that if pupils can tell a story with links across time this gives them a sense of real achievement. He says that it should be made clear, from the beginning of learning history, that this is what they are learning to do; they should be introduced to an outline of 'the big picture' they are going to find out about from the start.

The 'big picture' of the past must also be linked to the present, in order to make it relevant. We need to get children to see the past, not as separate from the present but ourselves as part of a continuum. What we aim to do is help children to make connections both within a period and across different periods. And, very importantly, a combination of related overview and depth studies is essential for time management, if children are to engage meaningfully with times in the past and also to relate them to a bigger picture. An overview might start with the Stone Ages until the present day. It usually takes the form of a timeline, with visual images, of key people and events and marked in units of time, which can be constantly referred to and ideally is created by children.

Themes

Themes are key concepts, which can be traced throughout the 'big picture', linking the past to the present day. We need to trace change and continuity over a long period, in ways that link past and present. Themes that might be built into planning and discussed might be: conflict, everyday life, links with other countries, power and democracy, or they might be the themes suggested by Dawson (below). The National Curriculum (DfE 2013) suggests that a theme might be a study over time extending pupils' knowledge beyond 1066, by tracing how several aspects of national history are reflected in the locality or a study of a theme in British history, such as the changing power of monarchs, changes in social history such as crime and punishment, the artistic and literary legacy of Greek or Roman history up to the present day. A chronological framework and a non European society that contrasts with British history should be extended to include an overview of early civilisations.

Depth studies

Depth studies need to be enquiries that are selected to reflect and deepen understanding of some of the key themes. Dawson (2009) suggests a depth study may be introduced as a story, which can be introduced in one session as a hypothesis to be reformulated through depth enquiries. This might, for example, explore the story from different perspectives. The depth enquiries show the interconnectedness and significance of events. We need to see the past as a series of interconnected stories, not as disconnected episodes.

It is also through the depth studies that children can begin not just to create sets of the visual aspects of a period (dress, furniture, houses), but also begin to 'get inside' the mind sets of a Roman, the Iceni, a Saxon, a Viking, and so to build up a sense of period.

Links between themes and depth studies

Dawson (2009) shows how enquiries about everyday life can be linked to the big picture, the key themes, the big questions. He sets this out under the following headings, for investigations in each period to be concluded at the end of a unit. These could be addressed in groups.

Time

- What were the key dates for this in depth study?
- When does this period fit into a sequence of periods?

Daily life

- **What would you have seen:**
- What did people wear?
- What kinds of buildings?
- How did they travel/communicate?
- What kinds of machinery/power?
- What kinds of work did they do?
- What did they do for fun?

What did they know?

- About science and technology?
- About other cultures and peoples?
- About medicine and health?

People and events

- Who lived then?
- What happened then?

Ideas and attitudes

- Who had a say in government?
- What did they expect rulers to do for them?
- Were all people equal?
- Were they tolerant of other religions?
- What justified war?
- Were they afraid of having nothing to eat?
- What did they think caused illness?

Banham (2000) argues that more time should be spent on depth studies than breadth studies because they are memorable and this is a more time efficient and historically valuable way of organising the curriculum.

Activities for long term assessment

- Provide a set of still or moving images and ask pupils to sequence them then write the voiceover that makes links with the period.

- Provide the story so far and ask children to provide the next image and voiceover.

- Jigsaw: sort pieces into sequence, identify any changes or continuities; reasons for changes and continuities.

- Start with a story about monarchy and develop an everyday life study from there.

- Picture sorting: sort images according to period. Why do you think so?

- Stand on a timeline as key characters (real individuals rather than events). Each person tell your story, then move on to the next person.

For more activities exploring time visit www.thinkinghistory.co.uk.

Case study 1, Year 6

Concepts of time

Concepts of time include continuity and change, cause and consequence, similarity and difference (DfE 2013). I explored these concepts of time and change over 6,500 years with a Year 6 class, on two very hot summer afternoons, in a school in rural Cumbria, encouraging them, in a fairly rudimentary way given the time constraints, to make connections, draw contrasts, analyse trends and frame historically valid questions (DfE 2013). I began by explaining that we were going to use four timelines. I had used these previously, when working with adults. Ideally children would have constructed these themselves. I said that we would use the timelines to ask and try to answer questions about changes, why things changed and how this might affect people's lives, discuss their ideas and make structured notes about them. The following day they would work in groups, using their notes to present their ideas as a piece of writing.

Some quick time questions

I began with a few quick questions to gauge the children's understanding of the measurement of time and time calculations. They were able to explain key terms: chronology, century, decade, A.D., B.C., CE., BCE. And they could calculate and compare durations of time over centuries. Well done Mrs Ager (the teacher) and her colleagues!

Interrogating the timelines

The four timelines were made from different coloured spools of florists' ribbon (bought for my niece's wedding), and the centuries were marked using 50 cm to represent one century, over a period from 4,500 BCE to the present. The themes for the timelines were central to history: beliefs, agriculture, houses and land transport. Since it was a lovely day we went into the playground and the children, in four groups, unrolled the timelines in parallel and secured them with sticky tape. They were amazed to see a visual representation of how far 6,500 years extended. 'Before the Romans!'

I had made picture cards by cutting significant images from a Key Stage 3 history textbook (These are very reasonably priced because so many are sold – lucky authors), and sticking them onto blank postcards. On the reverse I stuck the information caption from the book, including the date, or dates. The children were asked to work in four groups, to share out the cards related to their theme and to place them where they thought they belonged on the timeline, using the small piece of Blu Tack on the back. Then they were to discuss the questions on a note-taking frame (see table 7.1) then note their answers. The questions were:

- What did not change much for a long time?

- Between what dates was there not much change?

- How long was this?

- Can you think of some reasons why there was little change?

- How do you think this affected people's lives?

- What changed in a very short time?

- What do you think changed quickly?

- When? Between ? and?

- How do you think this changed people's lives?

- What changes do you think were an improvement?

- What changes do you think were not an improvement?

Jen Ager and I answered questions and offered clues when asked. We also moved between the groups, jotting down some of the discussions we overheard.

Oracy: snippets of overheard discussions

- **Disagreement – music to my heart!**

  Three boys sitting on a step were talking to the head teacher, who had come to see what they were doing. 'We're having a really interesting disagreement . . . '

- **Questioning the questions**

  Girl asks, 'But how long IS a short time? – 300 years – or not . . . .?'

  Group of boys. 'But some things in transport did not last for a long time or a short time. They *gradually* improved – like improved carriages, then improvements in trains, 1830 experiment, steam – then diesel . . .

■ No Whigs here!

I was surprised that most children did not have a Whig view of history; the idea that things continuously improve. Two children expressed this view, with valid reasons. 'Some things changed for the better, like living longer and better health treatments . . . '.

Others replied that, 'Things get better for some and not for others. There are always some poor people'.

One group of boys argued that they would 'rather have fought on a battlefield with lances and axes than in today's warfare'. 'And women and children weren't involved in those days. They were far away from the battlefield'.

'Why did they build all these little houses (prefabs) when most people already had brick houses'

■ Continuity between past and present

This discussion led to an awareness of continuity between past and present. 'Warfare has got far worse . . . kills more people . . . and it's going on in Syria AT THIS VERY MINUTE.' (Jorn Rüsen, the proponent of the idea of 'historical consciousness', would be impressed! This concept, which is dominant in, for example Germany and Brazil, emphasises the importance of understanding the past in order to understand the present and so to make decisions about the future.

■ Stimuli for further investigations

J. was intrigued by a picture of a 100 AD Iron Age horse masque (Stanwick Horse Mask, www.britishmuseum.org) and discussed with me the importance of the horse as a symbol, in the Iron Age. He considered the fact that we do not really know what it symbolised. He immediately enthused his group to want to 'find out more about the Iron Age'.

J. was anxious to point out that there were other concurrent more advanced civilisations, during the time these timelines described and planned to do a timeline for Greeks and Egyptians and to find out more about Cambodia, which he had found interesting when studying the Vietnam War in a topic on the 1960s.

■ Were changes an improvement?

'I'd rather have grown my own food and been able to walk to see my friends than having to buy it and go by bus to see them.'

■ Making connections

The transport group discussed connections between the inventing of steam power, steam trains, steam power to drain mines and mine coal and to make iron.

■ Issues

A. brought me pictures of a farm house and a suburban terrace house, both with the same range of dates. Question – 'Why do they have the same (mid nineteenth century) dates, then discovered that there were two other houses with these dates – Why? This led to a discussion about differences between town and country and different social and economic status, which became increasingly apparent in the Victorian period.

■ Different rates of change

I discussed with R. the reasons why there was a picture of a steam-powered threshing machine, introduced in the mid nineteenth century and also one of farm horses working on the land in the 1940s.

■ Continuity and change – overlaps

C. showed me a picture of a nineteenth-century farm house and said that she lived in a house like that and 'I was born in 2001', which led to further discussion about continuity.

■ Making connections

'Why did they have these little chapels in the nineteenth century when all the towns and villages already had a big church?' This led to making links with people's move to towns and work in mines and factories and their need for different kinds of worship.

■ Is it OK to *guess*?

The group working on 'beliefs' engaged in animated discussion about the role of 'guessing' in history, when we cannot know and to what extent this was valuable.

'We think they took so much effort over so many years that they (stone circles and henges) must have been to do with their beliefs. Were they about the seasons, sun worship, a meeting place for believers? We shall never know.'

All of this discussion took place in constructing the timelines and in filling in the note-taking frames – clear evidence of the importance of teachers listening and observing quietly sometimes, as well as of engaging in discussion in response to questions.

But we cannot pretend that everyone is 'on task' ALL the time.

Teacher: What are *you* thinking Alice?

'I was wondering if her (HC's) dress is white or pink . . .

Note-taking

The note-taking frames were designed to challenge children's thinking about change and to categorise their ideas about it and reasons for it, as shown in table 7.1. The numbers in the left-hand column suggest new paragraphs when developed as extended writing and the letters in the right-hand column refer to pictures from the timeline, which could illustrate the points being made.

Translating notes into extended writing

We cannot pretend that everything always flows smoothly, as planned. There were groans at the expectation of 'extended writing' the following day. Indeed the children's preparation notes were fairly brief and did not reflect the quality of discussion that underpinned them (table 7.1).

TABLE 7.1 Extract from Christian's, James' and Ryan's notes on the timeline for farming.

Preparation notes for TV programme / magazine article/ interview on...............

for the series ...*ITH News* Christian, James, Ryan M

			Picture reference
1.	What did not change much for a long time?	Farming 6000 years	A
	Between what dates was there not much change?	4500 BC 1500 AD	G
	How long was this?	6000 years	
	Can you think of some reasons why there was little change?	a) The Systme worked fine b) people were rougher c) technology wasnt advanced d) e)	
2	How do you think this affected people's lives?	they were resilliant	
3	What changed in a very? short time	The Flyl Size size changed sheep cattle	DEF
	When? Between 185 and 1900		
	Why do you think this changed so quickly?	a) because technology was more advanced b) The mass product Shon changed fast c) d)	C

But when I explained that the writing could be in the form of a TV or radio interview, a magazine article or a PowerPoint presentation, they rushed to their computers with enthusiasm.

However, children were anxious to get on with 'televising' the interviews without preparing them in writing first. Jen suggested that it would be helpful to give them a model to show them how the information in their notes could be developed and written in a different genre. So the following day she and I read an interview I had written the previous evening based on one group's notes and employing all our dramatic skills. The class was greatly entertained by this and children were then keen to start writing – all using electronic means as you would imagine – groans at suggestion of handwriting.

One thing that interested me was that all the groups were anxious to explore and expand the information they had been given on the timeline, mainly using the internet, and to incorporate their research into their writing. This research was in response to what interested the children and to questions raised in discussion. For example the radio interview below adds the information, which had been researched, that farming began in Egypt, long before the start of the timeline the children had been given. And I liked the way the presenter flagged a following programme on the Iron Age, which is what he had desperately wanted to research for this programme.

Extended writing

It was interesting to see how naturally children adopted the style of media interviews. These could have been considerably extended, had time allowed.

A radio interview: changes in farming

The layout and font were as selected by the children.

Parts

Presenter 1 – C. J. (Bob Hale) Main presenter of the HHH news

Presenter 2 – J. W. (Charles Smith) Agriculture correspondent for HHH news

Curator of the British Museum – R. M. (Dr. Geoffrey Moreson)

Script

Presenter 1: Hello and welcome to HHH News. I am Bob Hale and today I will be meeting Charles Smith, our Agricultural correspondent, and one special guest, Dr. Geoffrey Moreson, Curator of the British Museum.

Presenter 2: Oooh here he is!

Presenter 1: Let us welcome to HHH News today Dr. Geoffrey Moreson, Curator of the British Museum!

Geoffrey: Hello Bob!

Presenter 2: So Dr. Moreson, I have read in your recent article in The Times *that farming didn't change for a long time, more than one thousand years?*

Geoffrey: A lot more than that!

Presenter 2: Really? Blimey, how much more?

Geoffrey: Between 4500 BC and 1500 AD, about 6,000 years.

Presenter 2: So please tell me, why didn't farming change for such a long time?

Geoffrey: The main reason was simple, people didn't want or need to change, they had a perfectly good system as it was and they were a lot tougher, so they could do a lot more of the physical labour themselves.

Presenter 2: But we must remember that farming started over 10,000 years ago, in Egypt?

Geoffrey: Yes it started when the ancient hunter-gatherers settled down in one place and started planting and harvesting crops.

Presenter 2: But when did things change? I mean, it's hugely different today!

Geoffrey: It first started revolutionising when the Tudor sheep farmers kept huge flocks of sheep and started to export their wool. Although it only really took off in the 1700s when rich landowners bought up huge tracts of land and experimented breeding larger animals and growing corn in new ways. And by the 1800s people started mechanised methods, for example steam powered threshing machines. But farming was only fully mechanised in the 20th century and horses were still used to plough up to the 1940s.

Presenter 2: And the last question I'm going to ask is for the viewers, how do you think that the changes in farming have affected our lives today? (Long pause)

Presenter 1: Well thank you Geoffrey!

Geoffrey: A pleasure Bob!

Presenter 1: Well I think that every viewer enjoyed that fascinating interview and I will thank Geoffrey once again.

Geoffrey: Goodbye Bob!

Presenter 1: Goodbye Geoffrey! (Long pause as Geoffrey exits)

Presenter 1 Well I think all of our listeners learned loads, I certainly did!

Presenter 2: Yeah!

Presenter 1: I especially liked the fact that from the early Iron Age and late Medieval Ages farming hardly changed! Over 6000 years! And also farming changed so much in just under 500 years with steam threshers and everything!

Presenter 2: Yeah it's amazing!

Presenter 1: Well bye listeners and stay tuned for next week's episode on Iron Age forts.

Nevertheless, it was interesting to see that, while the boys who wrote the notes in table 7.1 had much to say orally about impact of changes in farming on lives today they took no notes on this and, very cleverly, the interview ran out of time before this was discussed. They concluded their radio interview by asking the viewers this question.

PowerPoint presentations

It was interesting that the children themselves differentiated their choice of written presentation. Those who were less good writers chose to make a PowerPoint, finding their own images to illustrate the points they were making in the headings and notes. And sometimes they focused on a shorter period.

One enterprising presentation was called 'The Horrible Historians Show'! It promised that, 'Here you will find out the basic history of mysteries hidden, deep, deep in the past.' The first slide, a picture of a horse pulling a hoe, with a reference to Jethro Tull's *Horse-Hoeing Husbandry* (1733) was followed by two information slides. The first slide (below) considers similarity and difference between now and 'then' and links the authors directly with former times, adding some researched information about horse-hoes.

We have it easy these days, all that farming back in the olden days – (4000 BCE–1500 CE) –really took blood, sweat and tears! We would all still be walking up and down fields having a horse pulling

The second slide has information about how the changes came about, with sympathetic concern for people who suffered for it at the time.

Because of the people that realized that there was money to be earned through the industry of farming, many people became rich and people that were poor had all their land bought off of them. This left them homeless, cold & very hungry.

The fourth slide has two images, illustrating changes since 79 AD. The images are captioned 'THEN'.

'Harvesting wheat in 79 AD with a sharp tool that can cut wheat', connected by an arrow to 'NOW', 'Harvesting wheat in 2013 with a huge machine called a combine harvester.'

Case study 2, Year 3

Significance: Romans in Britain

It was another hot afternoon at the end of the summer term. I had been told that the class had 'done a topic on the Romans'. I wondered what they would argue was 'most significant' about the Romans in Britain. The teacher told me that they had loved everything about the Roman Army, perhaps not surprising since the class consisted of twenty-two boys and seven girls – although I hoped they might have found other aspects 'significant', as well. They had been to the Vindolanda Army Museum. They had also visited the farm where one member of the class lived, in which an unexcavated Roman fort had been discovered. As a result a professional archaeologist had worked with the class, explaining what archaeologists do and helped them to 'dig' in huge sand-trays, carefully brushing away the layers of sand and recording their finds. They had been very enthusiastic about a Time Team programme on Roman excavation, made an aqueduct out of Lego and watched a Doctor Who programme in which he went back to Pompeii in the Tardis.

Following this the children has researched Vindolanda, discovered that the A6 road outside their school had been a Roman road, then written stories about the Romans who may have walked along it. They had made a variety of models connected with Roman Britain at home – always a sign of enthusiasm. They made an exhibition of these and the other classes had visited the exhibition, which each group of model-makers explained to the visitors, as they walked around. So there had been lots of research, activities and talk. The teacher told me, however, that these boys were reluctant writers.

What do historians mean by 'significant?'

I explained to the class that the curators at the Carlisle Museum were thinking of creating a special exhibition on 'the Romans', but that they had very limited space, so my friend, who is a museum consultant, had been asked to recommend what was most significant about the Romans in Britain, so that the exhibition could focus on this.

We discussed how it is impossible to include everything we know about the past in an exhibition – or a book – so historians select what they think is most significant, most important. They may decide on a person or an event or on people's beliefs, on changes or on aspects of people's everyday lives. We agreed that historians must have reasons for what they decide is most 'significant', that different historians might have different ideas about what is most significant and also why people at different times might come to different conclusions. They might consider what had most affected the lives of people at the time, how many people and which people, or they might argue that the things that still affect our lives today were the most significant. A hot afternoon and still everyone engaged – well done!

What the children thought was significant

So what did these Year 3 historians think was most significant about the Romans?

Lots of hands raised. I recorded children's key ideas as headings in blue on the electronic whiteboard and listed additional ideas related to the key ideas under the headings in green. Supporting reasons had to be given; because . . . They discussed their ideas enthusiastically with 'talking partners' for a couple of minutes. Then shared them with the whole class. I was delighted that things other than the army were seen as significant. Table 7.4 represents extended explanations. The word hygiene, for example, encapsulates discussion of Roman methods of tooth cleaning and toilet habits and fitness refers to the need for Roman soldiers to have small stomachs and 'small butts' (yes, I needed further explanations here too). Half an hour later the board looked like this – only not so neat (Table 7.2).

Working in pairs of children who had chosen the same 'most significant thing' they recorded their ideas about why they thought this was most significant, supported by at least four reasons.

Break time!

Planning the letter to the museum consultant

Tables 7.3 and 7. 4 show how children's writing about significance was scaffolded.

TABLE 7.2 Suggestions for the most significant aspects of 'the Romans'

Farms	*Army*	*Baths*	*Roads*	*Viaducts*	*Villas*	*Hadrian's wall*	*Myths*	*Emperors*
Cattle Crops Food	Turtle Fitness of Soldiers Forts Weapons Armour	Spring waters Hot/ Warm/ Cold baths	Mile-stones Ditches How roads made Taverns	Aqua - ducts	Hygiene Pottery Mosaic floors 'Fridges' Hypocaust	Mile-castles Mile-turrets Watch towers	Romulus Remus Venus Mars Mercury	Caesar Augustus Nero Julius Caesar Hadrian

TABLE 7.3 Shows how a child planned his letter arguing that the exhibition should be about the Roman Army.

We think the museum exhibition about the Romans must include	
army	
This is significant	because
helped make empire	*famous*
Also	because
protected empire	*protected Rome*
Another reason is	because
clever attacks	*formation weapons*
Finally	because
	organised brave
For these reasons, we hope that your Roman exhibition will be about	
the army	

Different arguments about what was most significant

The 'significance' distribution in the letters was:

Farms (8) (these children lived in a rural community)

Because they needed crops: to feed the army and feed the animals and they ate the animals and make bread; they feed people in the towns; to sell to the empire. They could buy things they needed like horses and chariots with the money.

TABLE 7.4 Shows how another child planned her letter arguing that the Roman gods were most important.

We think the museum exhibition about the Romans must include	
Roman Gods	
This is significant Mars	because helped win battles
Also Venus	because helped to get married
Another reason is Neptune	because stop storms at sea
Finally Jupiter	because controlled all Gods
For these reasons, we hope that your Roman exhibition will be about	
Roman Gods	

Emperors (5)

Because they are important leaders; they commanded the army and ruled the Empire; some of them were made gods and so people respected them.

Gods (2)

The gods supported them in difficult situations.

Roads (3)

Because they needed to walk from place to place; they helped them to stay on the right track; they went straight between places and were built of stones and they could go quickly; we still use the roads; they connected forts and cities.

Army (3)

Because they made the Empire one of the most famous and the largest ever; they protected Rome and the rest of the Empire; they were clever in ways of attacking and made good weapons; they used a very clever formation in battle and were nearly always successful, because they were organised and brave.

Baths (3)

Because they were heated with a hypocaust so they were hot; they also invented underfloor heating; there were three baths, cold, warm and hot. They scraped themselves clean with a strigilis and oil.

Villas (1)

Because they could be safe at night if the locals invaded; they had comfortable furniture.

Letters to the museum consultant

Each letter was beautifully written. The children were given school headed paper, so that they could focus on presenting their ideas in a letter format. The letters developed from the scaffolds for the proposing the Roman Army as the most significant focus for the exhibition (table 7.3) was developed into a letter (figure 7.1). The letter developed from the arguments (table 7.4) advocating a focus on Roman gods is developed in figure 7.2.

The reward of a response

It is important that children write for a purpose, or for an audience or an identified readership. So of course class 3 were delighted to receive in the post this encouraging response from Mrs W.

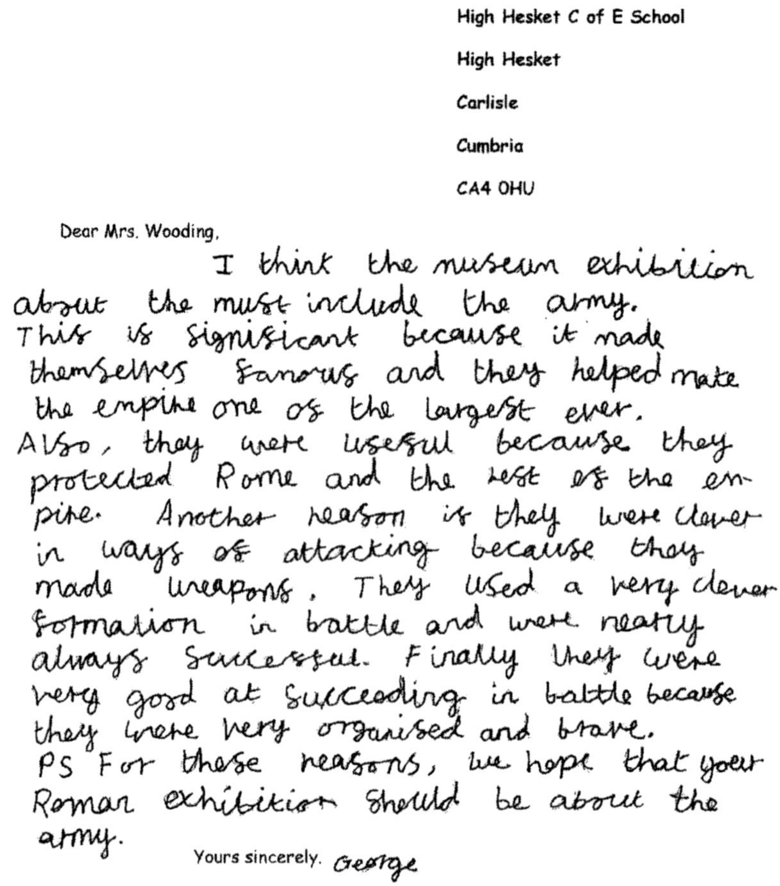

High Hesket C of E School

High Hesket

Carlisle

Cumbria

CA4 OHU

Dear Mrs. Wooding,

I think the museum exhibition about the must include the army. This is significant because it made themselves famous and they helped make the empire one of the largest ever. Also, they were useful because they protected Rome and the rest of the empire. Another reason is they were clever in ways of attacking because they made weapons. They used a very clever formation in battle and were nearly always successful. Finally they were very good at succeeding in battle because they were very organised and brave. PS For these reasons, we hope that your Roman exhibition should be about the army.

Yours sincerely. George

FIGURE 7.1 George's letter proposing the exhibition should be about the Roman Army.

Dear Class 3,

I read your letters, recommending the focus for an exhibition about the Romans, with great interest. You had such a lot of different topics which you think would be important to include in the exhibition (farms, roads, villas, temples, emperors, myths) and I was very interested in the reasons you gave for your choices. Clearly you have done a lot of work on, and enjoyed finding out about the Romans. I agree with you that these themes are all important, so I shall recommend to the curators at Carlisle Museum that when they plan a new Roman exhibition they take all your suggestions into account. Thank you all very much for writing to me . . .

Conclusion

These case studies, since they preceded the introduction of the 2013 National Curriculum, are merely exploratory. Indeed at present, there is insufficient evidence of how children can

High Hesket C of E School

High Hesket

Carlisle

Cumbria

CA4 0HU

Dear Mrs. Wooding,

We think the museum exhibition about the Romans must include the Roman Gods. This is significant because of Mars. Mars helped the Romans win their battles. Also because of Venus. The Goddess of love would help the Romans when they wanted to get married. Another reason is Neptune. The Romans prayed to Neptune for no storms when they were at sea. Finally Jupiter. Jupiter was the Roman king of Gods and he controlled all the Gods. For these reasons, we hope that your Roman exhibition will be about Roman Gods.

Yours sincerely. Alex and Tom

FIGURE 7.2 Alex and Tom wrote a letter arguing for an exhibition on Roman gods.

construct and interrogate chronological frameworks. Since the recent National Curriculum for History at Key Stage 2 emphasises the importance of developing a chronological framework in which overview and depth studies are combined this should become clearer. The new curriculum leaves teachers a considerable amount of freedom in the ways in which they do this. There is no requirement that history is taught in chronological sequence, the curriculum is expected to continue after 1066 and it is not stated that the study units must be equally weighted. There are many ways of developing and sequencing the statutory content and many interesting discussions to be had in doing so. It could be argued that it is logical for the first four units (Ancient Britain, Roman Empire, settlement of Anglo-Saxons and Scots, Viking and Anglo-Saxon struggles) to be taught in sequence over Years 3–6, perhaps for one term each, to establish a framework, a British history theme beyond 1066 in Year 6 in preparation for Key Stage 3, and the remaining four units, in no especial order, taught during the second or third term of each year. It is hoped that this chapter has indicated some of the possibilities of linking depth and breadth studies, however the history curriculum is structured.

References

Banham, D. (2000) The return of King John: using depth to strengthen overview, *Teaching History*, 99: 22–31.

Cooper, H. (2012) *History 5 – 11: a guide for teachers*, Abingdon: Routledge.

Dawson, I. (2008) Thinking across time: planning and teaching the power of time and democracy, *Teaching History* 130: 14–23.

Dawson, I. (2009) What time does the tune start? *Teaching History*, 135: 50–56.

Department for Education (DfE) (2013) The National Curriculum in England, available online at https://www.gov.uk/government/collections/national-curriculum.Department for Employment and Education (DfEE) (1999) *The National Curriculum: handbook for primary teachers in England*, available online at http://webarchive.nationalarchives.gov.uk/20130401151715/https://www.education.gov.uk/publications/standard/publicationDetail/Page1/QCA/99/457 (accessed 12.02.2014).

Howson, J. (2007) 'Is it the Tuarts and then the Studars or the other way round?' The importance of developing a usable picture of the past, *Teaching History*, 127: 40–47.

It depends on your point of view

Exploring different representations of the past

Penelope Harnett, Sarah Whitehouse and Jane Carter

Interthinking

Littleton and Mercer (2013: 1) explain how spoken language enables people to 'think creatively and productively together'. They call this *interthinking* and discuss how this process reflects an important evolutionary stage, when humans began to recognise the power of collective solutions, rather than seeking individual courses of action. *Interthinking* occurs when people *interact* with each other. It requires people to utilise language in dynamic ways, both to express their understandings and also to reach new and original understandings, as a result of their *interthinking*.

In order to evaluate the talk being undertaken in collective activities, Littleton and Mercer propose three levels of analysis: linguistic, psychological and cultural. Linguistically, they draw attention to looking at different types of talk as texts: disputational, cumulative and exploratory. These involve learners in different roles and forms of interaction. At the psychological level Littleton and Mercer consider how talk contributes to joint thinking and action through analysis of the forms of interaction. Culturally, they remind use those important contexts, the occasions when talk occurs and the opportunities for dialogues, which are presented and which are denied. In this chapter we discuss opportunities for *interthinking* as children engage in historical enquiries and we consider the range of talk that supports the development of their historical understanding.

Understanding representations of the past

Learning about different representations of the past has been a feature of the National Curriculum for History since its introduction in 1990. The National Curriculum revised in

2000 required pupils at Key Stage 2 to 'recognise that the past is represented and interpreted in different ways, and to give reasons for this' (DfEE/QCA 1999; 104–105). The National Curriculum (DfE 2013) continues to acknowledge the importance of interpretations and includes, amongst the aims for teaching history, that all pupils should, 'understand the methods of historical enquiry, including how evidence is used rigorously to make historical claims, and discern how and why contrasting arguments and interpretations of the past have been constructed.' (https://www.gov.uk/government/uploads/system/uploads/attachment_data/file/239035/PRIMARY_national_curriculum_-_History.pdf)

These requirements have marked a shift in traditional ways of thinking about how history may be taught to primary aged children. The single story about people and past events has been replaced by a range of stories with different emphases and details. We want to encourage children to think that people in the past had different views about events and that there are different versions of what happened. We also want to encourage children to think about how stories about the past have been constructed in a variety of media – books, films, images and so on; why and how interpretations differ and how they might be evaluated. Children are thus involved in making their own judgements and analysing evidence to support their own views.

In this chapter we discuss three case studies, which provide examples of how different teachers developed strategies to support children in exploring a variety of representations and interpretations of the past. We indicate how these studies, (World War II and its aftermath, a local history study of the Tonypandy riots and European exploration and settlement in North America), relate to the subject content of the history National Curriculum for England, and in the second case also that of the history curriculum for Wales.

Case study 1

Who benefitted from World War II?

World War II and its aftermath

This unit was planned for a Year 6 class at the end of the summer term. Children had completed their Standard Attainment Tests and were preparing for their transfer to different secondary schools. The unit contributes to the National Curriculum requirement to study an aspect of British history that extends pupils' chronological knowledge beyond 1066 and enables children to study the 'complexity of specific aspects of the content' (DfE 2013: 191). It also provides opportunities for children to contextualise their knowledge of British history in the aftermath of World War II within a world context, through learning about peoples' experiences in the USSR, the USA, Japan and Germany.

Historical novel; the aftermath of war

The class was reading *I am David* (Holm 1963) in their literacy lesson. This is the story of a twelve-year-old refugee boy who escapes from a labour camp in Eastern Europe with few possessions and some directions on how to reach Denmark. It recounts his travels across Europe and provides vivid images of daily life during the early post-war period. The teacher wanted to provide children with a greater understanding of the historical background, to enhance their understanding of the story, through learning about ways of life in Europe after the war. She also felt that through looking at the stories of individuals (whether fictional or real life), the children would gain a greater appreciation of the effects of the war on people's lives. This is an example of where productive links may be developed between history and other aspects of the curriculum.

The teacher wanted to help the children appreciate some of the devastation that occurred during the war and its aftermath. She was concerned that children might have the impression that when war ends and peace is concluded, everything returns to normal. A main aim of the unit was to question and challenge children's perceptions. Children are confronted with many images of the World War II, but rarely do they learn about its aftermath.

Framing an overarching enquiry question

Activities were planned within a broad enquiry question, which would enable children to explore perspectives of different people who lived during the war and also to think about how representations of their experiences are constructed. Children were asked to consider the question, did any country benefit from World War II? This enquiry question directed children's enquiries and also involved them in making some evaluative judgements at the end of the learning unit. The question was sufficiently open-ended to encourage children to express their opinions and to evaluate a range of evidence to justify their viewpoints.

Smaller enquiries

Within the overarching enquiry question, smaller enquiries were planned where children researched what happened in different countries (UK, Japan, Germany, USA and the USSR) following the war. After learning about one of the countries, children wrote one or two paragraphs on the effect of the war, before moving on to consider another country. This enabled them to keep a record of their learning, which they could draw on, when they wrote their final piece of writing, asking them for their opinions on whether any country benefitted from the war. It provided them with opportunities to practise writing sentences putting their own points of view, using explanatory frames, which were first modelled by the teacher. Children had opportunities to 'try out' different ways of constructing sentences, focusing on the clarity and purpose of their writing.

Cremin and Myhill (2012:76) suggest such scaffolding, rather than using restrictive writing frames, enables children to see writing as something they have control over, in terms of 'design', with a reader in mind. Not only did this provide the children with a purpose for writing – but it also demonstrated to the children how their different pieces of writing could accumulate and act as sources of information, to enable them to answer the main enquiry question at the end of the unit. The purposes for their writing are not always apparent to children and organising their work in this way, made this more explicit.

The activities described below are a selection of those utilised by the teacher as she encouraged children to explore the involvement of different countries in the war and what happened after peace was concluded.

Starting points: encouraging discussion and debate

Opportunities were created for children to share their opinions at regular intervals during all lessons. A variety of devices to encourage children to explore their own ideas and also to listen to each other's views was used. This was important since it gave children the chance to rehearse what they had learned and to refine their explanations, so that others could understand. It also required children to listen carefully to each other and to respond to each other's opinions. Partner talk was used effectively and all children had the opportunity to explore and to respond to different sources of information about the war. Skilful questioning by the teacher enabled the children to utilise different forms of talk as texts, described by Littleton and Mercer (2013) above. For example in an activity before assembly, the class was asked to discuss the questions *Should governments alone have the right to decide about going to war? Why can't people of a country vote for or against war? What do you think?* (www.goodmorningchildren.com/search/showplc/d/11579). Such questions have contemporary resonance and the children had many suggestions to make. There were opportunities for disputational talk, as children argued their own points of view. However, some consensus was finally agreed, when children acknowledged that there would always be too many conflicting ideas on whether a war should be started and therefore it might be better to entrust questions concerning war and peace to the government.

Questions were often open ended, permitting children to explain and justify their own points of view. For example, having learned about how Germany was divided following the war, children were asked if it was justifiable to treat Germany in such a way. Whilst some children felt that it was important to teach Germany a lesson, other children reflected different views and showed some appreciation of the diversity of opinions, held by Germans living at the time, in their answers.

> *I disagree. Everyone was punished for a few peoples' actions – they shouldn't have been treated like that.*

And

> *Not all Germans wanted to support Germany in the war – why should they be punished?*

Photographs were used to stimulate discussion and the exchange of different views. Children were presented with a selection of pictures, showing the devastation and ruined buildings from a number of different countries. They were asked to match the pictures against a list of European countries. The pictures were all very similar; it was impossible to identify where the photographs were taken. Questions such as, what stories should be remembered? What do all these images have in common? Can you match the country to the picture? helped children to develop their understanding that people in all countries had suffered as a result of the war and that there had been devastation throughout Europe.

Such activities were instigated in an atmosphere where all children felt confident to express their views; questions were open ended and opinions listened to – a reminder of how cultural contexts may influence talk, as described by Littleton and Mercer (2013).

Extracting meaning from different sources of information

Children were encouraged to explore a variety of sources of information about the war and its aftermath (written texts, photographs, films, newsreels, propaganda, cartoons and oral accounts). The strategies that children used to read the texts and identify key points necessarily varied, depending on the text. This provided opportunities to teach reading comprehension, 'situating' the teaching of comprehension in a valued and purposeful task (Duffy *et al.* 2010). As they were confronted with different sources, children were asked to describe the information that was provided and also to consider why and how these different sources had been created and survived. Such considerations enabled children to question the veracity and reliability of different sources of information and to explore different interpretations and representation of the past. This process matches the new requirements of the 2013 National Curriculum Programmes of Study for English, which states that pupils in Years 5 and 6 should be taught to summarise and identify main ideas, as well as to distinguish between fact and opinion across a range of texts.

Propaganda posters

Propaganda posters, linked with the World War II, provided opportunities for children to consider audience and to develop their awareness of hidden messages within the text. Children were asked to think why the messages might be important and to consider the effectiveness of different posters. Such discussion then led into children designing their own posters and to thinking about how they wanted to present their message to different audiences. The activity provided a useful stimulus to look beyond what was immediately apparent in texts and to question more deeply the purpose of the texts. The following website provides a useful selection of posters to work with: http://www.businessinsider.com/world-war-two-posters-keep-calm-2012-6?op=1.

Documentaries and films

Documentaries were also viewed as other sources of propaganda and children were encouraged to reflect critically on their messages. As they watched documentaries about different events, children were asked to think about how the documentary had been created; what messages were the filmmakers wanting to convey and how reliable were they as representations of what actually happened?

Selected clips from a documentary

Here Come The Yanks (http://www.youtube.com/watch?v=2lgAF41BB5M), which describes the role of the US in Germany after the war. Before they watched the film, children were asked how the US might have been feeling towards Germany in 1945 and what message the filmmakers might be wanting to convey to a wider audience. Children's comments about the filmmakers' positioning (*They might have felt sorry, They might have felt a bit smug*) indicate that they were able to recognise some of the beliefs and values that underpinned their films.

Discussion of why particular incidents were selected for filming

Children also discussed why particular incidents had been selected for filming.

They watched the opening scenes from *This is America – Germany Today* (http://www.youtube.com/watch?v=kjSBZLSpD8Q) and noted how the opening clips focused on key monuments, '*All the really important buildings were bombed to make them surrender*', '*People in Germany must have been really hungry*' (a response to watching people digging up potatoes in the Tiergarten, which had once been a public park). They noted how the commentator spoke about Germany on the film and thought carefully about the impression that was conveyed, through listening to the background music. Such activities enabled them to analyse how life in Germany after the war was being represented.

Documentary depicting the same event in different countries

A further activity involved children viewing a documentary which depicted the same event in different countries. Clips from the documentary, *USA and USSR after World War II* (http:// www.youtube.com/watch?v=CZ1es0rhKwg) depict the homecoming of US and Soviet troops after the war. In terms of individual stories and human emotions, there were many similarities in both nations. Soldiers were hugged by family and friends and there were huge crowds of well-wishers welcoming them home.

However, there were also startling differences when the cameras moved outwards to show what life was going to be like for the soldiers after the war. The increasing consumerism in the US was contrasted with the devastation in the USSR in the immediate post-war years. Whilst the documentary showed similarities in peoples' emotions, it also provided powerful reminders of peoples' different lived experiences in the two countries.

More recent films were also used to develop children's awareness that the past is continuously being represented; that there are no final conclusive interpretations of what happened. Selected clips of the film, *Enemy at the Gates* (2001), a war film directed by Jean-Jacques Annaud, were watched by the children. The film is a fictional story set during the Battle of Stalingrad in World War II. Children were asked to think about how the film was constructed and the messages that the filmmaker was trying to convey. An awareness that film is 'authored' in the same way as a written text is an important step in children's growing understanding of visual literacy (Bearne and Wolstencroft 2007). Understanding the choices that the filmmaker makes raises children's awareness of how the visual world can direct and even manipulate their views and ideas. Stafford (2011), along with resources from the British Film Institute, provides teachers with approaches to using film in this way.

Using photographs

A Berlin street after the war

Similar critical analyses were undertaken as children responded to different images of the war. Pictures have an immediate impact on children's thinking and children of whatever ability are able to make comments on what they see. Photographs were used as sources of information to extend children's knowledge and also to support the development of critical thinking.

Using a picture on the whiteboard, the teacher modelled how children might use pictures as sources of information, before she gave each pair of children a picture to talk about. The picture was a photograph of a street in Berlin with destroyed houses and people rescuing their belongings. In pairs, children talked about what they could see in the picture and were then asked to report back on their observations to the rest of the class.

Following the class discussion where they shared ideas, the children were asked to note down around the edge of the picture all they could see. This enabled children who were unsure what to write to build their notes on what had been said in the class discussion and also orientated all the children into looking more carefully at the picture.

Once the notes were completed, children were asked to draw some conclusions from their notes and observations, to answer the question – What was Germany like after the war? What does this picture show us? Following paired discussions, children provided thoughtful comments in their answers to the whole class once again.

Paired talk and whole class discussion supported the children as they made their notes. Children utilised disputational and explorative talk in the early stages of their research and as they drew conclusions, their talk became more cumulative.

The example below illustrates how one pair of children moved on, from describing what they could see in single words, to phrases and notes, as they drew inferences from their observations (figure 8.1).

First impressions written close to the photograph included:

> *Sad, pillows, destroyed, people, bricks, afternoon, trees, buildings, ruins, rubble, homeless people, rubbish, bags, wood, furniture, jobless, carpet.*

In the outer frame away from the photograph, children used these initial impressions to draw some conclusions about what was happening.

■ people outside homeless;

■ not back to normal even though the war has ended;

■ moving out or they're refugees;

■ starting fresh;

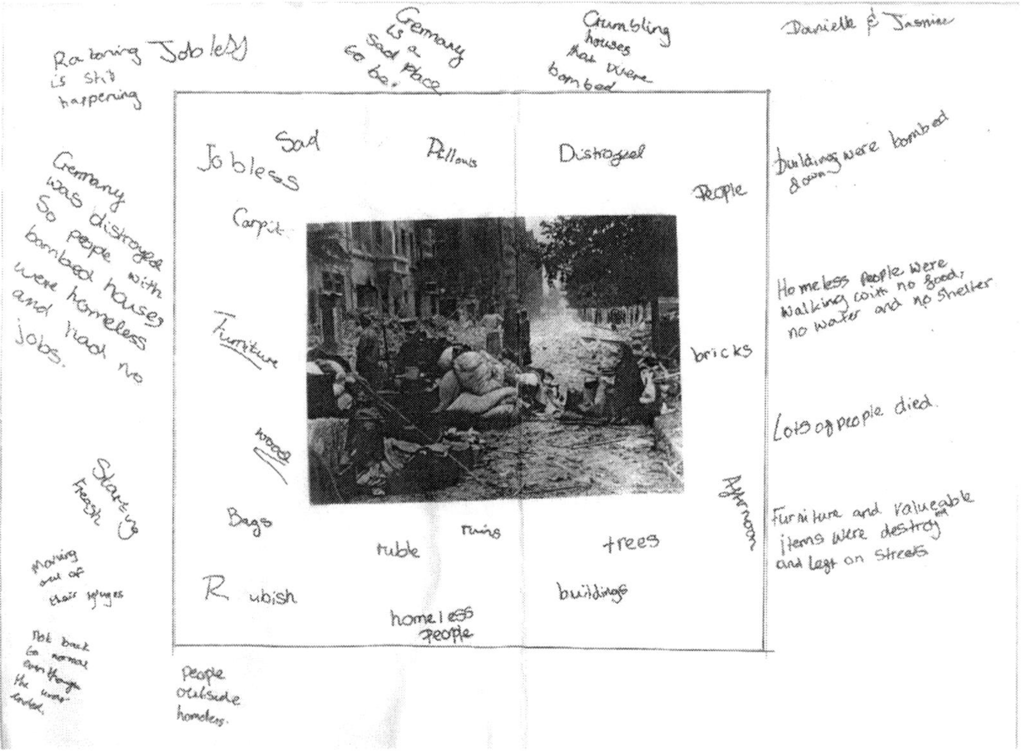

FIGURE 8.1 Illustrates how children in pairs moved from single words and phrases to drawing inferences.

- Germany was destroyed so people with bombed houses were homeless and had no jobs;

- rationing is still happening;

- Germany is a sad place to be;

- crumbling houses that were bombed;

- buildings were bombed down;

- homeless people were walking with no food/no water and no shelter;

- lots of people died;

- furniture and valuable items were destroyed and left on the streets.

The above example indicates how children moved from writing single words to writing phrases, which then, in turn, were then used to support more extended writing in their topic books.

The atomic bomb

Photographs were also used to enable children to raise their own questions and to think about the reliability of the photographic evidence in other ways. They were asked to frame their observations within facts (features that could be described in the picture), statements (some conclusions about what the picture represented) and questions (what further information it might be useful to know). This structure provided another strategy to help children to move beyond simple descriptions to more critical analysis. This sequence is further described by Stafford (2011) in relation to reading the visual image. When accompanied by considering the different language features and grammatical structures of the talk about the pictures, children can be introduced to the metalanguage of the grammar choices of critical analysis (Myhill *et al.*: 2013).

The picture below shows the mushroom cloud following the dropping of the atomic bomb.

- Facts: The atomic bomb has been dropped. A mushroom shaped cloud has appeared.

- Statements: This was how the war ended. I can see the after effects.

- Questions: What was America thinking? Why would America do this? Who chose to drop the bomb?

Understanding the past through people's different stories

One of the key aims of the unit was to help children understand the many different stories that may be told about people's lives in the past; to recognise diversity and to question the stories which were told. Reading *I am David* in their literacy lessons provided one such opportunity. How did Anne Holm know what to write – which elements of the story might be true and which elements were derived from her historical imagination? These were questions that children explored as they discussed the story and thought about how it was constructed. The careful analysis of a writer's craft (rather than the cold dissection of a text) enables children to see the choices that writers make and in particular how those choices affect the reader.

FIGURE 8.2 Children annotate a photograph of the dropping of the atomic bomb with questions, facts and statements.

Children were also encouraged to construct their own stories through responding creatively to visual images. Looking at a picture of the devastation caused by bombing, the children were asked to record what they could see, touch and hear as well as to describe their feelings.

One child wrote:

Falling to the ground in smithereens, the building kills many innocent souls.

Helplessly the buildings fall and break the city's heart.

I am all alone watching people die slowly pleading their last words to the air, lost without words.

I run through the rubble trying to save people's lives.

I hear sorrowful voices calling for help but it's no use.

What is happening?

Another child wrote:

I could feel the breeze against my dirty face whilst I was sitting there, no idea as of what was happening.

As I looked left and right I could see no people, just piles of rubble and buildings, that looked like they had been stood on.

My rifle by my side with a dirty scope.

Dust filled my hair

And I could feel the mud and small bits of rubble in my boots.

Not far away I could hear constant gun fire

And the screams of innocent men, children and women.

I could tell death was not far for me.

These examples of children's writing indicate ways in which children may become involved in reading a picture and utilising their historical imagination to think about people's experiences. It could be argued that it is unrealistic to try and 'pretend' to live in the past – how can people in the present really understand people's emotions from the past? Indeed many of the criticisms for teaching about empathy have centred on this argument. However, even though developing empathy presents challenges, it cannot be ignored. Children do need to know about how events affected people. The strategy presented here, of anchoring children's responses through analysing a pictorial source, offers the opportunity for the development of more critical understanding.

The school was host to Laura, a student from Germany who was training to become a primary school teacher. She was a valuable source of information about life in Germany after the war and was able to tell the children stories, which had been passed down to her by her grandmother and father, about their lives. Details of these individual recollections fascinated the children. Following the construction of the Berlin Wall, her grandmother had hidden coffee in her daughter's pram, as she crossed into the east to visit relatives; as a teenager on a school trip her father had been held up for a whole day at a checkpoint, since one of the boys on the bus had made a silly joke, which the soldiers had not found funny, as they crossed the checkpoint into Berlin.

Laura also spoke to the children about the Berlin Wall and individuals who had attempted to cross the wall. These individual stories appealed to the children, who made posters recording what they had found out about some of the daring escapes. Creating the posters encouraged the children to think about their audience and the messages that they wanted to convey.

Bringing it altogether and answering the enquiry question – Did any country or person benefit from World War II?

During the year, the children had experimented in presenting different points of view through their writing. One of their earliest experiences had been to look at various opinions of Jack and the Beanstalk. Was Jack a hero or a villain? He'd killed the giant, made his mother happy, but was it really acceptable to steal from another person? On another occasion the children discussed whether the school should hold a sports day and evaluated the advantages and disadvantages of staging such an event. Consequently the children already had a range of experience of presenting different viewpoints and had learned a variety of sentence structures, which they could employ as they answered the enquiry question on the aftermath of the war. They had also learned the purpose of introductory paragraphs, to introduce key ideas, and how to write a concluding paragraph, to summarise their point of view.

Following each lesson about the aftermath of the war in individual countries, children wrote a paragraph about what they had learned. They were reminded of particular sentence structures that might help them express their ideas, such as the following, which refer to experiences in Germany.

Even though Germany lay in ruins, the country was divided into four sectors.

Many have argued that Germany is now a strong economic power because of the support of the USA and Britain.

Although Germany had lost over 6 million people . . . . . .

At the end of the unit children created a benefit and loss sheet with columns for each country, which would enable them to answer the question. They returned to the paragraphs that they had written about individual countries and wrote phrases /words on post-it notes to remind them of important points. The benefit and loss sheet thus acted as a planning tool for their subsequent writing.

The example below illustrates the benefits/losses that one child recorded on the post-it notes.

Benefits

- *Germany is now a very wealthy country.*

- *Women's rights – women went to work and got paid.*

- *Britain won the war.*

- *If someone's family died they would get a new life.*

- *Russia helped defeat Hitler.*

- *Freedom from the war and for the Jews.*

- *USA and Britain helped Germany stand on their feet.*

Losses

- *Families die and people split up – men sent to be soldiers.*

- *Japan lost their country (atomic bomb).*

- *Britain lost loads of money.*

- *Rationing continued for ten years.*

- *Germany lost a lot of land.*

- *Houses got bombed and people died. Refugees lost their families.*

- *Berlin Wall was put up so you couldn't see your friend for thirty years.*

- *No jobs, no money.*

- *Russia lost millions of people.*

- *Lost buildings from the bombs.*

The enquiry is particularly open ended and we can see here how one child is developing her ideas concerning this very complex question. The question really engaged the children, since it permitted them to articulate their ideas, which they had rehearsed throughout the topic in paired and class discussions. Consequently when the children finally came to write their answers, they felt confident and had plenty of information to support the points of view, which they made. Their enthusiasm sustained them until the very end of the summer term and children wrote long, detailed and well argued answers.

The example below illustrates how one child thought very carefully about her answer and the justifications that she used to support her points of view. Her introductory paragraph introduces some key ideas and explains how she is going to structure her answer. She supports some of her assertions by using 'for example'.

> *World War II was described as the most devastating war in the world. In fact, this war had caused so much damage; for example 60 million people were involved. Thousands and thousands of troops from all over the world fought in this great war. Countries had suffered really serious bombing, for example America dropped an atomic bombs on two cities in Japan, and so caused this tragic war to come to an end. So many countries lost and gained power. This essay will explore and help you to understand who benefitted from the war. It must be remembered that these stories shall never be forgotten. From looking back could there really have been any benefits for anyone?*

The writer then goes on to discuss her views on the effects of the war on different countries. She begins with Germany, followed by Japan.

> *In 1945 Germany was left in ruins. Cities were destroyed and abandoned. Over 6 million Germans were killed and thousands of women were left jobless and the men either imprisoned or dead. All they did was plant and dig for food. The German people were left supporting themselves and their children. Germany's devastating ruins left them in horror and shock. About 80 % of the country was bombed. When Russia took over half of their country, German was no longer independent. They were now being ruled by 4 different countries. To this very day Germany is still recovering. Do you really think they could have benefitted from all this destruction? Now Germany is a very powerful economy and is independent.*

> *The dropping of the two atomic bombs by America on Japan was devastating. Hiroshima was wiped out. About 350,000 innocent people were killed. Later on Nagasaki was bombed but this bomb was even more powerful. It killed about 500,000 people. What the Americans tried to do was to hide the fact that they had bombed a city. They said that it was a large military base, not realising that it had killed many innocent people. The effect of the atomic bombs was that it put an end to the war. . . . Even now the radiation caused by the dropping of bombs causes people to have cancer in these devastated cities. Could Japan have benefitted from this war? It must be remembered that now Japan is a technologically advanced and wealthy country.*

The concluding sentence in each paragraph reminds the reader to reflect on the current status of these countries and the writer uses this device as she writes about Britain, the United States and the USSR. Thus when the writer begins her concluding paragraph, the reader can see how her argument has developed.

> *After weighing up the options I can now see that my prediction was wrong. Every country in a way benefitted from this devastating war. For example all the countries benefitted because they had a much stronger economy and all the women and all the countries were able to work. Britain and its allies and enemies had been through terrible times. It has still taken a long time as people are still recovering from this war. However, the world would not be the interesting and advanced place it is now if it were not for the Second World War.*

The above excerpts illustrate how one child was able to argue her point of view convincingly. The examples of introductory paragraphs below illustrate how other children expressed individual opinions and selected information to support their views.

> Child 1: *Many people thought that the war was over, but it wasn't. Over 10,000,000 people's lives were affected by the war. Even the countries which weren't involved had refugees coming into their country, asking them for money. No one was happy. On the other hand, some people gained while some people lost. This war has changed people's lives in many ways. For example, people lost their homes, family, friends and their LIVES! That must not be right. My opinion is that no one benefitted from the war. This text will discuss both sides of the argument and come to an informed discussion.*

> Child 2: *World War II was described as a global war. In fact it is believed that almost 60 million people died during this tragic event. Even though people have stated that the war was a beneficial thing, other people believe that this is wrong and that the war was devastation. However, our opinion counts as well, so read on, if you want to be heard. In this text I will explore different countries and find out if they really did benefit from the war. Do you think that anyone could really benefit from the war?*

Children's conclusions differed.

> Child 3: *I think after much learning, reading and writing, I would say no one in the world benefitted from the war. 60,000,000 people died all over the world, and most of them were innocent. . . . All those children, babies and wives losing their families – so could anyone have benefitted from the war?*

> Child 4: *In my opinion I think only America and Japan benefited from the war because even though they lost a lot of people they still became very powerful.*

> Child 5: *After the war many countries lost and benefitted in a way from the war. Germany became a fairer country and has not had a dictator since the war, but the country was left in ruins and many families were destroyed. It was believed there might be a nuclear war as a result of weapons amassed after the war. Britain became a multi-cultural country but British people lost jobs and many had to live on the streets because of the bombs . . . In my opinion I think that every country had both benefitted and lost.*

These extracts reveal how the children really engaged with the enquiry question. Rehearsing their ideas through talk and having opportunities to think and interthink, children were able to write down their views within a logical argument and to weigh up different viewpoints. The quality of their writing is evident and importantly too, children really enjoyed the topic. The classroom buzzed with their ideas and the explanations that they offered.

Case study 2

Who caused the Tonypandy riots?

This case study provides an example of how teachers in South Wales planned a local history study unit. Strong feelings are still held in some parts of the Welsh Valleys about the riots and this study unit enabled children to 'tap' into community beliefs, as well as providing them with opportunities to consider their own emotional involvement.

Background

Mining has a long history in South Wales and the Valleys made a significant contribution to the British economy in the export of Welsh coal throughout the world. The Merthyr riots of 1831, the Rhondda riots of 1910 and later the Miners' Strike in 1984/85 have all shaped the culture and historical characteristics of South Wales. Stories about the mines are often discussed today and feature on the curriculum in many schools, as children are encouraged to conduct enquiries into their local area. Furthermore, 'History contributes to the curriculum Cymreig, by making local and Welsh History a focus of the study and helping learners to understand the factors that have shaped Wales and other countries today' (Welsh Assembly 2008: 8).

Local history enquiries are important since they provide opportunities for children to make sense of the past at first hand and to recognise how the past might have impacted on their communities. They also support children in developing their understanding of how changes in their local area might occur, through investigating the lives of different people or through a significant event. Children can also be encouraged to look outwards to develop an appreciation of how local events connect to the wider world and also the consequences of different events.

The Tonypandy riots are often referred to as the Rhondda riots, which took place in 1910 and 1911. The Tonypandy riot refers specifically to events of 8 November 1911. The Tonypandy riots followed long disputes between the miners and the Cambrian Colliery Combine – a business network of South Wales pits, about wages and price regulations. Miners went on strike and as the dispute escalated, violent skirmishes occurred between police and miners. The then Home Secretary, Winston Churchill, authorised troops to be sent to the Valleys to reinforce the police. This authorisation, and the consequent disorder and hardships suffered by the miners who gained little and returned to work after several months on strike, remains a highly emotive and controversial incident in Welsh history. Thus as teachers planned their work for this topic, they considered how they might need to deal with children's and their families' strong emotions and the sensitive issues that might need to be addressed.

This topic relates to Welsh National Curriculum and the 3–19 Skills Framework (Welsh Assembly 2008); this skills based curriculum allows the teacher to plan for historical progression by addressing key skills in history and wider skills, which include thinking and communication. The National Literacy Framework in Wales (Welsh Assembly 2013) has a key focus on developing children's writing across all subject areas and as such this topic allowed for children to develop their discursive writing.

The History National Curriculum for England also requires children to undertake a local history study, a feature of which might be 'a study of an aspect of history . . . dating from a period beyond 1066 that is significant in the locality' (DfE 2013: 207, a study of an aspect of history or a site, dating from the period beyond 1066 that is significant in the locality). In addition children are expected to learn about British history and learning about an event in Wales can contribute towards children's understanding of the histories of different countries within Great Britain.

Local history

As with any new topic it is important to access children's existing funds of knowledge (Andrews and Yee 2006). Children may already know key information about their local area and this information may provide an interesting way in for initial discussions. Stories passed down from grandparents and other family members may differ from official versions of the past and children may be encouraged to explore where there are differences and why these differences might occur. Such enquiries may provide insights for the children concerning the different opinions and values that are held about past events.

The unit was taught to two classes in upper Key Stage 2 (9–11 year olds). Class teachers shared their planning and taught together as a team. Team teaching across year groups enabled the teachers to build upon each other's ideas and strengths and to take responsibility together for resourcing and the organisation of visits to places of interest.

Planning for children's learning about the Tonypandy riots

Inspiration for this topic came from a very successful Welsh TV series, *Y Tŷ Glo* (Coal House), which featured Welsh families travelling back in time and living and working in the early twentieth century (http://www.bbc.co.uk/programmes/p00htnc2). The study unit focused primarily on the development of children's historical understanding through an enquiry approach similar to Roberts' four stages of enquiry (2003).

Roberts' framework for developing enquiries includes four essential aspects, which were adapted to provide a framework for the planning of this unit:

1   Creating a 'need to know' – finding interesting starting points to stimulate children's curiosity.

2   Using data – gathering information from a range of sources of information.

3   Making sense – interpreting and evaluating evidence to develop personal understandings concerning what happened in the past.

4   Reflecting on learning – evaluating learning and drawing conclusions.

Creating a 'need to know'; starting points for the topic.

The unit started with a visit to the Rhondda Heritage Museum (http://www.rhonddaherit agepark.com/). This historical site was once home to the Lewis Merthyr Colliery. Visits are often used in primary schools, and the visit at the start of the unit gave the children a focus to develop their historical understanding. The opportunity for the children to have first-hand experiences of visiting the mine shaft, helped children to appreciate what it would have been like to go down a mine.

The size of the cage (lift), which would have housed approximately fifteen men, helped them to consider not only what it would have been like, but also to experience the cramped conditions and the feeling of going underground in the dark for long periods of time. This prompted some purposeful questions and comments from the children, which helped shape the enquiry further. For example the children asked,

■   How long did they spend underground?

■   How did the men get out if it was an emergency?

■   Was it dangerous?

■   How did they eat their lunch?

Using data – What can we learn about the miners and their families?

The 1910 census was used to find out who lived in a street in Tonypandy at this time and what jobs these people did. The main source of employment identified from the census was the Lewis Merthyr Colliery, which the children had visited when they went to the Rhondda Heritage Park. The census provides information about the area at this time and children were asked to consider how useful this information was. Children were asked to look for the surnames on the census and identify those surnames that were most frequently noted e.g. Jones, Williams, Griffiths, Davies. The children were allocated a surname (e.g. Jones) and asked to find where the Jones families were recorded on the census. This enabled them to consider how families often lived very closely together with their extended families. Some surnames appeared only once on the census. From further investigation the children thought that a surname such as Smith, in a Jones' household, could indicate the family was taking in lodgers. The children began to understand the importance of lodgers at this time and also how people moved around the country and further afield in search of employment. The census revealed that some of the household members had come to South Wales from Australia as well as from other locations, including Bristol and parts of the south west of England. Careful questioning from the teacher supported children in recognising the importance of South Wales at this time, for its coal and mining communities. Employment was a key area for discussion throughout the unit and children considered changes in working patterns between then and now.

Children were asked to step back in time and imagine that they were employed in the early years of the twentieth century. They were allocated different occupations to investigate, such as the roles of fireman (the legal title of a deputy who holds a certificate to fire shots), lamps man (in charge of ensuring that the lamps were working properly), overman (underground foreman subordinate to the manager), clerk (managing wages and absenteeism) and banks men (those at the bank, or top of the pit who would unhook and empty the laden corves (trucks) from the mine into the carts and wagons).

Discussions around the different occupations followed and children investigated the roles of different workers.

Class teachers dressed up in role as the mine owners, and gave the children their wages. This proved to be a turning point in the unit, as the children recognised how important work was at this time and just how much people were dependent on their wages. The children also recognised the disparity between different jobs that the miners did and how this reflected in the quality of life that they could lead, varying from being barely able to survive to being 'better off'.

Children were immediately struck by the different opportunities offered to men and women. The boys went to work in the mines and the girls did not realise that they would not be in paid employment but would be expected to stay at home doing the housework. Children began to consider how the role of women has changed significantly since this time and also to think about the impact that these changes have had upon their own lives.

The men (boys) were also given the challenge of managing the family budget. They had to work out what their wages would provide and how much things cost at this time. The differences in wages highlighted the disparities in what the men could afford to provide for their families and children discussed how the jobs they did impacted on their families' well being. This was a useful starting point for later discussions, focusing on how the colliery owners' proposed new pay structures for their employees would eventually lead to the Tonypandy riots. Role play is often used as a strategy to develop children's appreciation of past ways of life and teachers modelled this approach as they encouraged children to think about the miners' families. They also used this as a formative assessment opportunity, which helped to shape the enquiry further. Teachers considered how they could support children in developing their understanding of the causes of the riots and how the proposed changes in the pay structures would have such an impact on the miners' lives.

The children watched an episode of *Coal House*, which featured families on payday and also how difficult life could be if anyone was injured at work. One mine worker had hurt his arm and as a consequence of this did not receive his full pay. He was not able to buy his family the customary Friday night treat of fish and chips. His fellow miners and their families responded in different ways to this situation. Some of the families joked about his circumstances, which led to jeering and jokes at the injured miner's expense; other families however, shared their own fish and chips with him.

After discussing the episode further key questions were added to a question wall. The children then acted out the role of families on payday. The 'poorer' families realised they would not be able to afford any luxury items; their wages would barely cover necessities. The recognition of what life was really like at this time was evident in children's role play and the discussions they held. Some families in the role play decided to 'barter' items such as home-made biscuits or home grown vegetables. This was unprompted and illustrates how children were beginning to take ownership of their assigned roles and find solutions to alleviate their poverty.

Making sense - interpreting and evaluating evidence

The unit progressed with a discussion on the different sources of information that were available, to find out about miners' lives. Children looked at a range of information, including paintings, contemporary newspapers, belts and helmets worn by miners, coal, poems and reference books. They examined a replica Davy lamp, which was taken into the mines to provide warnings for miners of the presence of explosive gases. Children were asked to consider when the lamp was used. How was it used? Why was it used? This was an opportunity for children to utilise exploratory talk, as they worked in pairs, developing skills in interthinking, (Littleton and Mercer 2013) to reach some conclusions.

The activity also led to further questions from the children. One child, John, asked, *Why did the miners continue to go down the mine if they knew it was dangerous? If all the miners refused to go down the mine owners would need to do something.'* John clearly recognised the potential power of the workers and this was useful in understanding the motivation behind the Tonypandy riots.

Discussion

A discussion followed, in which the children reflected on the impact that going on strike would have on miners' families. Working life was very dangerous and often men were injured or killed down the mines, yet despite these dangers they had to go to work to feed their families. If they went on strike their families might starve. The dilemmas facing the miners helped the children to appreciate that decisions are taken, often as a result of many factors. This would later help them with their discursive writing on the riots.

Teachers encouraged children to consider which sources were the most useful and why. Children looked at contemporary sources and also considered sources of information from more recent times. They were asked to consider the audiences for the different sources of information and to think about how the past is represented and why the past may have been represented in this way.

Reflecting on learning: drawing conclusions

Children were encouraged to evaluate critically the different sources of information. The short example below illustrates how one child assessed the reliability of accounts in the different newspapers.

> *A newspaper is a primary source of evidence although it is debatable whether it is a reliable source. There are many different people who write them. This is one reason why newspapers can be unreliable. Some journalists can exaggerate the truth. Another thing, newspapers can be biased, which means they can have an inclination or prejudice for or against a matter. Alternatively, newspapers can be extremely informative and give us detailed accounts of events. I believe that you should not rely on newspapers as sources, as the person who wrote it might have thought that something happened but it did not actually happen.*

This extract shows how Anna has been able to consider issues of reliability and purpose, the use of the word **some**, is particularly insightful as this shows a recognition that journalists hold different opinions and that they may have different purposes for writing. The use of **alternatively, prejudiced** and **unreliable** are good examples of key vocabulary which you would expect to see in writing of this kind.

Anna goes on to write about the census. She weighs up different points of view and uses connectives such as 'however' and 'nevertheless' effectively.

> *I believe a census is quite reliable because the information recorded comes from asking questions and gathering information from people who were around at the time of the event. However, you can't be 100% sure the information is totally accurate without talking to each person involved. Nevertheless, it is the closest you will come to being accurate and it is a legal document.*

At the end of the unit, the children were asked to reflect on the cause of the riots by looking at a range of perspectives: the miners, the mine owners and the police.

> *It started when the mine owners from the Lewis Merthyr Colliery lowered the miners' pay, the miners were not happy with this decision. Even though the mine owners were wrong to lower miners' pay, the miners should not have gone into Tonypandy and looted every single shop except for the jewellers and the chemist, this made the miners look bad. On the other hand I totally agree with the miners in some ways, the mine owners had no right at all to stop them from coming to work. In my opinion, I agree with the miners and feel that the mine owners caused the riots by lowering pay.*
>
> (Billy)

Billy's comments above illustrate how he has been able to see the event from different perspectives. He is able to empathise with the miners' predicament. However, he feels strongly that the mine owners' decision to close the mine ultimately resulted in the riots. He recognises that despite the miners' hardship they should not have behaved as they did by rioting and looting, which only undermined the miners' position.

> *I can see the mine owners' point of view, the mine owners thought the miners were working slowly on the seam, when the miners went on strike the mine owners could not fill their orders. In my opinion I think it was the miners who caused the riot as they wanted more money. They were offered a compromise. However the miners said no. It was their fault that the riots happened. The riots caused a lot of damage. I believe it was the miners' fault.*
>
> (Sasha)

Sasha's writing shows that although she is aware of the miners' issues about pay, she has been able to look at the riots from the perspective of the mine owners. Her comments about compromise and the fact that the miners caused a lot of damage clearly influenced her decision making in her writing.

The miners wanted their pay to be 2s 6d, on the other hand the mine owners wanted to give them 1s 9d. They were offered 2s 3d. The miners rejected this. Because the owners shut the mine the strike started. The mine owners were part of the cause; however the owners could only pay so much. The miners were not getting paid enough and they were in a tough space. My opinion is that the miners caused the riots because they wanted too much money.

(Ioan)

Ioan echoes the thoughts of Sasha. He is empathetic to the plight of the miners. However, he is able to see how the miners' behaviour influenced the miner owners' decision, which ultimately resulted in the riots.

I think it was the miners' fault for not taking the money and the mine owners for not paying the miners enough, they were both to blame.

(Bethan)

Bethan has opted for a slightly different response as she feels that both parties were to blame for the riots.

The above excerpts indicate how, through carefully structured activities, children were able to feel confident to express their own points of view in their final conclusions to the unit, and how, through scaffolding, they were able to express their opinions in writing.

Case study 3

Britain and the wider world: different viewpoints

This case study describes an approach used by a whole school to plan historical enquiries focusing on the exploration of North America and the expansion westwards of European settlers. The case study provides an example of an aspect of British history that extends pupils' chronological knowledge beyond 1066 (DfE 2013: 207) and also offers opportunities to fulfil the stated aims of the National Curriculum for History by ensuring that children know, 'how people's lives have shaped this nation and how Britain has influenced and been influenced by the wider world' (DfE 2013: 204).

Although this case study was undertaken with Key Stage 2 children, younger children could also study the arrival of the first Europeans in North America as events beyond living memory, which are significant nationally or globally (DfE 2013: 205). The teaching strategies used could, of course, apply to considering different perspectives of any person or group of people.

A further focus of this study was the application of literacy skills and knowledge for a real purpose and audience, using historical enquiry as an opportunity for children to apply genre specific learning within a literacy-based lesson. Guthrie and Wigfield (2000) identified a number of key elements of a successful writing curriculum: strategy teaching, so teaching organisation, language, vocabulary, transcriptional skills; having an intrinsic motivation to write, so writing in social contexts, an emotional engagement with the writing and a purpose to writing and significantly, for writing for historical enquiry purposes, curricular coherence. Ellis (2013) calls this 'teaching points that travel' or literacy-focused teaching, that is then 'nudged into independence' and used across the curriculum.

Planning a history topic – developing a whole school approach

Teachers within the school chose to plan their history as Key Stage topics – with children across a Key Stage focusing on the same theme or historical period. In schools where there is high mobility, with class configurations changing as numbers within year groups change, this approach ensures children do not repeat topics, or 'miss' key skills and knowledge in their journey through the school. In single form entry schools it also enables teachers to work collaboratively on a topic, sharing ideas, approaches and resources. In this school it also enabled the history subject leader, the school expert, to support all the staff in the planning, teaching and assessment process. This approach also highlighted progression in learning as it focuses teachers, at the planning stage, on the expected outcomes for each year group in terms of skills, attitudes and knowledge. The 'information' about a period of history is transformed into a progression in knowledge, where knowledge is viewed as an understanding, interpretation and application of this shared information.

Confronting stereotypes through language and reading comprehension

This topic, 'Birth of a Nation –the exploration of North America' was chosen by the subject leader as it was particularly useful in helping children understand about different interpretations. From initial discussions with children it was clear they already had a range of ideas about life in North America and firmly held representations and views of its people and places. Studying this therefore enabled children to both extend their knowledge and also to evaluate their existing knowledge.

Different perspectives

The Year 3 and 4 classes focused their learning on the impact of the arrival of the Europeans on the indigenous population. They began with a whole Key Stage event, which focused on encouraging children to empathise with both the settlers and the Native Americans. Initially the children saw this as a simple activity. Children were divided into two groups. Each group established their own game. The children shared and knew the rules of their game and were developing and playing them independently. Gradually children from one game were moved into the other game, with resulting conflicts and difficulties, with both groups believing their game was the 'right' game played in the 'right' way.

The discussion that followed introduced the topic, using the *Horrible Histories* series and some BBC Primary History clips. Children began to see that this topic could be viewed from different perspectives and that the same event could be viewed in more than one way – just as they had experienced in the 'games' event.

The initial discussions revealed children's views and representations of the Native Americans – who were seen by some of the children as one homogenous group and as uncivilised, warring peoples. Others had seen Disney or other Hollywood films (e.g. *Pocahontas* and *The Lone Ranger*) and so had different viewpoints. These discussions were supported by the Lyn Dawes'

Talking Points prompts (Dawes 2012). A 'Talking Point' board was maintained in the classroom and this began with children's initial views and ideas and developed as the project continued. They were encouraged to reflect on where their ideas and views originated from and to acknowledge that there were other sources of information that may influence their ideas.

Reading and different perspectives

The exploration of stereotypes of the Native Americans was continued through reading activities. The National Curriculum (DfE 2013: 14) identifies reading 'to gain knowledge across the curriculum' and a main aim in Years 3 and 4 has a comprehension focus that requires children to 'ask questions' of what they have read and to retrieve and interpret the information presented. In Years 5 and 6 this is extended to 'making comparisons' across texts, 'explaining' and giving 'reasoned justification' for opinions, as well as learning to 'build on their own and others' ideas and challenge views courteously'. The skills and strategies of reading comprehension were taught in focused literacy teaching and applied as part of the historical enquiry. Children had access to a range of books about Native Americans, published over a long period of time. Books were sorted by publication dates and the titles and chapter headings investigated. These revealed a range of terms, ('Red Indians', 'Native American Indians', 'Native Indians', 'Native Americans') along with a range of different tribe names and information. A range of text-based exploration developed from this starting point and children were asked some of the following questions:

- Look at the contents pages of each book – is there a difference between books? What could this tell us about the author's perspective? Is it possible to find out more about the author? What do the contents pages tell us about the intended audience of the book and its purposes?
- Find similar topics (events or people) in each book and investigate using some of the following questions (taken from Lewis and Wray 1997).

1   What is the subject or topic of the text?

2   Why might the author have written it?

3   Who is it written for? How do you know?

4   What values does the author assume the reader holds? How do you know?

5   Who would feel 'left out' in this text and why?

6   Who would feel that the claims made in the text clash with their own values, beliefs or experiences?

7   How is the reader positioned in relation to the author e.g. as a friend, opponent, someone who needs persuading, someone who agrees?

8   How is the text influencing you?

9   What assumptions about your values and beliefs does the text make?

Children in Year 5 and 6 were able to continue to explore these questions when investigating online texts, including Wikipedia, using their knowledge of the Wiki text form as being a collaborative text with the potential for multiple authors. They also extended the idea of a 'text' to film, both documentary and narrative.

Vocabulary and perspectives

The National Curriculum (DfE 2013) makes special mention of vocabulary teaching. Acquiring a 'wide vocabulary' is stated in the aims and this is further developed in the reading and writing programmes of study, with a particular strand of the writing programmes of study in each year group titled 'Vocabulary, grammar and punctuation'. Vocabulary plays an essential role in the process of understanding new concepts (Snow, Griffin and Burns 2005) and is a strong indicator of reading success (Biemiller 2003). With this in mind, children were encouraged to explore the vocabulary of the texts they were using – this included:

- Finding words and phrases that suggested the information given was fact or was an opinion.

- Investigating further the words and phrases that suggested an opinion was being given. An example of a grid for investigation is given in table 8.1.

Reliability of sources

The children went on to study a character that appeared in a number of their texts – Pocahontas. They read written texts, web-based texts, BBC 'Primary History Famous People' (http://www.bbc.co.uk/schools/primaryhistory/famouspeople/) and a series of representations of Pocahontas. Drawing on their prior knowledge of the Disney version children identified the many differences in the ways she was represented. They began to consider the 'reliability of sources'.

> Anyone can make up a website but the BBC have been going a long time. I don't think anyone made it up. They have facts. Most. . . . I'm not sure about all . . . are true.
>
> (Year 3 child)

Collating different perspectives

Children used the 'role on the wall' technique to gather and collect the different views of the representation of Pocahontas. This involves creating a life-size outline of the character on the wall where children can 'post' their thoughts and ideas as further representations emerge.

A variety of strategies could have been used at this point in the learning sequence: jigsawing of different accounts of the life of Pocahontas; using the 'read-pause' technique when reading about her life story from one perspective – reading a section, pausing to predict, discuss, make

TABLE 8.1 Grid for identifying fact and opinion and making connections.

Words or phrases	What does this tell us? (what lies beneath the words/what can we infer)	Connections
They were loaded like cattle	They were not seen as human They had no sympathy or empathy with the people	Reminds me of what happened to the Jews in World War II
Removal from their lifelong homes	The people had lived there for a long time Removal suggests they were forced	Bullying

connections, draw, retell or summarise. These 'pause' activities involve children in discussion and close reading. The activities can be recorded on a 'book mark', which becomes the journey of the reader, as they create their mental model of the text. This is particularly effective where two contrasting views or accounts are given and read in this way.

For younger children a variety of writing frames could be used to draw their ideas together for each representation of Pocahontas they had discussed.

This picture is a painting/ drawing/ statue of . . .

In this picture I can see . . .

This is a good/ poor representation of Pocahontas because . . .

A better way to represent Pocahontas would be . . . . this is because . . . .

Using drama to appreciate different viewpoints

The teachers wanted to support children in thinking about different viewpoints of people living in the past. Drama was an effective device to enable children to explore different views in relation to the life of Pocahontas. In the 'notes and guidance (non-statutory)' that runs parallel to the programmes of study in the National Curriculum (DfE 2013) role play and drama are identified as important approaches to supporting children in their search for meaning. Drama approaches immerse children in an event and are most effective when exploring historical events where children have had an initial exploration of the historical sources. In the 'imaginative' application of drama approaches it is important to ensure children do not 'revert' to their initial knowledge about a subject. Approaches used by the teachers included:

1   Gossiping in role e.g. what have settlers heard about the Native Americans? Children imagine they are a settler and are 'gossiping' with friends about what they know or think about the first settlers.

2   Hot seating the teacher in role as Pocahontas, Powhatan/ Wahunsonacock (her father), John Smith and John Rolfe. The teacher in role can be a more effective way of modelling the different perspectives of an historical figure, although the hot seating of children in role can provide powerful assessment evidence.

3   Freeze frame of significant moments in Pocahontas's life. Accompanying the freeze frame with thought tracking is also a successful approach to revealing perspectives. The teacher can also pick up on misconceptions here and require children to support their ideas with evidence from their research. The teacher shifted her questioning from 'What do you think?' when questioning a character in role, to 'What do you think and what makes you say that?' This was particularly important when the children were referring to one source of evidence only – this tended to be the *Horrible Histories* film clip they had seen. Children remembered the memorable 'funny moments' of the John Smith encounter with Pocahontas and seemed to be representing this as the only view, without recognising the author's viewpoint and purposes. Photographing the freeze frames and adding hearts (what the person is feeling), minds (thinking) and voices (saying) using post-its on the photos or on the interactive whiteboard, provided opportunities to extend thinking about different viewpoints.

4   Freeze frames can be brought to life for ten seconds (no more!); the freeze frame gives children a clear starting point to a piece of drama and a clear end point. The brevity of the ten seconds of action focuses children on the key event they want to represent. The continual reference back to evidence is important again at this stage and could be further developed if the children had been asked to create some stage directions rather like a film producer – providing the background for his or her actors.

5   Creating a number of tableaux to represent different perspectives of the same event – creating statues that represent feelings, themes and emotions. Each statue or tableau can be given a title, which supports children's skills in summarising a key event, emotion or theme. Again the teacher's skill in questioning and the classroom climate of children raising questions, challenging and presenting an alternative viewpoint, is important when using the tableau to ensure that there is authenticity and appropriate reference to evidence.

6   Conscience alley can be used to represent the differing viewpoints of an event, e.g. what could be going through the mind of the soldier given orders to move the Cherokee from their land to the reservations.

It needs to be remembered that it is not only the drama itself that supports children's developing understanding but the talk that surrounds it. Exploratory talk (Mercer and Littleton 2007) where children engage critically but constructively, building on ideas, challenging and counter challenging, justifying and offering alternative hypotheses should characterise the talk that accompanies drama used to develop historical understanding.

Drama leading to writing

The National Curriculum identifies the need for children to 'talk the text' before writing and throughout the programmes of study for each year group it outlines 'composing and rehearsing sentences orally'. The non-statutory guidance mentioning the power of working in role to do this. However, it is not a simple matter of children being able to write what they have said in role – writing is not talk written down. Very often we need children to move from the drama role in the first person to a third person account or from using the active voice of the drama to the passive voice of a more formal non-fiction text. It is important therefore to consider how to structure the drama activities so that they move more closely to the talk of the text type the children will be using for their writing.

Cremin and Myhill (2012) suggest a sequence for a diary entry: as a group re-enact through a series of freeze frames an event, they then work in pairs, telling the partner what happened – this could be a conversation over a meal or a phone conversation; then moving to monologue – a thinking over the day out loud as they get into bed. This final move to monologue is then close to the writing voice of the diary entry. As this process is moved through, key vocabulary can be recorded to support future writing. It is not only the key vocabulary of the subject content that needs to be considered. When moving to writing the metalanguage of grammar can be useful to support children's understanding of writing for a purpose.

The National Curriculum (DfE 2013) has a renewed focus on the teaching of grammatical terms. Research indicates that there is 'no correlation between grammar teaching and writing attainment' (Myhill *et al.* 2013). However, where grammar teaching is linked to writing for real purpose and audience, then there is a positive effect on writing outcomes. Discursive writing uses subordination to justify and explain each differing perspective; coordination to add and extend an argument; adverbials of time and place to support the orientation of the reader for example. Writing historical accounts and providing commentary involves the writer in a complex dance between tenses and can introduce children to the use of modal verb as they consider what might, could, should, ought to have happened. Providing children with the language to talk about their writing can be a powerful tool in supporting the developing writer.

Drama provided ideas for writing for different purposes and forms. The drama used by this school could lead to: stories; diary entries; letters; non-chronological texts – leaflets, museum guides; court case notes and many more.

The Year 4 children in the school decided to focus their writing on simple recounts, told from two differing perspectives.

Stimulus for writing from different perspectives

The stimulus for this writing was a book *Mirror* (Baker and Bennett 2010). This book recounts in pictures a day in the life of a family from Australia and a family in Morocco. The book opens at a central page and it is here that we imagine the metaphorical mirror. The Australian family's day is depicted on the pages as we turn left to right; the Moroccan and Arabic script and picture of the day in the life of the Moroccan family is depicted as we turn the pages right to left on the other side of the 'mirror'. This simple format allows the reader to see life from two perspectives at the same time. It was used as a starting point by the teacher to encourage children to look for similarities and differences in experiences of the Europeans and the Native Americans.

Children's responses

A lift flap book

Children then used this idea to create a lift-the-flap book, where one perspective is told in the main book and the alternative viewpoint is found by lifting the flap on each page. This approach also identified children's gaps in knowledge. One child had written about the settlers coming to trade but when she lifted her flap she was unsure of how a Native American may have viewed this. She thought initially they would be pleased because they were being '*given* nice things' but prompted by a peer she asked 'But what is trading?' It would have been easy to assume that the vocabulary was known to children but many terms are used by teachers and are found in the texts we use, but are not understood by children. Figure 8.3a shows the first page of one child's lift-the-flap book written from the perspective of the English and figure 8.3b shows the page underneath the flap (glued along the top edge) showing the Native Americans' perspective. The books have wonderful illustrations and continue for many pages. This book continues:

> Suddenly we saw some warrior looking men approaching us with spears in their hands. They looked very different because they had black skin and hardly any clothes. They couldn't understand our language so we moved on. We started to explore. We thought it was a great place to build new houses and make a fortune. We chopped down lots of trees to make wooden houses and started to grow our first crops . . .

Meanwhile, the indigenous people think *them* very strange, wonder whether they are approaching to attack them and whether they are going to destroy their land . . .

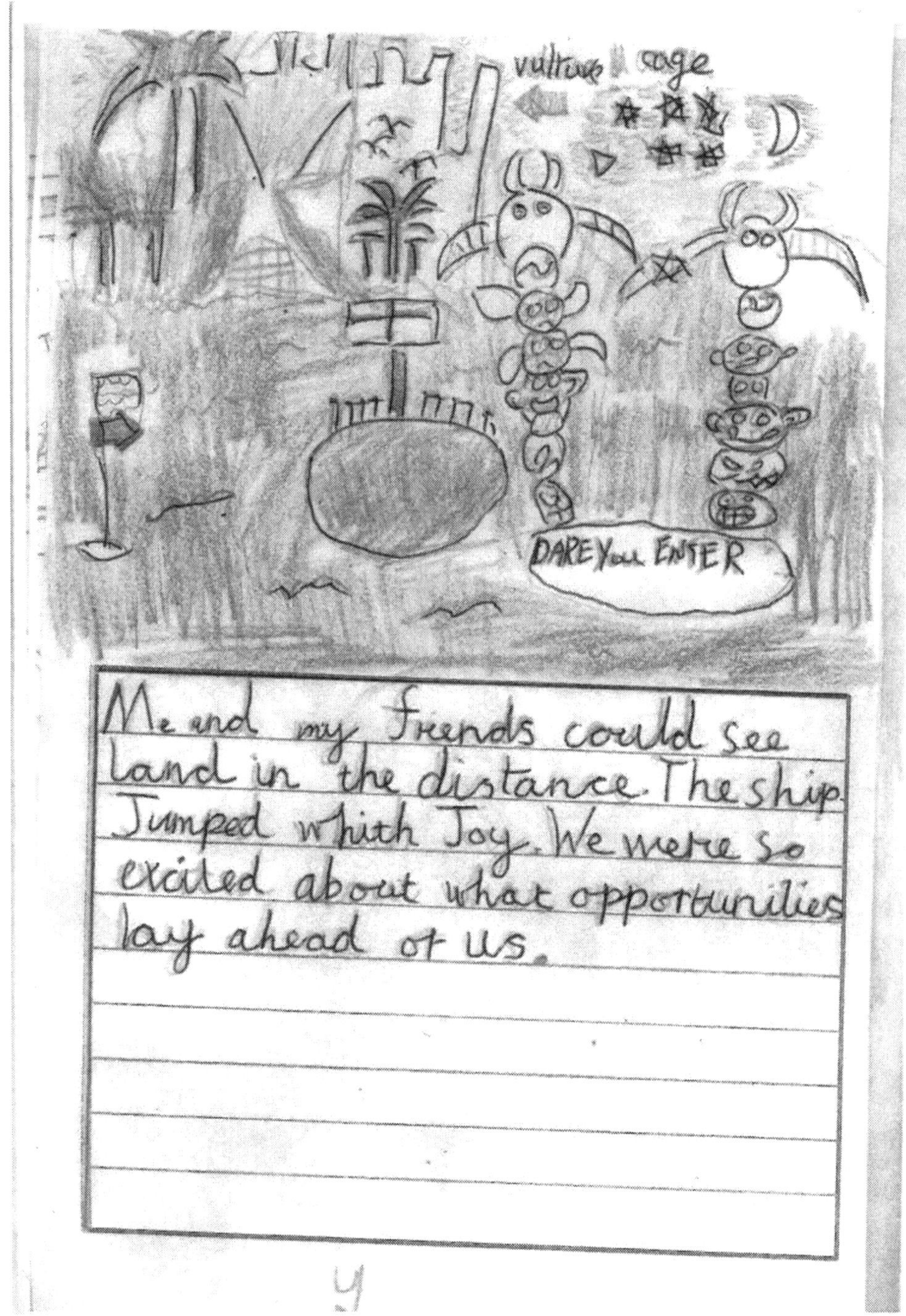

FIGURE 8.3a Shows the page of the flap book suggesting the English perspective.

FIGURE 8.3b The page beneath the flap, showing the possible thoughts of the Native Americans.

Perspectives cube

A similar idea was taken and extended by the Year 3 teacher. The multiple perspectives of the story of Pocahontas were represented in a 'perspectives cube'. This is a net of a cube (without the top section). In the centre section some common 'facts' are written about the event or person e.g. when, what, where, who, or as in the example in figure 8.4a, the key events the four people were involved in. Each other section then represents a different perspective of the event or person. In this example, are John Smith, King James, Chief Powhatan and Pocahontas. The reverse side of the net shows the name of each person whose possible perspectives are described in each square (figure 8.4b).

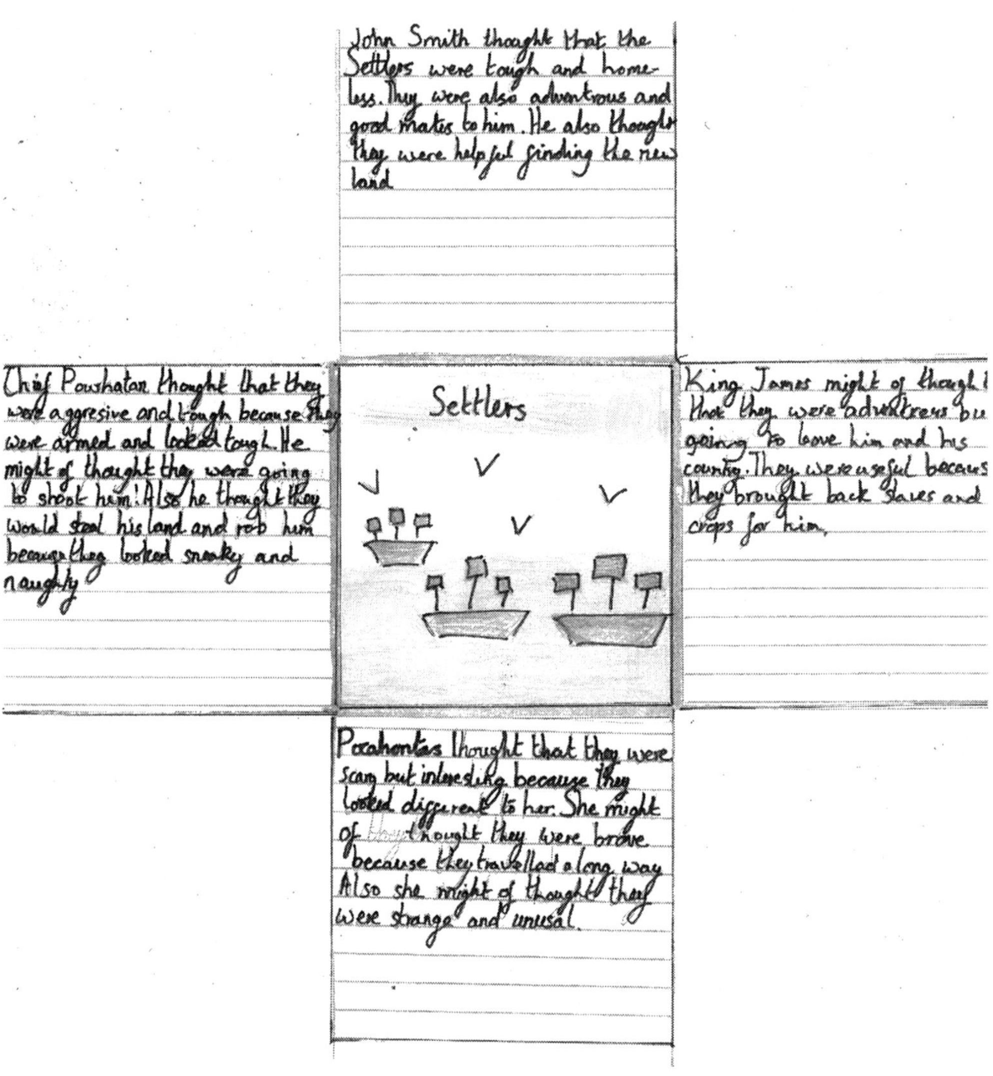

FIGURE 8.4a Net of the inside of the cube, showing the four different perspectives of those involved in the Pocahontas story.

FIGURE 8.4b Shows the outside net of the cube (on the reverse of the paper), with the name of each person, whose possible perspectives are described inside the cube.

Writing for an audience who may have their own perspectives

A further interesting way to develop the writing is to have a real purpose for the writing and a real audience who may have their own perspectives. Quadblogging (http://quadblogging. net/) is a fantastic way to do this and can help children see differing perspectives, particularly when children are blogging with children from different countries.

This was an ambitious topic to embark upon both in terms of subject matter and breadth! The range of approaches used began to support children as they developed their understanding of the past and in particular the differing perspectives of the same events. It is sometimes easy to minimise the complexity of the tasks children engage with in terms of the literacy demands placed on children in cross curricular learning. However, it is only the authentic application of literacy learning that will enable children to develop as confident and competent readers and writers of purpose, and historians with knowledge, skills and integrity.

Conclusion

The three case studies provided children with the opportunities to appreciate different ways in which the past is represented. They introduced them to some of the complexities and also to some of the excitement in trying to piece together what might have happened. In each of the case studies, talk was a central feature, which enabled children to explore their ideas and listen to other opinions. Opportunities to rehearse their ideas through talk enabled children to feel confident, as they approached their writing as well as stimulating their curiosity further.

Each of these case studies also involved reading and writing in many different genre forms and contexts and all the case studies teachers supported children, in a variety of subtle ways, and were rewarded with children's enthusiasm, and a high quality of thinking, resulting in some excellent extended writing.

All the case studies are relevant to the National Curriculum (DfE 2013). However, they model the many ways in which any exploration of different viewpoints about a person or an event can be explored with children.

References

Andrews, J. and Yee, W.C. (2006) Children's 'funds of knowledge' and their real life activities: two minority ethnic children learning in out-of-school contexts in the UK, *Educational Review*, 58 (4): 435–449. ISSN 1465-3397.

Baker, J. and Bennett, R. (2010) *Mirror*, London: Walker.

Bearne, E. and Wolstencroft, H. (2007) *Visual Approaches to Teaching Writing*, London: Sage.

Biemiller, A. (2003) Vocabulary: needed if children are to read well, *Reading Psychology,* 24: 323–335.

Cremin, T.C., Myhill, D.A. (2012) *Writing Voices: creating communities of writers*, London: Routledge.

Dawes, L. (2012) *Talking Points: discussion activities in the primary classroom*, London: Routledge.

Department of Education (DfE) (2013) National Curriculum in England, History Programmes of Study, available online at https://www.gov.uk/government/publications/national-curriculum-in-england-history-programmes-of-study/national-curriculum-in-england-history-programmes-of-study#contents (accessed 9/10/2013).

DfEE & QCA (1999) *The National Curriculum: handbook for primary teachers in England*, London: DfEE and QCA.

Duffy, G., Miller, S., Howerton, S. and Williams, J.B. (2010) Comprehension instruction: merging two historical antithetical perspectives, in D. Wyse, R. Andrews and J. Hoffman (eds.) *The Routledge International Handbook of English, Language and Literacy Teaching*, Oxon: Routledge, pp. 305–317.

Ellis, S. (2013) Pedagogies that support literacy, *The Strathclyde Early Years Educational Research Conference*, University of Strathclyde, Strathclyde (Sept 2013).

Guthrie, J.Y. and Wigfield, A. (2000) *Handbook of Reading Research*, Vol. 3, eds. M.L. Kalil, P.B. Rosenthal and P.D. Pearson, New Jersey: Lawrence Erlbaum, pp. 403–422.

Holm, A. (1963) *I am David*, Copenhagen: Gildendal.

Lewis, M. and Wray, D. (1997) *Extending Literacy: developing approaches to non-fiction*, London: Routledge.

Littleton, K., and Mercer, N. (2013). *Interthinking: putting talk to work.* London: Routledge.

Mercer, N. and Littleton, K. (2007). *Dialogue and the Development of Children's Thinking: a sociocultural approach.* London: Routledge.

Myhill, D., Jones, S., Watson, A. and Lines, H. (2013) Playful explicitness with grammar: a pedagogy for writing, *Literacy* 47 (2): 103–111.

Roberts, M. (2003) *Learning Through Enquiry*, Sheffield: Geographical Association.

Snow, C.E., Griffin, P. and Burns, S. (2005) *Knowledge to Support the Teaching of Reading. Preparing Teachers for a Changing World*, San Francisco, CA: Jossey-Bass.

Stafford, T. (2011) *Teaching Visual Literacy in the Primary Classroom*, Oxon: Routledge.

Welsh Assembly (2008) Skills Framework for 3–19 year olds, available online at Wales.gov.uk.

Welsh Assembly (2013) National Literacy Programme, available online at www.Cymru.gov.uk.

Pupils developing their interpretations of the past

Sue Temple

The school

This project was undertaken at Fellview Community Primary School, which is found in the small rural village of Caldbeck in North Cumbria. Nestled in the Northern Fells, this village is perhaps best known as the resting place of huntsman John Peel, immortalised in the song 'D'yea ken John Peel' but it was also a hive of industry just prior to the Industrial Revolution. It is now a popular destination for tourists looking for a place 'off the beaten track'. Many of the children in the project school live on farms in the area so the rural Anglo-Saxon way of life is perhaps closer to their own lives than the Roman theme, where there is often an emphasis on Roman soldiers, roads, towns and cities. The Anglo-Saxon period was also an era that I had little experience of teaching in school, so I was keen to rectify this.

The National Curriculum (DfE 2013)

The new National Curriculum (DfE 2013) strengthens the inclusion of the Anglo-Saxons in Key Stage 2, as they are mentioned in two of the statutory aspects:

- Britain's settlement by Anglo-Saxons and Scots

- The Viking and Anglo-Saxon struggle for the Kingdom of England to the time of Edward the Confessor (DfE 2013).

Although Sutton Hoo, the Anglo-Saxon, seventh-century ship burial site in Suffolk, is not mentioned specifically in the suggested content, it would fit well with the former of these aspects, in particular when considering:

- *Anglo-Saxon invasions, settlements and kingdoms: place names and village life* – Sutton Hoo demonstrates the kind of weapons used in this time

- *Anglo-Saxon art and culture* – the treasure illustrates the development of art and culture

- *Christian conversion* – the Christian and Pagan aspects of the burial demonstrate how these were combined and how some people moved between the two during this period.

The suggestion is that 'teachers should combine overview and depth studies to help pupils understand both the long arc of development and the complexity of specific aspects of the content' (DfE 2013: 189–192). The former Invaders and Settlers theme in the previous National Curriculum encourages teachers to introduce Romans, Anglo-Saxons and Vikings in an overview study and then to focus on one of these in more detail. This approach could still be taken. However, the new curriculum is also an opportunity to review and evaluate what we have done in the past and make changes and given the overall focus on pre 1066 it may be that schools decide to include a greater emphasis on these aspects in their revised history curriculum.

History at Fellview School

In the school prospectus the staff explain their approach to history.

> In history, we encourage pupils to be curious about the past in Britain and the wider world. Pupils consider how the past influences the present, what past societies were like, and what beliefs and cultures influenced people's actions. As they do this, they develop a chronological framework for their knowledge of significant events and people. Pupils will develop skills through visiting places of historical interest, researching, sifting through evidence and engaging in active discussion – skills that will prepare them for adult life.

The Anglo-Saxons

Using a timeline

The children have studied a range of different historical eras throughout their time in the school. These included Ancient Egyptians, Romans, Vikings, Celts, Tudors, Victorians, the Great Fire of London and Florence Nightingale. This has given them a good grounding in history, which became clear through this project. I decided, in conjunction with the class teacher, to begin with a general timeline, in order to help the children make links between what they already knew and the Anglo-Saxons. I used a piece of twine, stretched across the classroom, with a variety of laminated pictures to 'peg' onto this. Finding images on the Internet for this purpose is not difficult. However, I would urge caution, as several of the Viking illustrations included the double-horned helmets, which we now know to be a misconception. This demonstrates that we must be critical of the images and information we find on websites. The activity worked to an extent, but the less able children struggled to appreciate where to find the different dates, so I would use a paper or card timeline on the floor with the dates clearly marked, if I did this again. The majority of the pupils demonstrated a good grasp of the 'bigger picture' when I asked them to place different eras on a timeline. One boy was even able to explain that there was an overlap between the Anglo-Saxon and Viking eras. As this was something I had only relatively recently begun to appreciate myself I felt this was impressive!

On reflection it might have been a good idea, having established how long the period described as Anglo-Saxon is, to have also looked briefly at an Anglo-Saxon timeline (c. 400–1066 CE), as part of an on-going breadth study, within which a series of depth studies, similar to the Sutton Hoo project, could be related. For example, children could have been given paper tunics with key dates on and asked to line up in the correct time sequence before each new depth study, revisit what they knew, maybe adding notes and drawings related to each 'tunic', as they built up a coherent picture.

Introducing the Anglo-Saxons

Here, in Cumbria, schools have tended to focus on the Romans for their Invaders and Settlers theme, as we are so close to Hadrian's Wall. With its related museums and historic sites this makes an ideal location for a study of this era. For this project we therefore decided to explore the Anglo-Saxon era as a contrast to this. The children in this mixed Year 5/6 class had previously studied the Vikings and the Romans but had not examined the Anglo-Saxons at all.

I wanted to find a way to demonstrate to the children that we do have evidence of this era all around Cumbria, so we started by using a map of Northern Cumbria and trying to find as many place names with an Anglo-Saxon meaning as possible. The first Anglo-Saxon settlements would have been named after the leader or chieftain of the village. This demonstrated which tribe the people belonged to. These places often have the 'ing' ending in their name. Villages settled later on would have been more likely to be named after geographical features, for example 'ton/tun' meaning an enclosed village or farmstead (e.g. Wigton or Oulton).

The children worked in mixed ability pairs and small groups and were quickly able to see very clearly that there was evidence of small settlements, especially from the west of Carlisle through to the Solway Plain and around the Penrith area. We were also able to discuss anomalies such as Mere Tarn. 'Mere' is the Anglo-Saxon word for a small lake or pond and 'tarn' is the Viking word for the same geographical feature and so we have Mere Tarn, which translates to Pond pond! So there must have been places where both Anglo-Saxons and Vikings had lived.

TABLE 9.1 Anglo-Saxon place names.

Anglo-Saxon word	Modern Meaning	Cumbrian examples
ton/tun	An enclosed village/farmstead/manor	Wigton, Brampton, Kirkbampton, Dalston, Plumpton
leigh/lee/ley/by	Forest clearing	Rosley, Thursby, Ireby, Lazonby, Melmerby, Crosby, Langwathby
burgh/borough	Fortified place	Drumburgh, Burgh by Sands
mer/mar/mere	Pond or small lake	Windermere, Mere Tarn
ney	Island	Walney
ham	homestead	Sebergham

The loan box

We are very fortunate in North Cumbria to have a large local museum, Tullie House in Carlisle, which runs an excellent service for schools. This includes a loan box service. The Anglo-Saxon box was not often lent out but it contains an interesting variety of resources, including four complete replica outfits for the children to dress up in.

Anglo-Saxon dress

These outfits stimulated a lot of discussion exploring the types of materials used, the dyes that would have been available to the Saxons and the types of fastenings used during this period. There was much amusement at the broad laces that wound up the boy's legs – one explanation for these is they were to stop mice and other small creatures running up inside their trousers when they were busy working in their fields or small vegetable plots!

We also discussed what a replica was, why the originals would not have survived and what kind of evidence the clothing had been based on; illuminated manuscripts perhaps. We compared these clothes with those we wear now and considered whether we are now much more sensitive to the cold, as these items would not have kept you warm; they seemed to be a kind of linen. Internet research answered this question. Men might have worn linen but they also wore hip-length wool undershirts with long sleeves and woollen trousers and women wore a long-sleeved underdress of linen or wool. The women would have spun the wool and woven it into cloth themselves (http://www.tha-engliscan-gesithas.org.uk/education/anglo-saxon-clothes-men). It is good for teachers and children to say, 'I wonder' and to find out more together!

Giving due consideration to similarities and differences between our lives and those of the Anglo-Saxon ordinary people is an aspect that Ofsted (2011) feel is not dealt with well by teachers of history, so I felt it was important to encourage this kind of discussion and understanding of why their lives, and in particular, their clothes were similar or different. Children often develop the misconception that all people in the past were stupid; they need to realise their limitations in terms of materials, knowledge, understanding and technology within which people in the past worked. Spinning and weaving your own clothes from fleeces, making your own shoes out of leather is something none of us could do. Given their constraints, the solutions people in the past came up with were often very clever.

Reflection

However, I realised that the question I had asked the children, 'How do we know what Anglo-Saxon people wore?' was one I thought about later and realised I had no idea. There were plenty of pictures on the Internet, but they were all replicas. So what were they based on? Eventually I found a fascinating book that answered my question (Owen-Crocker 2004). Her research began with a PhD in the 1970s when, it seems, nobody knew much about what ordinary Anglo-Saxons wore, for the reasons the children gave; very little evidence had been found. Owen- Crocker collected fragments of cloth from grave goods, in areas where the conditions were favourable (including Sutton Hoo). There is some visual evidence in metal work and carved stones, in Icelandic poems and, after conversion to Christianity, there is increased evidence, on sculpted crosses and in seventh and eighth century manuscript illuminations, for instance in the *Book of Kells*, in Trinity College Dublin. I learned that the

Gosforth Cross in Cumbria shows a woman with a knotted pony tail. Other evidence comes from poetry, wills, laws and – indeed – from *The Anglo-Saxon Chronicle*. Owen-Crocker gives an exhaustive list of Old English names for items of clothing: clapes – a garment for either sex, gidweb – something made of precious cloth, skyfel – a woman's hat or hood, prawing spinel – a hairpin, belt . . . a belt. I think this is one reason why I love teaching; sustained, shared thinking (Siraj-Blatchford et al. 2002)! But back to the loan box.

The loan box

The loan box also contained a variety of replica artefacts and pictures. Following a short discussion about what we might count as evidence and how we might interpret evidence the children were organised into mixed ability groups, where they examined a range of replica articles or pictures.

Artefacts

Actually handling the artefacts was very important to some children. One group, who had a medium-sized, decorated pot to explore, quickly identified thumb-prints, where the pottery had been formed by hand. This pot was also carefully decorated with simple indentations. The children discussed why and how the pot would have been decorated. Suggestions included using knifes and thorns. The pupils then had a productive discussion about what might have been kept in this kind of pot. They came up with a long list of possible items, which may have been kept in a pot like this. There was much support for the idea of ashes, if it was a burial urn, but other suggestions included berries, herbs and spices, coins, jewels and gold and special drinks. The children were also sure that the pot belonged to someone important due to the decoration, or that it may have been a gift for a 'Very Important Person'. One child hypothesised that it may have held 'berrys for die' – berries for dyeing. This shows how children made links between these items and the previous discussions about clothing in Anglo-Saxon times.

Coins

A different group had a small collection of replica coins to examine. There were three different kinds of coins here, which led the pupils to surmise that they were 'from three different tribes' (Angles/Jutes/Saxons) because, 'there are three different pictures'. They also noted that some of the letters and symbols used on the coins were familiar but others were not. 'I couldn't read some of the words because some of the letters were the same and some were different.' One child also recognised the name, 'ALFRED' from their previous work about the Vikings.

Visual sources

Images can be very useful when working with children with Special Educational Needs and this is true for all children, in history lessons. We have to ensure that we demonstrate to the children how observant they need to be and how the interpretations they make can be just as valuable as those of the adults in the room. An enlarged picture of an illustrated version of Bede's *Ecclesiastical History of the English People* was shared with one small group. This is a very detailed picture and the children found a range of aspects interesting. It depicts a group of people gathered around a man in a large chair all playing musical instruments. The pupils thought the group might have been worshipping the man sitting on the 'throne' or he may be their leader. They also commented, 'even though it is small it is very detailed' and (the artist) 'must have put a lot of effort into this picture. He must have had both skill and patience.' One child even remarked that 'all the faces are mostly the same'. This demonstrates that these children took the time to look very carefully and then came up with their own interpretations of the illustration. I had not noticed how the faces were similar but the child was quite right.

A second illustration of a feast was used with another group. The children thought that two of the men who were leaning down holding 'cababs' (kebabs) were probably slaves. The other three people, 'probably men who were lords, entertaining warriors, in some kind of grand hall', were being offered more food. (Note the use of probably – it is very important to make no unfounded claims in history.) They also noticed that there were no forks in the picture but at least one man in the picture had six fingers on one hand. Comments were also made about the gathered tablecloths and hanging tapestries behind the table. The pupils commented on the strange letters at the bottom of the page – these are the runic alphabet. They also noticed that some of the clothes worn by these people were similar to the outfits worn by the children in the earlier activity.

Sutton Hoo

Storytelling

The second session began with a 'storytelling' approach to the Sutton Hoo burial site, dating from around 700 CE. The Sutton Hoo site in Suffolk is a collection of mounds, or more correctly *barrows,* of various sizes. I illustrated the story with pictures on the whiteboard. There were local legends about these mounds containing treasure. Sutton Hoo House and the surrounding land were owned by Edith Pretty and her husband. When he died she resumed one of the interests of her youth; archaeology. Some of the barrows had been subject to episodes of digging and burrowing but no proper archaeological dig had taken place. Mrs Pretty approached Ipswich Museum and they recommended a local man called Basil Brown. I told the story up to the point where Basil Brown began to uncover the treasures buried there. Bage (1999) suggests to storytellers that the story should be paused at certain points to encourage the children to explore aspects of the narrative in more detail, i.e. not just accepting that this is one version or interpretation. Introducing the session in this way helped to capture the children's interest and imagination and we built on this by using a thinking skills activity I had adapted, before returning to the story and examining photographs of some of the treasures found.

Thinking skills activity

I have successfully used this approach with several classes of children. I find it engages the pupils at a deeper level than simply showing them a picture, and they have to use their observation and oracy skills carefully. Children need to engage with historical enquiry, so that it becomes part of what constructivists call their own 'mental map', enabling them to build on their prior knowledge and gradually understand the situation and concepts of each era. Although the treasure uncovered on this site is truly awe-inspiring I did not want to focus on this and ignore the rest of the site. The archaeological dig itself was so carefully undertaken by Basil Brown that the original shape of the ship, which was 27 metres long, was still visible, despite the fact that it had decayed and disintegrated with only the rivets surviving. I find this remarkable. The burial also contains a variety of other artefacts, as well as the more famous helmet and jewellery; these give us additional clues about the person who was buried here and the customs and beliefs of that time.

I split the class into groups of four and asked the children to number themselves 1–4. Each group was given a large sheet of A3 plain paper and one pencil. The children numbered 1 then come to the front to examine the picture, in this case a photograph of the reconstruction of the Sutton Hoo burial chamber.

I gave the children a minute to examine the picture and then they returned to their group and carefully described what they have seen in sufficient detail for child no. 2 to draw it. After a few minutes child no. 2 then came up to examine the picture before returning with child no. 3 drawing this time. The numbering is important to ensure that no child who has actually seen the picture is drawing until the very final pairing. Three of the groups produced reasonably accurate depictions of the photograph. However, one group started a new picture each time a new child began describing the original photograph. I found this a fascinating interpretation of my instructions as this has never happened before! I was very careful to respond in a positive way to this more creative interpretation of the activity. The purpose is to develop their oracy and thinking skills; the final product is not so important, so this was perfectly acceptable.

The Sutton Hoo treasure

Following this activity we returned to the whiteboard and my storytelling. I showed the children photographs, taken at the time, showing the ship being uncovered and explained how the dig came to national attention and more notable archaeologists joined the site. I also explained how this was 1938-9 – immediately before World War II broke out and that there was concern and pressure to move the treasure to a more secure site, because war was understood to be imminent. During World War II the treasure was kept in sealed boxes in an underground station used by the British Museum. I showed the children photographs of how the helmet looked when it was excavated (basically a lot of rust fragments!) and the process it went through, including misplacing a box of the pieces when the helmet was originally reconstructed, before the famous replica helmet was made much more recently. As most of the helmet had been made of iron it had rusted badly but because of this, when the roof collapsed, it did not do the major damage that would have been caused if it had been whole at this point. The roof of the ship had collapsed in on itself, probably about 100 years after the burial, and this had caused damage to some of the other grave goods. The eyebrows, nose, mouth and moustache had been made of bronze so these were recognisable as being part of some kind of face mask.

We also discussed the conditions in the barrow and how this affected the different items in the site, including the body. No body was discovered when the site was excavated in 1939. It was only when the site was reopened in 1965–7 that soil samples were taken, which confirmed it was highly likely that a body had indeed been buried here. Archaeologists now believe that the nature of the soil in this area and the body being placed in the ship under the mound of earth would have led to water draining into the ship, forming an 'acidic soup' around the body, which would have led to its complete decay. Luckily much of the treasure was not affected by this process; gold, silver and the precious stones all survived. We also discussed how the ship must have been dragged up from the river to this site and so the site itself might have had significance to the Anglo-Saxons. The artefacts themselves also revealed connections to various parts of the then known world. For example, there was silver from the Byzantine Empire, Frankish gold coins and a gold buckle similar to Gaul designs. Scandinavian influences were also evident in the boat burial custom, the helmet and the shield. This burial site illustrated that the heroic poems, such as *Beowulf*, did have some truth in their descriptions of life for the upper tiers of the society.

Interpretations

I had been careful to present the evidence to the children and not make any comments about who might have been buried there, as this was what we wanted the pupils to think about. Given the evidence from the site, what kind of person could this have been? The pupils should be helped to understand that interpretations of the past must be based on the evidence available and be able to justify and explain their thoughts and ideas. The National Curriculum (DfE 2013: 206) states in its overarching aim for Key Stage 2 that 'They (the children) should understand how our knowledge of the past is constructed from a range of sources' and that different versions of past events may exist, giving some reasons for this. As we have only fragmentary evidence of some eras it is important that the pupils understand this important strand of how historians work.

Planning the writing frames

There are many different writing frames available in both books and on the Internet. The most important aspect the teacher needs to consider is the purpose of the writing frame and how it is going to support the writing of the children in the class. You need to find a balance between supporting and encouraging the children and allowing them the freedom to be creative within that framework. This is an important consideration as you can be too restrictive and end up with every piece of work being more or less the same. You must allow for the children expressing their own ideas, and demonstrating their own abilities, within the framework provided. A writing frame needs to be designed to support those children in particular to whom a blank piece of paper is too daunting; it guides and encourages these children but should not hold them back either.

Our aim in the writing following these activities was to encourage the children to consider the evidence they had examined and outline their interpretations of what kind of person was buried here and, more importantly, justify this. We therefore decided to use an explanation writing frame but we adapted this to differentiate within the class. Some pupils find non-fiction writing problematic, so scaffolds such as these can overcome this initial difficulty. The EXEL (Exeter Extending Literacy Project, Lewis and Wray 1997) suggested that the use of writing frames should be modelled by the teacher, followed by a joint activity with the class, then a scaffolded writing activity (e.g. using the frame), finally ending with an independent activity. Although this project was almost twenty years ago, and writing frames have fallen out of favour, this seemed like a good model to start from. In this project the teacher supported the children with their writing more than I did, as she knew her children's abilities and was much more able to encourage and challenge the children to think about how to improve their writing – in particular with the use of connectives and more ambitious vocabulary. As is always the case, a class teacher who knows her children well, can support writing more effectively than a visitor in the classroom.

As we were focusing on the explanation genre and asking the children to justify their views – i.e. *why* they thought whatever they did, the use of the word 'because' became extremely important. We therefore decided to remove this word for the more able children in the class and encourage them to use a wider range of connectives but to leave the less able children with 'because' included in their frame. Figure 9.1 shows a less able child's writing and figure 9.2 shows a more able child's writing

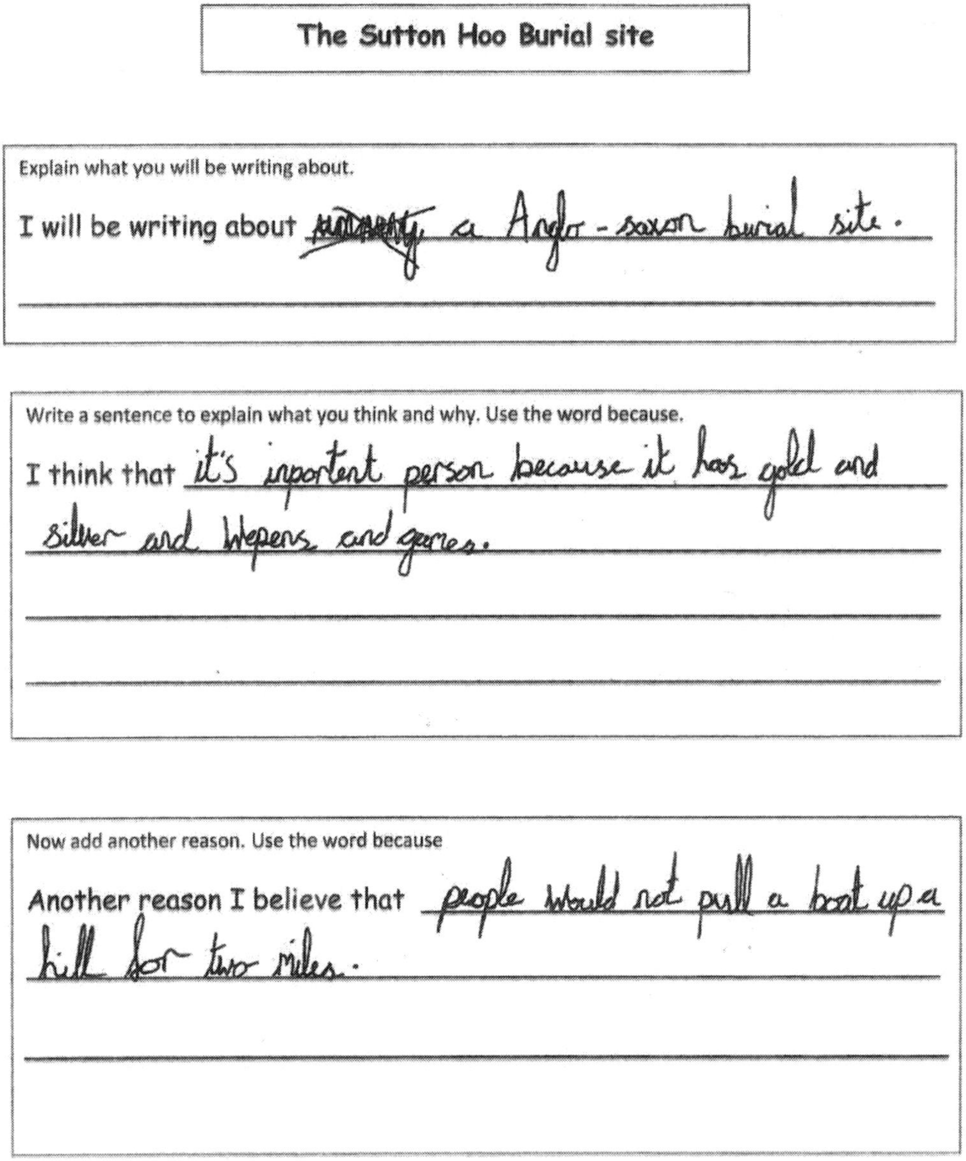

The Sutton Hoo Burial site

Explain what you will be writing about.

I will be writing about ~~anxiety,~~ a Anglo - saxon burial site.

Write a sentence to explain what you think and why. Use the word because.

I think that *it's inportent person because it has gold and silver and wepens and games.*

Now add another reason. Use the word because

Another reason I believe that *people would not pull a boat up a hill for two miles.*

FIGURE 9.1 Less able child's writing.

The Sutton Hoo Burial site

Explain what you will be writing about.

I will be writing about _the Sutton Hoo Burial site_

Write a sentence to explain what you think and why. Use the word because.

I think that _The Sutton Hoo burial site is a very important burial because he has lost of nice things like jewels, spears and alot more preshes thing._

Now add another reason. Use the word because

Another reason I believe that _And his helmet looks very posh so I think he is a king._

Consequently these facts show that this man was very important

FIGURE 9.2 More able child's writing.

Assessment

In order to assess children's work I feel it is useful to go back to the Attainment targets in the 1999 National Curriculum (DfEE 1999). These give reasonably clear guidance of what level a child is working at and therefore where they need to go to make progress. Without a simple method of assessing children's work in history I strongly feel that it may be difficult to ensure progression particularly for those teachers who are not confident in teaching history. Progress might then become limited to the literacy work and not in the skills, knowledge and understanding of history.

TABLE 9.2 Assessing the children's writing.

Attainment target	*Examples from the children's writing*
Level 3: They use sources of information in ways that go beyond simple observations to answer questions about the past	*It might have been for storing berries.* *It was pinched because you can feel the finger marks.*
Level 4: They show some understanding that aspects of the past have been represented and interpreted in different ways.	*I thought that the pot would have been handmade and because it has patterns it must have been made for the chief.* *I think that it was a chief's burial because it had spears, pots, armour, statues and shields.*
Level 5: They know that some events . . . have been interpreted in different ways and suggest possible reasons for this.	*Bede seemed to have put a lot of effort into this picture. He must have had both skill and patience.* *I think that the coins are from three different tribes because there are three different pictures.* *I think that he was important because he was buried with gold, silver, games, armour and weapons, therefore he was rich.* *Another reason I believe that is because they dragged the boat a long way up a hill which they would not do for a normal person.*
Level 6: They examine and explain the reasons for, and the results of, events and changes.	*I think that the Sutton Hoo burial site is a very important burial because he has lots of nice things like jewels . . . Another reason I believe this is because his helmet looks very posh so I think he was a king. . . . Consequently these facts show that this man was very important.*

The class teacher is able to use this information to plan her future lessons, both in history and literacy, to ensure that she is challenging, as well as supporting, each of the children in the class.

Differentiation

The majority of Special Educational Needs children do not really seem to need radically different approaches. These pupils need more time to think, talk, explore and consider, and more support to get to the same points as 'mainstream' children. I feel it should be more about giving the children good historical experiences and activities that make them think, helping them to make sense of their thoughts and feelings and then using the writing frames to support them, as they record these accurately, before they lose their train of thought. Once these ideas are recorded as notes it will be easier for the child to produce a piece of extended writing, as they have these notes to refer to – though depending on the child, this may have to be done in shorter time blocks to keep their concentration levels up. This is all hard to organise, in a busy mainstream classroom, but the sense of accomplishment for the child can be so great. Alternative ways of recording could also be used to encourage the engagement of these children, through the use of technology (e.g. PowerPoints or podcasts). Similar structures to the writing frames could be used to support the pupils in their development and thinking.

I often suspect it is our expectations that need to be considered much more than the children's abilities. The children I have worked with over the years have frequently surprised me with their insights and understanding – sometimes appreciating things or highlighting aspects that I had just not thought a child would suggest – and sometimes things I had not appreciated either!

Conclusion

Of course, if you live near London you could see the Sutton Hoo treasure in the British Museum (http://www.britishmuseum.org/explore/online_tours/britain/our_top_ten_british_ treasures/the_sutton_hoo_ship-burial.aspx).

If you live in Suffolk you could visit the burial site (http://www.nationaltrust.org.uk/ sutton-hoo/).

And if you live in Staffordshire you could relate the enquiry to recently discovered Staffordshire Hoard, now exhibited in a seventh century mead hall (http://www.staffordshire hoard.org.uk/news/striking-new-exhibition-places-anglo-saxon-treasures-in-an-ancient-feasting-hall).

Or you could use similar teaching strategies to find out background information about any number of people, artefacts or situations, particularly those in the Stone, Bronze and Iron Ages about which we have no written evidence but about which children enjoy making rich, imaginative interpretations, which are valid if they conform with what we know, is possible and when there is no contradictory evidence. Techniques described in this chapter could be applied in many other contexts, to encourage children to create different interpretations, supported with evidence.

References

Bage, G. (1999) *Narrative Matters: teaching and learning history through story*, London: Falmer, 2/e London: Routledge.

Department for Education and Employment (DfEE) (1999) The National Curriculum: handbook for primary teachers in England, available online at http://webarchive.nationalarchives.gov.uk.

Department for Education (DfE) (2013) The National Curriculum in England, Key Stages 1 and 2 framework document, available online at www.gov.uk/dfe/nationalcurriculum

Lewis, M. and Wray, D. (1997) *Extending Literacy: children reading and writing non-fiction*, London: Routledge.

Office for Standards in Education (Ofsted) (2011) *History for All*, London: Department for Education, available online at www.ofsted.gov.uk/resources/history-for-all

Owen-Crocker, G.R. (2004) *Dress in Anglo-Saxon England* (revised and enlarged edition), Woodbridge: Boydel Press.

Siraj-Blatchford, I., Muttock, K., Golden, R. and Bell, D. (2002) *Researching Effective Pedagogy in the Early Years* (Research Report 356) Annersley: Department for Education and Skills.

Useful information for teaching about Sutton Hoo:

BBC 2 Chronicle: Sutton Hoo (16.08.89), available online at http://www.bbc.co.uk/archive/ chronicle/8622.shtml

The Historical Association:

Reference

http://www.history.org.uk/resources/primary_resource_3865.html

Lesson plans

http://www.history.org.uk/resources/primary_resource_3738.html

http://www.history.org.uk/resources/primary_resource_3866.html

http://www.history.org.uk/resources/resource_3738.html

Primary History **Case Studies on the Saxons**

Spring 2008:21– 4; spring 2009: 21– 4; summer 2010: 34–37.

Discursive and reflective writing – into the classroom

Jon Nichol

Classroom culture, genre and pupil composition

Chapter 2, Genre and children writing history – reflective and discursive learning, argues strongly that reflective and discursive [R&D] composition/writing does not occur in a vacuum. It is embedded in a teaching process that enables such writing to occur (for one aspect of this, see chapter 3, Oracy: speaking and listening). The teaching process is part of a history education pedagogic culture whose warp and weft are Nuffield Primary History and Cognitive Acceleration learning principles, see p.00. These principles underpin pupil understanding of what 'Doing History' involves and upon which all forms and levels of their writing depend, from single words and phrases to extended pieces. In the case studies in this chapter we examine some R&D writing that ensued from R&D teaching, drawing upon examples taken from different categories of genre (table 10.1).

TABLE 10.1 'Doing History': genres of case studies in this chapter.

Case	Genre	Topic – title
1	Police report Historical fiction – an account	Investigation of the contents of a mystery suitcase
2	A travel brochure of Celtic Britain A spy account of Caesar's army	Celtic Britain and the Roman Army
3	A newspaper report	An archaeological investigation of a body discovered in a Danish peat bog
4	Anglo-Saxon poetry [see pages 27–32 and 165–166]	The destruction of England's Roman towns
5	Historical recreation – a short story	A Tudor feast

R&D writing is embedded in our history *schemes of work*, which usually last from six to twelve ninety-minute lessons. At every point, in the schemes of work we challenge the pupils individually, working in pairs or as small teams to investigate, discuss, debate, speculate, hypothesise, reach conclusions, defend them and write about what they have learned.

An interview with two nine-year-old pupils illuminates the process. They told the interviewer about how they, as a team of four archaeologists in a classroom simulation of an archaeological dig, had excavated a Viking burial mound in the Isle of Man. The team uncovered a sacrificed slave girl's skeleton in the mound and a coffin and its contents in a pit below the centre of the mound. Using history topic books and the Internet the pupils then investigated the clues, their significance and their historical context. This enabled them to use their informed imaginations to write an archaeological report of the excavation – their interpretation:

Interviewer:	What did you find out about the Vikings and all the things that they believed about, such as death? Were they same as us?
Pupil 1:	One thing I found out, that was quite interesting, was that the Vikings believed in the god Odin and he was the god of poetry and war and he rode a horse with eight legs . . .
Interviewer:	That's brilliant, right, and so there's the funeral and what's this now [pointing at the diagram]?
Pupil 2	This is a coffin with his weapons broken up and . . .
Interviewer:	That's his coffin is it?
Pupil 2:	Yes.
Interviewer:	Right, so now why has this person got weapons in his grave?
Pupil 2:	Because of his new life in heaven. So they broke them all up so they couldn't hurt him and no one would want to rob him of them.
Interviewer:	So what kind of person was this?
Pupil 2:	Well, he was an important person.

Case 1: The Mystery Suitcase – The Police Report and a World War II Short Story – historical fiction

Introduction

The Viking Burial Mound is one element in a series of twelve one-and-a-half-hour lessons scheme of work [SoW] on Roman, Saxon and Viking England, which follows an introductory lesson. The SoW's introductory lesson was on 'What is History?' in which the pupils, as history detectives, investigate the contents of a mystery suitcase, to find out about its owner. The enquiry ends with them writing either an *investigative report* or a *fictitious story* about the suitcase's owner – a school child.

The children in this mixed ability class of thirty-two Year 5 and 6 [nine to eleven-year-old] pupils investigating the suitcase were adequate to good readers and writers. Their private, personally chosen reading books showed that there were no 'weak' readers. In terms of writing, their composition books showed they all could write at length, reasonably accurately, grammatically and with an understanding of genres, i.e. they were all functionally literate.

FIGURE 10.1 Spider web diagram to plan investigation about who Rose was.

The teaching phase: investigating the suitcase

In chapter 3, Oracy: speaking and listening, pp. 47–51, we examined how the class investigated the mystery suitcase in the first six episodes of the lesson. This enabled the pupils to build up detailed knowledge and understanding of the owner of the suitcase, Rose. We now move on to writing about Rose. Episode 7 picks up the story where we left off on p. 51. The pupils had produced concept webs about Rose (figure 10.1) to accompany their report sheets about her (see p. 48).

EPISODE 7

The writing phase: the police report and the short story–historical fiction
Concerning genres, we told the pupils that they had a choice of either writing a *police report* about Rose or a short story – historical fiction as if they were Rose. Each pupil had to think carefully about the genre they chose:

Tenor – Who was the author, what was his or her purpose and who was the intended audience?

Field – The content of the piece: what information would it contain, both its overall context and its detail?

Mode – What form the writing would take, its mode. What kind of language would they use: how would they structure and organise their writing: how would they open and conclude it?

Culture – The overall cultural context for their writing, in this case, their knowledge of police enquiries and of children's fiction.

Getting ready to write

The pupils were told that they could either plan out their writing or, if they had a clear idea of what they wanted to write, to begin without any formal planning. Pupils and adults have different writing approaches; they range, on a spectrum, from free, spontaneous composition to detailed, meticulous planning – we wanted to retain that level of freedom.

Writing phase

Drawing upon their police reports, spider webs and what they had learned from discussion and debate the pupils spent the next half an hour in writing about the owner of the suitcase. The extent, variety and relative sophistication of the writing was very pleasing – we had deliberately worked within two genres that the pupils had already extensively experienced, i.e. historical investigations and using the informed imagination to write historical accounts, i.e. historical fiction. What was fascinating was how the fiction writing drew upon our previous scheme of work on *World War II* that had focused on the Blitz. This included the class being evacuated from their school in Tiverton to Exeter by train, each pupil clutching a suitcase and a gas mask.

Running away [short story – historical fiction genre]

I am scared. It is the war and I am running away to escape the bombing. Oh, by the way, my name is Rose Nichol.

I think that if I hadn't decided to run away I would have been evacuated. Any way I just packed my suitcase and I am on the train to the country. As I exit London I feel sad about leaving my family. Yawn. Now I think I will just have a little sleep . . . 5 hrs. later.

The train has just pulled in to a station. Right, this is where I get off. After a couple of hours walking I eventually find a nice warm place to sleep. It is behind the bakers, in the shed where he leaves his bread to cool. I can get in behind these racks and snuggle down in this corner by the window. I open my case and pull out my doll. She is called Mary-Anne. She has lovely golden curls with a dark red dress and a matching bonnet. As I cuddle into her, I heard a bomber plane fly overhead. I wish more than ever that I was back with my parents.

Report on Rose Jenkins [police report genre]

Hallo, my name is Constable Hill. I have been told to give you a report on a girl I met the other day. Her name is Rose Nichol. Rose is a very funny and happy girl. She lives at 541, Sylvan Road, Exeter Devon. Her telephone number is 01392 73946. She is a short brown haired girl with a pale face.

Her hobbies are skipping, playing recorder, horse riding and drawing. She attends Stoke Hill 1st school in Exeter. She learns French there. Rose is a very clever girl. She has one friend called Gemma. She has a dog and cat. She has 2 sisters called Ellie and Kitty. She likes playing with her Barbie Doll. She is 6 years old. She likes the beach and she went on holiday to the Isles of Scilly. When she grows up she will be very rich. Thank you for listening.

Commentary: The pupils' compositions

Historical fiction – running away

The tenor is clear – the writer [name not on paper], is writing for either herself in diary form or a close, intimate friend. The piece opens with a clear statement – 'I am scared.' It ends with a logical conclusion to the story: 'I wish more than ever that I was back with my parents.' She has taken the idea of the suitcase to write a story based upon their previous scheme of work – World War II, where they simulated an evacuation from their school near Tiverton, Exeter, to Exeter by train. She places her story in its overall setting: 'the war . . . escape bombing . . . . Evacuated . . . train to the country . . . Exit London . . . finding shelter . . . with her doll . . . hears a bomber plane.'

The police report – report on Rose Nichol

Mathew has taken the role of a policeman, Constable Hill, with a clear concept of tenor – the author in relation to the audience and the writing's purpose. The writing opens with setting the scene in relation to purpose and audience, and concludes in the same way. In the body of his report Mathew selects from the clues in the suitcase to provide a connected, well argued report about Rose. He links judgements to evidence, writes in short, clear sentences and builds up a full, rounded picture of her. Running away is a fascinating account.

REFLECTION

Consider how the writers have drawn upon their understanding of what genre involves, to write contrasting pieces.

- The authorial voice in relation to the piece's purpose and the intended audience.

- The mode – the form the writing takes, with its organisational patterns and conventions.

- The field – content: what have they drawn from the content in their compositions.

- The cultural context that helps shape their compositions.

Case 2: Roman Britain: Conquest and settlement – a travel brochure about Celtic Britain and a Spy Account of Caesar's army and a Spy Report

Introduction: the travel brochure

After the mystery suitcase lesson, the Year 5 and 6 class of nine to eleven-year-olds moved on to studying Roman Britain – invasion and settlement. The Roman Britain scheme of work was for four lessons and included two main compositions: a multi-media travel brochure and an eyewitness account of Caesar's army, prior to its invasion from Gaul, modern France. Each of the teaching and writing phases for the brochure and the spy report lasted for two one-and-a-half-hour lessons.

The teaching phase: the travel brochure

We worked for the first lesson intensively upon what a Celtic village would have been like, using a range of activities to study our sources:

- an artist's recreations of one village;
- a map of Celtic Britain;
- a timeline;
- a contemporary Roman account of Celtic Britain.

We [the class teacher and I] introduced the idea of the Celtic travel brochure by moving from what children knew and interested them to the topic we were studying. We asked the class: Would they like to go on a holiday to an exciting place of their choice? How would they find out about it? We brainstormed their replies, listing them on the board. The class mentioned the Internet, travel brochures: Emily's contribution – 'travel agent' resulted in my response: 'excellent!' On the board we then used a grid to pose questions, field answers and ask for a new question about each place (table 10.2).

The class worked through the genre elements of a modern single-sheet travel brochure that folded in to three sections, i.e. six in all.

Author[s]	Who wrote and produced the brochure [the firm's instructions to the authoring group – the writer, designer and production team]?
Purpose	What was the purpose of the brochure, i.e. what was it for?
Audience	Whom were the authors writing for?
Field – content	What each side of the brochure contained. They came up with a list that we put on the whiteboard.
Mode – form	Next we talked about how the pages were designed: pictures – beach, bedroom; where it is; where you can fly from; guides; cost; leisure facilities; climate.
Culture	What were the overall cultural factors reflected in the brochure about the role and nature of holidays in modern British society?

TABLE 10.2 Grid for posing questions, in preparation for writing a travel brochure.

Where?	*Why chosen?*	*Questions about it*
Alaska	Adventure	What do they grow for food?
Ibiza	Hot	Why is the sea so blue?
France	French food	How do they make the food so good?

TABLE 10.3 Storyboard produced by teacher and children, as a model for writing travel brochures.

CELTIC TRAVEL GUIDE BROCHURE template			
Visit the diamond isle Land of ancient customs and ways of life	Celtic life	Visit a hill top town	Have a go at making jewellery
Wide choice of location [For further details, see back cover **[INSERT MAP]**	Take a walk on the wild side	Learn about the celtic year	Have a day out with the local boys – mini skirmishes guaranteed
Atrebates – chief Caractacus Stay on a small farm Sleep under thatch	Take a day out hunting & see the flora and fauna of the region Attend a festival	Weather	Night life
Front page – 1/3rd of A4	Page 2 back of cover	Folds onto page 2	Folds onto page 3

The writing phase

The teacher and class then modelled the brochure to produce a storyboard, joint composition, for the pupils to use as a framework for their own Celtic brochures. These they produced during the week after the lesson.

The spy report

Introduction

Work on the travel brochures meant that when I arrived for our second Celtic and Roman Britain lesson, the travel brochures were on display! The pupils knew, from the story about Harry and Hermione visiting Caractacus, that Caesar was about to invade Britain, so our focus was for the class to find out about how the Romans fought to repel Caesar's invasion. The cultural ambience for the teaching was the Harry Potter phenomenon: nearly all the children had read a Harry Potter novel or seen a Harry Potter film.

The teaching phase: finding out about the Roman Army

The resources for the lesson were:

- A short clip of the opening battle scene from the film *Gladiator*.
- A spy report sheet for the pupils to complete.

- A short story about Harry Potter and Hermione's journey to the village of Caractacus, chief of a major Celtic tribe whom Caesar threatened – the Atrebates. Harry and Hermione were in role as Celtic children – in the village they met Caractacus's children, Dylan and Emma. Caractacus decided to send Harry, Hermione, Dylan and Emma as spies to find out about what a Roman army was like and how it would fight.

We told the class that in teams of four they were to find out about how Caesar's army fought. The class read through the Harry and Hermione story of their visit to Caractacus's village and the decision to send Harry, Hermione, Dylan and Emma as spies to witness Caesar fighting the Gauls.

The Roman Army at war

How could she do it, thought Dylan. How could Emma have dropped them in the space between the two armies! On one side stood the Roman catapults and troops, on the other they could hear the trumpets and howling battle cries of the Gauls, as they swarmed through the forest. Thank goodness the invisibility cloak was also a shield that nothing could damage. Now Emma and Dylan would find out how the Romans fought. The Roman general roared the order to fire the catapults – the battle had begun. A giant Roman arrow bounced off the top of the invisibility cloak and soared towards the forest. The children could hear screaming, the roar of the burning forest, the wild neighing of horses and charging feet . . .

The teams of four had to think of questions they would ask about Caesar's army. These we pooled and the most important listed.

1 How many soldiers did they have?

2 What types of weapons did they have?

3 Where will the soldiers attack first?

4 How many weapons?

5 What did the soldiers wear?

6 What armour did the soldiers have?

7 Where are the soldiers fighting?

8 What strategy is planned?

9 What explosives did the soldiers have?

10 How did the soldiers camp?

The learners wrote these on their spy sheets (see below).

We then played the battle scene from the film *Gladiator*. Great excitement, only for one child to tell us that it was a 15 certificate film and we shouldn't have shown it! Reassurance came from the class teacher's comment that a clip was fine. Also, pleasingly, two-thirds of the class had already watched the whole film.

The class completed their spy sheets. Here is Harriet's spy sheet (table 10.4)

TABLE 10.4 Harriet's spy sheet.

The Roman Army Spy Sheet	*Name: Harriet [aged 8]*		*Date 3/2/03*
???????????????s	**Answers**		
What armour did Roman soldiers wear?	*Helmets, mail*		
What weapons did Roman soldiers have?	*Spears, swords, catapults, bows and arrows*		
What were the shields of Roman soldiers like?	*Big with their arms on the front and a hole for a spear to go through*		
How did Roman soldiers fight?	*On horse and by foot* *standing and firing arrows*		
What did Roman army camps look like?	*Dirty, little food, smelly*		
What would you hear, smell, see and taste on a visit to a Roman army camp?	*Hear* *Smell* *See* *Taste*	*Battle cries* *Fire, sweat* *Men fighting and dying* *Stuffy air, a stench of death*	
What words and phrases would you use to describe a Roman army on the march?	*Fierce, solemn, sinister, sad, overcoming*		
The Enemy Army Spy Sheet			
???????????????s	**Answers**		
How many enemy soldiers are there?	Thousands		
What weapons do they have?	Bows and arrows, swords, catapults, spears,		
Where will they attack first?	The nearest village after the woods		
What did they wear?	Armour, helmets		
What armour did they have?	Helmets shields swords		
Where are they fighting?	The woods		
How did they camp?	Out of battle range but moveable		

The writing phase: the Spy Report

Now the class were ready to write their Spy Reports for Caractacus. Although they already had extensive knowledge of the genre, from the school's literacy programme, we worked out the structure, a model of it, for their reports. Our action research diary for the lesson's fifth episode reads:

Focus: writing the report

Break went on a long time and an assembly followed, in which it seemed that every child in the school received an orienteering certificate! But, back to work with 45 minutes to complete the lesson. We wanted to make sure that the report was as fully and carefully structured as possible. I did not have a 'model' report to demonstrate and analyse – I assumed that they had already worked extensively on this particular genre.

We were conscious of the need to provide triggers for the field of the report – its content. The Roman Army Spy Sheet has trigger words and smart words to help in the writing. The final section was designed to make the children think clearly about how to use their information.

We decided next to go through what was involved, so we worked out the structure of the report genre on the blackboard. This covered three elements:

- setting the scene;

- details of what we would write about;

- the advice we would give to Caractacus.

In working out the report genre of the framework, we stressed tenor throughout, identifying the authorial perspective [Dylan and Emma], the writing's purpose for a specific, clearly and fully defined audience [Caractacus]. For details see table 10.5.

TABLE 10.5 Spy Report Genre Frame.

SPY REPORT: CAESAR'S ARMY REPORT GENRE FRAME

Name: ____ Date: _______________

1 Set the Scene

- Place – where ■ Setting the scene ■ When (date – day, time)
- You are there
- Feelings

Audience: who is the report going to? (Caractacus the Celtic King)

Author: Emma or Dylan

2 Detail

* armour * weapons * explosives * camp * campaign

* battle plan – tactics * smells * where marching to

3 Advice to Celtic King – Conclusion

TO HELP YOU WRITE YOUR REPORT, THINK ABOUT

- **Trigger words**

Armour, boats, camp, catapults, cavalry, charge, fight, general, legions, march, officers, spears, swords, tunic

- **Smart words**

Then, another point, because, finally, first, I think, in conclusion, next, we saw

- Look at your Roman army spy sheet: put the points in the order you want to write about them.

Episode 6: focus – writing

The pupils then wrote their reports, using the Spy Report sheets (table 10.4) and the Spy Report Genre Frame (3), to guide them, which was similar to the one below. This is from a previous teaching of the scheme of work where pupils had reported on Caesar's camp, having investigated in groups of four, seven detailed pictures of the Roman Army, how it was equipped, camped, marched and fought.

Commentary

We analysed the children's spy reports and mapped the different elements that they had included. There was comprehensive coverage of the topic, drawing upon the pupils' knowledge, developed during the reflective and discursive teaching, and their existing understanding of what writing in a genre like the Spy Report entailed.

REFLECTION

Consider how the teaching and learning principles of Nuffield Primary History and Cognitive Acceleration underpin the teaching and learning that resulted in the pupils' Celtic travel brochures and Spy Reports.

Case 3: The Body in the Bog – A Newspaper Report

Introduction

A pupil investigation of a body found in a Danish bog is a long established, iconic element in the teaching of history in England, since its first appearance in the early 1970s as an element of the introductory *What is History?* teaching programme of the Schools Council History Project [SCHP], aka the Schools History Project. The SCHP revolutionised history teaching in Britain. The SCHP investigation was of Tollund Man. We researched the idea and discovered that there was another body, that of *Grauballe Man*, which involved a genuine history mystery – there were two possible interpretations of who the person was and how and why he had died. The teaching of *Grauballe Man* involves the pupils, as archaeologists, investigating the body. The teaching can take many forms: researching the sources as a set of separate hard copy clues, as a computer database or as a double page spread of a textbook.

In chapter 2 (pp. 40–45), we reported on the teaching phase until the point when we could prepare the class for their discursive and reflective writing.

Teaching phase [continued]

Pupils as archaeologists investigate the body. The pupils in teams of four worked on the following sources:

- a set of clues about The Body in the Bog and a network of connections between them;

- photographs of the bog where the body was found and the body in the ground: as www. downloads, see https://centres.exeter.ac.uk/historyresource/mysteries/bogbody/start.htm and http://en.wikipedia.org/wiki/Grauballe_Man

- a history novelette in the Harry Potter genre – *Red Christian Goes Missing* – as a class reader.

Each pupil team had a reporter, organiser of resources, note taker and observer. During the teaching phase the learners had, as archaeologists, investigated how, when and why the man had died, producing lists of questions, words and phrases, as well as discussing, in their teams of four, the clues, their hypotheses, interpretations and conclusions.

The final pre-writing element was a class debate about what might have happened to the body found in the bog. Each group's reporters gave their group's conclusion and what it was based upon, followed by a whole class discussion:

- two groups decided a local farmer had killed Red Christian in a row over a girl friend;

- two groups decided that an old, local man was responsible for Red Christian's death;

- two groups decided that Red Christian had fallen into the bog when going home drunk, one group could not decide and gave three possible scenarios;

- the final group to report argued, 'We don't think it's Red Christian. The cauldron's from the Iron Age. It could have been a Roman, because Tacitus wrote about them.'

The class then debated the different interpretations: they were now ready to write up their conclusions.

Writing phase: a choice of genres

In chapter 2 we introduced the idea of a writing generator, p. 23, which we developed for pupils writing about the Body in the Bog mystery. The writing generator enabled the pupils to create their own genre, through combining one entry from each of its three columns of author, mode and audience, in relation to the field – the mystery's factual content.

Two pupils chose to write from the perspective of journalists, one for a local newspaper report, the other for an international publication.

TABLE 10.6 The writing generator enables pupils to create their own genre.

Writing generator: The Body in the Bog		
Content/field: The mystery of the body found in the bog and evidence relating to it		
Choose ONE **relevant** category from each column to provide the unique writing genre		
Author	*Mode*	*Audience*

THE DANISH TIMES

The Battle of the Scientists

Science correspondent

On July 17th a body was found in the peat in Nebelgard Fen, near the village of Jvostrup, and this has sent rumours flying around the town. Local evidence has suggested that the body may be that of Red Christian who went missing on June the 3rd.

Local historian, Dr. Balsey, has said that you can see the fingerprints so it is modern. The other evidence is from an old lady [who refused to be named], that it was Red Christian in the photo but other experts disagree.

There is evidence from the ancient scientist Strabo that the body may be Iron Age.

Strabo's research said that Iron Age sacrifices were placed over a cauldron and their necks were cut matching the cut on the body, above, an engraving from the cauldron. No one knows for sure if the body is likely to be Iron Age.

THE MOON

Bog-Buried Body

By an International Reporter

Yesterday Friday 13th of January a body was found by local peat cutters of Nebelgard Fen, assumed to be Red Christian. [a local man]. Is this true?

A local woman looked at the body and recognized him as Red Christian.'you can see his nails; always used to bite them. And around the time he disappeared he was suffering from tuberculosis. The body has a pinched face, so I really think the body is Red Christian.'

A local historian also examined the body and said it seemed the body had been in the peat for less than a hundred years.

Red Christian was a poacher and it is assumed Karl, a local farmer is one of the suspects, as Red Christian used to poach there.

Officer Carlson is also a suspect, as he came back angry from the pub the night Red Christian disappeared, and Red Christian had been treating his girlfriend badly.

It is also possible that the body is from the Iron Age, evidence that suggests this is: In (the) Iron Age they had sacrificial ceremonies where priestesses would slice the throat of the victim over a large tub. It is possible it is this, as there is a long thin scar down the man's head.

Other Iron Age bodies have been found in Nebelgard Fen but none as well preserved as this. Carbon dating was carried (out) on the body, and it has been recognized to be hundreds of years old. So it isn't long before further tests are (to be) carried out to find the exact age of the body, but could this be Red Christian?

Commentary

These two pieces are in some ways quite remarkable examples of the kind of reflective and discursive writing ten and eleven-year-old pupils can produce.

The Battle of the Scientists account opens succinctly, directly and to the point with the date a statement of what was discovered, where and the local response, including the identification of the corpse. The second paragraph provides corroborative evidence – and then the author introduces the alternative interpretation that it was an Iron Age body, drawing not only on a contemporary written source but also citing the engraving on the Gundestrop cauldron. The conclusion is balanced and judicious.

Bog-Buried Body also starts with a pithy title – and like The Battle of the Scientists sets the scene succinctly, ending with a question as to whether the local explanation that it was a local man's body, Red Christian's, was true. The account continues with a summary of three different local pieces of evidence about the corpse being Red Christian's, and why he died.

The penultimate paragraph examines the hypothesis that the body was an Iron Age sacrifice, summarising the evidence that it could have been. The report ends with a reference to Carbon 14 dating, while leaving the issue open as to whether the body was from the Iron Age or Red Christian's.

This was perfectly appropriate because at the time of discovery atmospheric testing had made Carbon 14 dating unreliable for the short period of high levels of radioactivity the nuclear tests had caused.

REFLECTION

Consider what kind of thinking the pupils are demonstrating in their two newspaper accounts and whether they show that they are capable of the analysis of evidence, the balanced discussion of interpretations and the reaching and support of conclusions.

Case 4: Anglo-Saxon poetry

Introduction

In chapter 2 pages 27–32 introduce how pupils prepared to write their own short Anglo-Saxon poems about the destruction of a Roman city, as described in the Saxon poem *The Ruin*. Using the evidence from *The Ruin* the pupils annotated their pictures of a Roman City, St Albans, and its forum in its heyday, see pp. 38–39, to show its destruction.

In the next phase of preparing to write an Anglo-Saxon poem we modelled the structure and composition of *The Ruin's* genre, looking at tenor [author-purpose-audience], the mode [structure of the poem], field [content] and overall context [culture]. For mode we looked at:

- alliteration;

- rhythm of the poetry, with split, two-part, balanced lines;

- the use of adjectives;

- metre – line length;

- paragraph/section length;

The pupils then wrote their own six to ten-line poems about a destroyed Roman city, drawing upon what they had learned about the end of Roman Britain, the description in *The Ruin* of a ruined Roman city and their annotated picture of the wrecked St Albans. On page 31 you can read examples of the children's Anglo-Saxon poetry.

Commentary

The pupils had a clear sense of *register* [*tenor*] – they were writing as if they were Romans still living in Britain, at the time of the city's destruction, to their friends in Rome, telling them about the city's devastation. The poems remarkably reflect *the mode* of Saxon poetry with its structure, rhythm and cadences. *The content* [*field*] is full, clear and accurate while the poems show a grasp of the overall cultural context of the period of invasion following the end of the Roman Empire.

REFLECTION

Consider whether the critique that primary school children are unable to think in a sophisticated and complex way in dealing with abstract ideas, causation and abstract ideas is reflected in the evidence from cases 1–4.

Case 5: Henry Unton – a Tudor feast: historical recreation

Introduction

The final case of reflective and discursive writing was in many ways our most ambitious: to use a scene from a Tudor painting, of the life of a Tudor courtier Henry Unton, as the basis for the pupils' composition. In many ways the painting is a comic strip of separate images, one for nine phases of his life from his birth to his death and funeral. One scene shows Henry Unton presiding over a banquet while a masque of Mercury and Diana is performed, accompanied by musicians (http://www.npg.org.uk/collections/search/portraitLarge/mw06456/Sir-Henry-Unton).

Teaching phase

We decided to use the Unton picture with a class of thirty mixed ability seven and eight-year-olds. The majority of the class were in their early stage of writing, with the ability to write short paragraphs. The more able could write long pieces of connected prose. For the first two lessons we worked on the story of Henry Unton's life, first creating a timeline of its nine main phases. With the class we talked through what each scene showed starting with his birth, school days and studying at Oxford University and ending with his death and funeral. Then we used drama to connect the nine scenes together into a coherent story.

To dramatise Henry's life the teacher and I divided the class into nine teams of three to four pupils, one group for each image. Each pupil in each team then took on the identity of one person in their scene. The team's task was to plan, work out and produce a tableau of that scene. We then joined up the scenes as an expressive movement montage – moving from one scene to the next as we told the story of his life.

The drama sequence involved each team in considerable discussion, debate, organisation and cooperation, to organise a tableau based upon their section of the painting. In the next lesson we moved on to the writing phase: we wanted the class to recreate, on paper, the banquet, masque and music scene.

The writing phase

We decided to use a passage from an Enid Blyton style novel (see below), as the genre that would provide a framework for the children's own account of the Tudor feast scene. In a short twenty-five-minute lesson the class worked intensely in pairs, small groups and as a whole class upon the Blyton text, using Textbreaker (table 2.4, p. 24), to develop understanding at word, phrase, paragraph and whole text levels, of what the scenes were about and filling in the accompanying Textbreaker grid, below the piece from the Enid Blyton novel.

> **Your title:**
> ....
>
> Are you all looking forward to a party, like the one we planned? We would like you to tell us a story about the party that Henry Unton held in his house. To help you make up your own story about Henry's party, we can read about a children's party. Four boys and girls, Philip, Jack, Dinah and Lucy, went to the party. It takes place in an old farmhouse. Mr. Evans the farmer greets the children:
>
> He led them to the farmhouse, and, when the door was flung open, what a welcome sight met the children's eyes! **[a]**
>
> A long, sturdy kitchen table was covered with a snow-white cloth, and on it was set the finest meal the children had ever seen in their lives. **[b]**
>
> A great ham sat ready to be carved. A big tongue garnished [decorated] with bright green parsley sat by its side. An enormous salad with hard-boiled eggs sprinkled generously [a lot of] all over it was in the middle of the table. Two cold roast chickens were on the table too, with little curly bits of bacon set round. **[c]**
>
> The children's eyes nearly fell out of their heads. What a feast! And the scones and the cakes! The jams and the pure yellow honey! The jugs of creamy milk! **[d]**
>
> I say, are you having a party or something?' asked Jack. **[e]**

TABLE 10.7 Grid for children to record information about the party.

Finding out about the party			
Who was there?	**What kinds of food were on the table?**	**What words tell you what the food was like?**	**What colour do you think each kind of food was?**

We discussed how all stories like the Blyton exemplar genre centre on a problem or problems to solve, something we returned to the next week when the children wrote stories about Henry Unton's feast. Using the idea of the writing generator, p. 23, we wanted the children to write a story of the feast from the point of view of one person who was there, taking the Enid Blyton genre as its model. We taped the lesson: the transcript for its opening phase reads:

Episode 1: Introduction to storytelling – demonstration and modelling

There was a detailed laying out of what the lesson's writing was about but first a recap of the Enid Blyton feast lesson.

1   Settled class with pens/pencils and paper. Told the pupils that:

- We are going to write a story about the feast scene taken from the Unton picture.

- We will write the story as if we are a person in the feast picture, as if we are there at the time.

- We will give you a small picture of one person in the feast picture with whom you will identify – you will take the role of that person.

2   Before we do that we are going to look at the Enid Blyton story we read last week, do a little bit of work on that, and:

- See how the writer makes up her story.

- What we want to do is to try and copy how she made up that story.

- We start off with that story, last week's, then we move on to this one about the picture.

- And then we end up by writing a story about this picture.

Episode 2: story as mystery and problem solving

Focus: getting the idea of children building their story around solving a problem

Now every story has some idea of a mystery in it, some kind of problem in it.

Can we all look at the Unton picture that is in front of you, everybody look at the picture please.

And, begin to think of something that might happen in this scene . . . Something that causes a problem.

Pupil 1 Somebody might have dropped the food on the floor.

Pupil 2 Somebody spilled their wine.

Pupil 3 Somebody played the wrong tune / music.

Pupil 4 Somebody gets bad tempered.

Pupil 5 Somebody causes an argument.

Pupil 6 Somebody could have fallen over while they were dancing.

Pupil 7 Somebody could have cooked the wrong food.

The pupils now 'read' the picture of what the feast picture showed: Bethany, an able pupil, filled in her grid (table 10.7). Her entries are italicised:

TABLE 10.8 Bethany's notes about John Unton's feast.

READING the feast picture – look at the Henry Unton feast. Write down what you think in the spaces				
The scene	*Who is there?*	*What clothes do they wear?*	*What objects do they have?*	*What are they doing?*
The feasters The musicians The dancers	*Henry Unton* *Lady Unton* *feasters* *musicians* *dancers*	*posh clothes* *collar* *shirt ruff dress* *skirt hats* *tiara*	*sceptre* *flute* *napkin* *banjo/guitar* *violin* *cups plates*	*dancing* *playing music* *eating* *speaking* *laughing*
Sounds you can hear	*Laughing, giggling, clapping, crunching, music, speaking, scratching, gulping, cutting, munching, feet*			
Smells	*burning: cooked food, chicken, eggs, soup, bread dust smoke people, flowers, fire*			
Colours	Red, black, white, grey, silver, brown, purple, orange, mauve, yellow			

TABLE 10.9 Bethany's storyboard for the Upton Feast.

THE UPTON PARTY – STORYBOARD			
Who am I: musician		**Who is my story for: mum & granny & grandpa**	
The scene *Party at the table* *The people near me* *Other musicians* *Dancers* *People at the table* *Servants*	What is happening now? *Playing the banjo merrily*	What problems might there be? *Spoiling the song by playing the wrong tune* *Someone gets drunk and starts a fight*	What might happen next in the story? *Henry gets mad and everything went quiet*

The next phase in the pupils' writing was for each of them to complete a storyboard to plan their stories. The storyboard was based upon the story genre. Bethany's indicates how she planned her tale (table 10.8).

In the final part of the lesson the pupils wrote their stories: even the most vestigial set the scene, introduced a problem and its consequence and ended with a conclusion. Bethany's story reads:

The Best Feast Ever!!!

<u>1580 Wedding</u> One day Henry had a party. I was a musician back then. The smell of the food was delicious but musicians did not get any food. We were all sat at the table and everyone was near me and other musicians, dancers, servants – everybody was near me. I was playing the banjo happily when suddenly another musician ended up playing the wrong tune. It was a very sad tune called Montoanisia. It made everyone cry except for Henry who got mad. Very mad, he got so mad he smashed the glass on the floor and shouted STOP!!! Everything was quiet, apart from the fire. It was going mad but apart from that everything was quiet. Late on Henry's old friend went and tripped the dancers up and they all fell on top of each other. After that everybody laughed and the party ended happily ever after.

Commentary

The writing is coherent and clearly written – drawing heavily upon the Enid Blyton genre, while drawing its content from the Henry Unton picture. The story follows the outline of the storyboard plan. Bethany centres upon a problem, and interestingly solves it through the medium of the dancers being tripped up, which meant Henry's bad temper disappeared and everyone was happy.

> **REFLECTION**
>
> Having read through the chapters and its five cases, what ideas has it given you about how you might develop your pupil's writing in the context of them learning history?

Conclusion

Writing this chapter has convinced me that reflective and discursive writing cannot occur in a vacuum – it must be the outcome of a pedagogy that at every stage is social, interactive and encourages the enquiry, problem solving, discourse, thinking and understanding that makes such writing possible. The learning outcomes of the Caesar Spy Report lesson indicates what is involved.

The children:

- gained a detailed understanding of the Roman Army, its weapons and fighting methods;

- were able to use and synthesise a range of sources to construct their understanding of a past situation;

- developed skills in questioning and discussing evidence;

- deepened their understanding of the report genre; they organised a plethora of information to write well-structured, vivid and accurate reports.

Afterword

I think that children should have the last word. Eight-year-old Helen and Emily decided write a poem, after listening to the teacher's reading Julius Caesar landing in Britain.

> And now the standard bearer of the tenth legion cried, 'Leap down men, unless you want to abandon the eagle. I at all events shall have done my duty to my country and my general'. Uttering these words, in a loud voice, he threw himself overboard . . . Eventually the Britons were put to flight.
>
> Caesar's *Gallic Wars*, Book 4,
> chapter 25 (www.classics.mit.edu.Caesar/gallic.4.4)

Caesars Battle

Round the cliffs,
Boats come in.
British scream, "we'll win, we'll win!"
as they come in.
Romans in their armour
Shining as the sun
THEY altso shout, "we'll win, we'll win"
British in there furs
dont have many weapons . . . .
So Caesar Wins.

Helen's and Emily's poem based on the text from Caesar's *Gallic Wars*.

Index